P9-CRM-579

THE RESCUE OF MISS YASKELL

OTHER BOOKS BY RUSSELL BAKER
Washington: City on the Potomac
An American in Washington
No Cause for Panic
All Things Considered
Our Next President
The Upside-down Man
Poor Russell's Almanac
So This Is Depravity
Growing Up

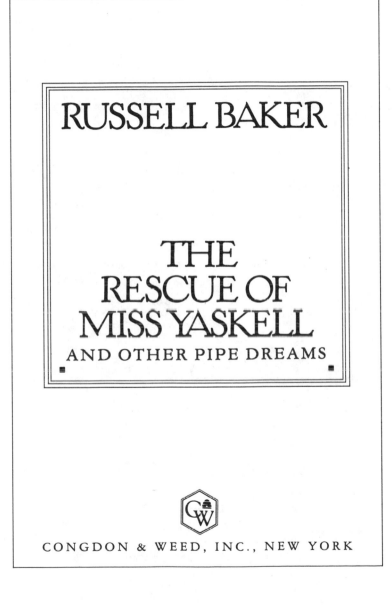

RUSSELL BAKER

THE
RESCUE OF
MISS YASKELL
AND OTHER PIPE DREAMS

CONGDON & WEED, INC., NEW YORK

All material appeared in the author's "Observer"
column in The New York Times *and his "Sunday Observer"*
column in The New York Times Magazine. *Copyright* ©
1975, 1976, 1977, 1979, 1980, 1981, 1982, and 1983 by The New York
Times Company; reprinted by permission.

Copyright © 1983 by Russell Baker

Library of Congress Cataloging in Publication Data

Baker, Russell, 1925–
The rescue of Miss Yaskell and other pipe dreams.

Consists of material from the author's columns in
the New York times and the New York Times magazine.
I. Title.
PS3552.A4343R37   1983   814'.54   83-14303
ISBN 0-86553-098-X
ISBN 0-312-92730-4 (St. Martin's Press)

Published by Congdon & Weed, Inc.
298 Fifth Avenue, New York, N.Y. 10001

Distributed by St. Martin's Press
175 Fifth Avenue, New York, N.Y. 10010

Published simultaneously in Canada by Methuen Publications
2330 Midland Avenue, Agincourt, Ontario M1S 1P7

All Rights Reserved
Printed in the United States of America
Designed by Barbara Huntley
First Edition

CONTENTS

CONTENTS

CONTENTS

CONTENTS

THE RESCUE OF MISS YASKELL

REGIONS OF
THE PAST

A VISIT
WITH THE FOLKS

Periodically I go back to a churchyard cemetery on the side of an Appalachian hill in northern Virginia to call on family elders. It slows the juices down something marvelous.

They are all situated right behind an imposing brick church with a tall square brick bell-tower best described as honest but not flossy. Some of the family elders did construction repair work on that church and some of them, the real old timers, may even have helped build it, but I couldn't swear to that because it's been there a long, long time.

The view, especially in early summer, is so pleasing that it's a pity they can't enjoy it. Wild roses blooming on fieldstone fences, fields white with daisies, that soft languorous air turning the mountains pastel blue out toward the West.

The tombstones are not much to look at. Tombstones never are in my book, but they do help in keeping track of the family and, unlike a family, they have the virtue of never chafing at you.

This is not to say they don't talk after a fashion. Every time I pass Uncle Lewis's I can hear it say, "Come around to the barber shop, boy, and I'll cut that hair." Uncle Lewis was a barber. He left up here for a while and went to the city. Baltimore. But he came back after the end. Almost all of them came back finally, those that left, but most stayed right here all along.

Well, not right here in the churchyard, but out there over the fields, two, three, four miles away. Grandmother was born just over that rolling field out there near the woods the year the Civil War ended, lived most of her life about three miles out the other way there near the mountain, and has been right here near this old shade tree for the past 50 years.

We weren't people who went very far. Uncle Harry, her second child, is right beside her. A carpenter. He lived 87 years in these parts without ever complaining about not seeing Paris. To get Uncle Harry to say anything, you have to ask for directions.

"Which way is the schoolhouse?" I ask, though not aloud of course.

"Up the road that way a right good piece," he replies, still the master of indefinite navigation whom I remember from my boyhood.

It's good to call on Uncle Lewis, grandmother and Uncle Harry like this. It improves your perspective to commune with people who are not alarmed about the condition of NATO or whining about the flabbiness of the dollar.

The elders take the long view. Of course, you don't want to indulge too extensively in that long a view, but it's useful to absorb it in short doses. It corrects the blood pressure and puts things in a more sensible light.

After a healthy dose of it, you realize that having your shins kicked in the subway is not the gravest insult to dignity ever suffered by common humanity.

Somewhere in the vicinity is my great-grandfather who used to live back there against the mountain and make guns, but I could never find him. He was born out that way in 1817—James Monroe was President then—and I'd like to find him to commune a bit with somebody of blood kin who was around when Andrew Jackson was in his heyday.

After Jackson and Abraham Lincoln and the Civil War, he would probably not be very impressed about much that goes on nowadays, and I would like to get a few resonances off his tombstone, a cool *frisson* of contempt maybe for a great-grandchild who had missed all the really perilous times.

Unfortunately, I am never able to find him, but there is Uncle Irvey, grandmother's oldest boy. An unabashed Hoover Republican. "Eat all those string beans, boy," I hear as I nod at his tombstone.

And here is a surprise: Uncle Edgar. He has been here for years, but I have never bumped into him before. I don't dare disturb him, for he is an important man, the manager of the baseball team, and his two pitchers, my Uncle Harold and my Cousin-in-law Howard, have both been shelled on the mound and Uncle Edgar has to decide whether to ask the shortstop if he knows anything about pitching.

My great-grandfather who made guns is again not to be found, but on the way out I pass the tombstone of another great-grandfather whose distinction was that he left an estate of $3.87. It is the first time I have passed this way since I learned of this, and I smile his way, but something says, "In the long run, boy, we all end up as rich as Rockefeller," and I get into the car and drive out onto the main road, gliding through fields white with daisies, past fences perfumed with roses, and am rather more content with the world.

THE BOY
WHO CAME TO SUPPER

For a long time I used to eat supper. "Supper's at 5 o'clock and you'd better be here," my mother would say. We lived in the rural South then, but later we moved to New Jersey and kept right on eating supper, though sometimes it was as late as 6 o'clock.

In fact, I was still eating supper at the age of 22 when I started working for an Eastern newspaper. Since it was a morning paper, the work hours extended from 3 P.M. to midnight with an hour off to eat, and at 7 P.M. an editor habitually notified me that it was all right to go to dinner.

Since all the other reporters racing for the first martini were also going to dinner, I went to dinner, too. In this way I gradually became a dinner eater, though the transition was confusing. On days off, since I was still living at home, my mother insisted that I eat supper, though it was often served as late as 7 P.M. now.

For a year or two, I remained in this transitional stage—a dinner eater at the office, a supper eater at home. Since I was eating dinner five nights a week and supper only twice, however, the dinner habit began to enslave me and tensions developed at home.

"When are we going to have dinner?" I would ask my mother. "Supper will be ready as soon as I finish frying the potato cakes," she would say. We were drifting apart. Something basic we had once shared had now eroded. I was moving into another world, the world of the dinner eaters, while she was firmly anchored in the world of supper eaters. I left home and have been an incorrigible dinner eater ever since.

This distinction between Americans who eat supper and those

who eat dinner is one of the most striking divisions in the national life, yet nobody has ever persuasively explained the difference between the parties, though many sociologists have tried.

Andy Rooney, for example, holds that it defines the difference between political parties. Democrats eat supper before sundown, he states, while Republicans eat it at 8 P.M. and call it dinner.

If this is so, how does he explain why headwaiters in New York keep me waiting at the bar past 10 P.M. while influential Democrats arriving in limousines are promptly ushered to the dinner table I thought I had reserved for 8:30?

Calvin Trillin has a theory that the distinction has something to do with American regionalism. His three tests for identifying an Eastern city are: "a place where nobody on the City Council ever wears white patent-leather shoes, where there are at least two places to buy pastrami" and "where just about everybody eats supper after dark and calls it dinner."

Trillin's theory is not supported by my experience in Newark, N.J., and Baltimore—indisputably Eastern cities, in which I lived for 15 years among people who almost universally ate supper. In fact, the notion that anybody could eat dinner at the end of the day, except in the movies, never occurred to me until the age of 22.

Until then, in my experience, dinner was eaten only once a week, always at 3 o'clock on Sunday afternoon. When somebody invited you to dinner you assumed it would be eaten at midafternoon on Sunday and the menu would be chicken. Having seen Jean Harlow and Wallace Beery in "Dinner at Eight," I realized there were unique people who put on tuxedos and gowns to eat dinner at the hour when normal people were taking their prebedtime cocoa, but the idea that I might ever doll up in order to tuck into the potato cakes seemed as far-fetched as the possibility of picking up Claudette Colbert on a Greyhound bus.

When I was in the transitional stage, learning to eat dinner with veteran journalistic dinner eaters, I first assumed that dinner was distinguished from supper by the beverage that came with it.

Supper had always been accompanied by iced tea, a glass of milk or, in cold weather, a cup of coffee, all of which were designed to wash down the potato cakes. At dinner, the prevailing drink seemed to be gin, which was designed to help you forget you were eating potato cakes.

This may explain why I was converted so easily, but it does not explain anything more profound, since deeper investigation showed that many supper eaters partake regularly of beer, and even bourbon with ginger ale, while many dinner eaters are content with soda water, a few ice cubes and a slice of lime.

Long investigation of this division among Americans forces me to dismiss as myths such popular theories as: (1) that blue-collar people eat supper while establishment people eat dinner; (2) that people with good digestion eat supper while people prone to gastric distress eat dinner; and (3) that people with hearty appetites are supper eaters while people with jaded palates are dinner eaters who are really just going through the motions so they will have an excuse to lap up the wine.

My studies have produced only two illuminating facts: first, that a real supper eater wouldn't be caught dead with a Cuisinart in the kitchen; second, that dinner eaters are five times less likely than supper eaters to faint dead away if you serve them an artichoke.

▪ HECK ON WHEELS ▪

Norman Rockwell and I never saw things eye to eye when we worked together on The Saturday Evening Post. Norman was illustrating covers and I was trying to sell the finished product. The selling was hard labor.

I would strap on my roller skates, sling a canvas bag containing two dozen Saturday Evening Posts over my shoulder and begin by ringing doorbells. The sales pitch was simple: "Want to buy a Saturday Evening Post?" As the week progressed, it became tinged with subtle pathos: "You don't want to buy a Saturday Evening Post, I suppose?"

During the final day or two of each week's sales campaign, when the imminent arrival of next week's batch of Posts loomed like the *Wehrmacht* massing on the borders of the soul, I would post myself at a strategic traffic light and dart among idling cars shouting, "Saturday Evening Post!"

In good weeks, the sales profit ran as high as 25 cents, which, even though a nickel could buy three apples in those days, did not strike me as the kind of revenue that was going to induce J.P. Morgan to put out the red carpet when I arrived to establish a line of credit.

It was clear to me that the fault was largely Norman's. Although I was only eight, or nine, or ten at the time, I had seen enough of the mass market to realize that Norman's vision of reality was hopelessly askew. The world whose doorbell I rang hungered for tales of illicit passion, gore and depravity, and was shameless about saying so.

Mounting three flights of stairs on wheeled feet, banging at an apartment door, flashing Norman's vision of America, I would be met by a slattern in beer fumes declaring the only magazine she wanted was True Confessions.

Men sat around the house in their undershirts growing whiskers in that America. Permanent unemployment tends to make a man indifferent to the dictates of Gentlemen's Quarterly and sour of temper toward midgets on roller skates peddling Norman's wholesome folks.

"Why don't you sell something good like True Detective?"

". . . Spicy Adventure?"

". . . Doc Savage?"

I never told Norman what the world was really like out there. The Saturday Evening Post did not tolerate its business officers trying to interfere with its editorial content. Consequently,

Norman never drew a boozy woman in bare feet at the front door announcing her preference for tales of adultery, nor the look in the eye of an unshaven man in his undershirt when he tells you that he'd really rather look at pictures of mutilated bodies (preferably female).

The disagreement between Norman and me was never expressed. As a result, Norman went on painting dogs as winsomely lovable pooches instead of nasty, snarling carnivores ready to pounce at the first sound of a roller skate wheel on the front porch.

Long afterwards it occurred to me that if I had gone to him and said, "Look, Norman, I'm dying out here trying to sell these wholesome characters and phony mutts you're painting," he would have smiled and painted me as an apple-cheeked nine-year-old with a patch on my corduroy knickers and innocence sticking out all over my cowlick. He was that insistent about refusing to see the world as it is instead of as it should be.

At the time of his death, people who have to comment on such things stated that despite his mass audience—perhaps the largest any painter has ever had—he was not an artist but an illustrator. I don't know. There are many definitions of art. Somebody has said that art is a lie that helps us to perceive the truth, and it seems to me that this pretty well expresses what his work was about.

His paintings are graphic fairy tales about Americans. They speak of a people unbelievably decent and innocent. That we were not during the age he painted is beside the point; the fact is that Americans in that time thought of themselves as such. And, indeed, acted on that assumption when the age culminated in World War II.

In "Not So Wild a Dream," one of the definitive books for students of World War II, Eric Sevareid writes that he was frequently astonished and appalled by the innocence in which American soldiers went to death for a purpose of which they understood nothing except that it was fundamentally decent.

This old sense of innocence, which we have now lost, had bleak political consequences, beginning with our refusal to set realistic war aims in the 1940s and ending with the triumph of the notion that the alternative to innocence must be cynicism.

I didn't understand Norman's significance in the old days. All I could see was that he didn't know what it was like trying to sell The Saturday Evening Post on roller skates. He saw things truer than I did. It was an honor to work with him.

GROSS ROOTS

Watching the reporters take off in battalion strength for Plains, Ga., to search for the roots of Jimmy Carter in the summer of '76, I finally realized why I have always shrunk from running for President. Splendid though the honor would be, I wouldn't dream of subjecting my home crossroads to the indignities which necessarily occur when the press descends in force to do its sociological study of the candidate's roots.

It would surely take these ferrets no more than a day or two to unearth the fact that, as a toddler, one of my most memorable achievements was the discovery that my Uncle Bruce hid his whisky in a Mason jar behind the barrel of whitewash in the rear of my grandmother's house. Or that my grandmother, on being shown the evidence by me, threw the whisky on the woodpile and gave Uncle Bruce such a lecture that he never touched the stuff again for several days.

Uncle Bruce is dead now and beyond public humiliation, but I cherish his memory too closely to want to see the story laid out in Newsweek under an old snapshot of him, merely to authenticate my early rustic credentials for the Presidency.

Moreover, since the episode occurred during Prohibition, making his possession of the stuff a criminal enterprise, and since the only surviving snapshots of Uncle Bruce show him with several days' growth of whiskers, he would be bound to emerge from the presentation as a distinctly sinister character.

He was not, of course. Almost everybody at the crossroads who was male shared his taste for moonshine, while almost everybody who was female spent a good bit of time emptying Mason jars on woodpiles. I shudder to imagine what character assassinations this would produce in the press encampment, and now that I think of it, I am not altogether certain it would help my campaign to have The Chicago Tribune discover that the first skill I mastered was capping the bottles of my father's home-brew.

The exception to the prevailing contempt for the 18th Amendment was Uncle Irvey. He was a church deacon and a Republican, which was permissible, at least for deacons, in this particular region of the shallow South. In 1928 he had persuaded my Uncle Harry to vote for Herbert Hoover, and when the Depression arrived shortly afterward, Uncle Harry held Uncle Irvey personally responsible for it.

I don't know what the network sleuths would make of the fact that for years thereafter Uncle Harry never spoke to Uncle Irvey except in anger, but I suspect there would be nasty suggestions that ours was an eccentric family. This would be totally misleading.

Although not a member of the Peace Corps like Mrs. Lillian Carter, my mother was equally adventurous and taught school in an area that was always called "up there along the mountain." Through her school connections, one of my earliest heroes became a boy named "Eleven." The story had it that Eleven was his parents' 11th-born child, that when he came along they were at a loss for a name they hadn't already used, and so decided to improvise.

I don't know what became of Eleven. All I know is that I don't want to be sitting before the television some night surrounded by Secret Service men when suddenly Mike Wallace appears, interviewing a man named Eleven about my early deficiencies as a maker of mud pies. I'd rather not be President.

Nor do I want to pick up The New York Times and read a full description of my grandmother's various supernatural beliefs. These would doubtless strike the contemporary electorate as amusingly batty, and there was nothing, absolutely nothing, batty about my grandmother. She was a force of nature, and she lived in a world of coal-oil lamps that made night a time of grotesque shadows. Lighting her way to bed one night, she saw her long-dead son, Raymond, on the stairs, and when she returned to report it to a room of adults, no one laughed.

Once, a bird came down the chimney and flew into the house and she announced that it was an omen that someone would die, and no one laughed that time either. Dying was still a commonplace then. Antibiotics were still undiscovered, and even the young lived in dread of pneumonia, fevers, blood poisoning.

All this is just a moment back in time, before rural electrification and asphalt paving finally finished off rustic America for good, yet it already seems a world away. I wouldn't want the political reporters digging it up to find my roots. They are fiercely capable fellows when it comes to finding the Uncle Bruces of America, but they are not geared for the important things, like detecting the way a June morning smelled in 1934 or what the wind sounded like in the chimney that December.

RIGHT
SMART O' WIND

Watching television weather reporters rave about the wind chill factor always reminds me of my Uncle Bruce and what a loss his passing was to the art of cold-weather reporting.

Neither the wind chill factor nor the TV weatherman had been invented in Uncle Bruce's lifetime. All he had to work with were nerve ends and instinct, but with these primitive gauges he could give a flawless reading on how cold you were going to be outside on a winter morning.

At the edge of the mountains in northern Virginia where we lived, winter could be "pretty cold," which was the entirely adequate report he often brought back after returning from a dawn trip down across the orchard to the barn where he milked the cows.

"How cold is it out there this morning, Bruce?" my grandmother would ask him.

"Pretty cold," was his most common report in deep winter.

Everybody knew from this two-word report precisely how much discomfort to dress for. Clothing had to be slightly thicker than what you wore when he reported "just a little ice around the spring," but not as heavy as you'd need when he answered, "mighty cold."

Blizzards often howled down off the mountain when it was "mighty cold," and when Uncle Bruce came back banging the snow off his knee-high rubber boots his weather report was expanded to take note of the howling.

"How cold is it out there this morning, Bruce?"

"Mighty cold," he would say, then add: "There's a right smart o' wind."

"Mighty cold" with "a right smart o' wind" meant the cold was as terrible as humans could possibly stand without turning brittle and cracking.

These four gradations of coldness were completely adequate for our survival purposes in winter. "Just a little ice around the spring"—a tolerable day. "Pretty cold"—winter will always be with us. "Mighty cold"—button up tight. "Mighty cold" with "a right smart o' wind"—well, man is born to suffer.

Uncle Bruce's right smart o' wind was intended to warn us against what is now called the wind chill factor. Doubtless the wind chill factor is a measurement of great scientific value, but for nonscientific purposes it is not in the same class with a right smart o' wind.

The electronic weathermen going on and on each winter about incredible wind chill factors tend to sound like the boy who cried wolf. On rising one winter morning recently I was astonished when one of them said that though the temperature was only zero or thereabouts, the wind chill factor would assault me with a frigidity equal to 55 degrees below zero if I left the house.

It took some courage, but I left the house anyhow. What a disappointment. I don't doubt the wind chill factor made the outdoors feel as if the temperature were 55 degrees below zero, but there was no noticeable difference between the cold I felt in this amazing scientifically measured condition and what I felt when Uncle Bruce reported those childhood mornings as "mighty cold" with "a right smart o' wind."

Despite the ballyhoo about the astounding coldness, I had felt this same degree of chill off and on many times from the cradle without realizing that anything incredible was happening.

It made me feel like that boob in the Molière comedy who discovers in his middle years that he's been speaking prose all his life and is so delighted he can't resist boasting about it. Since childhood I had been routinely surviving wind chill factors of 55 degrees below zero while supposing that I was merely living through "mighty cold" days with "a right smart o' wind."

Uncle Bruce's weather reporting, of course, was just that: reporting. He didn't have to oversell winter to avoid losing a transmission-repair sponsor. He went at it like an honest old beat reporter who has felt it all, hot days and frigid, and was beyond gussying up the facts to sell a humdrum story to the city desk.

Gee-whiz stories like "coldest winter since the 19th century," which entrance today's TV weather reporters, would have baffled Uncle Bruce, for these are based on minute variations in thermometer readings and he paid little attention to the thermometer.

My grandmother kept one nailed to her front porch, but it was only there as a status symbol. (She was an important woman thereabouts and had too much taste to put a cast iron deer on her lawn.) Nobody ever consulted this thermometer before deciding how to dress on a winter's day.

Everybody knew that 10 degrees Fahrenheit was a relative thing that could be either tolerable and harmless or make your ears drop off, depending on whether the quality of wind motion was negligible or right smart.

Naturally Uncle Bruce noticed that some winters were harder than others. He didn't need scientific instruments for that. In a really hard winter the popcorn ran out before March.

■ ANY HUMANS THERE? ■

A machine purporting to be the Rev. Jerry Falwell had written a strident letter asking me to send it $5, $10 or $25 immediately, and signed itself breezily as "Jerry."

I don't know Mr. Falwell but in my associations with men of the cloth I have never overcome the awe and respect for their calling that Uncle Irvey taught me as a child. Accordingly, I felt duty bound to warn Mr. Falwell that a machine was writing letters over his name and trying to cadge money from strangers.

I knew Uncle Irvey would have wanted to hear about it if the machine had surreptitiously written to a perfect stranger, asked for $5, $10 or $25 immediately, and signed itself "Irv." In my childhood Uncle Irvey was the superintendent at the Shinar Lutheran Church and, as such, became my model of sound churchly behavior.

Machines, for example, had no place in churchly doings. Though he owned an automobile, Uncle Irvey preferred the horse and buggy when he went to church, at least until age, infirmity and the decline of the horseshoe overtook him. He chose to approach the Lord's house in a peace undefiled by the clattering of soulless machinery.

He would have considered it indecent to ask anyone to put a $5 bill in the plate, and obscene to press for $10 or $25. Any plutocrats hoping to pass through the eye of the needle by dropping a princely $1 bill were expected to conceal their shameful wealth in sealed envelopes.

A machine putting the muscle on people for sums of $5, $10 or $25 would have been an abomination of Satan, in Uncle Irvey's view. If the preacher was hard pressed for money or the church needed repairs, he was not above putting the muscle on certain well-to-do farmers during pious chats by the corncrib, but if a machine calling itself "Irv" had gone public all across the county, he would have wanted to know about it.

I assumed Mr. Falwell would want to know about it too, and I had just started to write a letter to him when the telephone interrupted. A woman's voice said a machine wanted to speak to me. Would I talk to it?

"Does it call itself 'Jerry'?" I asked.

No, the woman said, it was the voice of one of Elvis Presley's closest friends. The machine came on the line. It spoke in a gooey cornpone voice. It had heard I was a devoted Elvis fan. Would I like to hear a message from Elvis?

"Look here," I said, "I am not that much of an Elvis fan, and I am busy writing to the Rev. Jerry Falwell about a machine that's sending out letters over his name, and I don't have time to . . ."

"Before he died," said the machine, "Elvis told me he wanted every one of his fans to enjoy the greatest bargain in recorded music . . ."

I hung up and returned to my letter. "Dear Mr. Falwell: I am sure you will be as outraged as I to learn that a certain machine, calling itself 'Jerry,' is trying to cadge sums of $5, $10 or $25 . . ."

The phone rang again. A machine spoke. It had the affidavit voice of an F.B.I. agent.

"Are you the person who just hung up on the machine bringing you a message from one of Elvis Presley's best friends?"

"Is your name Jerry?" I replied.

"I'll ask the questions," the machine said. "How long do you want to live?"

"Are you threatening my life?" I asked.

"Are you aware that a new physical fitness program designed by foremost physiological scientists can add years of glowing health to your life? This life-enhancing miracle is now available exclusively for only $39.95 . . ."

I hung up and waited for the next ring. This time it was a machine under the misapprehension that I had received some mail-order aspidistra plants and refused to pay the bill after four warning notices. I hung up before it threatened to haul me into machine court.

"Dear Mr. Falwell," I began again. "You probably never heard of my Uncle Irvey, but . . ."

Telephone. "I am one of Uncle Irvey's longtime associates," said a machine. "Before his death Uncle Irvey spoke to me down by the corncrib. He had just put the muscle on me for $5, $10 or $25 to buy shoes for the preacher's little children, and he said, 'Wouldn't it be nice if there was a wonderful machine somewhere that could just reach out to all the wonderful people in this good old world of ours and tell folks to send in $5, $10 or $25 immediately?' "

I was too stunned to argue. "This is Jerry, isn't it?" I whispered.

"Send me $5, $10 or $25 immediately," it said. "Yes, sir," I said. I meant it at the time, but next day I saw things more clearly and sent Mr. Falwell a note.

"If you and the missus are pinched for food money," I said, "let me know and I will bake you an apple pie and send it along."

I'm pretty certain that would have been Uncle Irvey's way.

THERE IS
NO THERE HERE

▪ ▪

LANCASTER, Va.—For nearly 400 years Americans have spent their history getting from There to Here and usually found Here unsatisfactory after they arrived. Sometimes, as now, they have been so disenchanted with Here that they want to go back to There and start over again.

This is one impulse behind the Reagan movement with its varied urges to go back to one of those forks in the road and take another route. Which fork we want to go back to is not so clear. The religious fundamentalists look back to Victorian social morality, the economists look back toward the business imperium of the 1920s and the military and foreign policy people yearn for the age of the battleship and unchallengeable American power around the globe.

Whether the goal is 1890, 1928 or 1946 may be unclear, but one point on which there is agreement is that today won't do. Some place back there, there was a good There and we made a terrible mistake in coming Here.

How we got from There to Here, however, is finally a question for each of us to answer individually. A country like this does not move like a vast army but travels a path that is the sum of millions of individual decisions, accidents, strokes of good fortune and small disasters.

One of the more durable Theres in my own journey was located here at Lancaster Court House, a Tidewater town near the Rappahannock River. Calling it a town is overstatement. It is a few houses, a schoolhouse, a small store and a courthouse along the side of the road and, as a cousin of mine puts it, "if you blink twice while you're driving through, you'll miss it."

Here my maternal grandfather and great-grandfather lived the life that now seems so desirable to those who are angry about the environs of the 1980s. My great-grandfather practiced law here before and after the Civil War, and if the testimony of the Confederate war monument can be trusted, did some service to the cause of perpetuating slavery in the 1860s.

My grandfather followed him in the practice of the law, thus perpetuating a family tradition. This business of the son carrying on his father's work probably strikes many of us as one of the happy characteristics of life back There. The necessity to defend slavery clouds this happy picture a mite.

My grandfather lived less than a mile from the courthouse. He had a big house, a farm and timberland off the left side of the road that runs down to the river. His two daughters and seven sons were all born there just before and after the turn of the century.

In this bucolic There, there was no birth control. Certainly no abortion. My grandfather was a pious man. So pious, in fact, that he refused to buy life insurance. He said insurance was a sacrilegious betting with God.

Whether the corporate tycoons who surround the Reagan philosophers would approve of going back to this particular There seems doubtful. I rather fancy they would disapprove of the old gentleman's refusal to invest in America, but surely he would cut a fetching figure for the folks of the Moral Majority.

Whatever the case, God called for him in his uninsured state one May day in 1917, and he passed from the sweet There of Lancaster Court House to the Hereafter. He and my grandmother are buried under a shady tree behind White Marsh Church about two miles from their home place.

I stopped by there the other day. It is everybody's dream of the country graveyard: The plain brick church built in 1848 on the ruins of another built in 1792. The white dogwoods flowering, the spring breeze rippling the grass. Not like those hateful new burial factories being constructed like high-rise apartments on the outskirts of today's cities.

My grandfather's death ended my own chances of ever living in that particular There. He had left little but debts. His house, farm and timberland were lost, his children scattered down many roads, as American children have always been scattered by happenstance, and traveled from There to many Heres.

His grandchildren were born and shaped along those many roads, some in Richmond, others in Baltimore, New York and California, and the old There ceased to exist. I went looking for it after visiting his grave. His house had sat at the far end of a long lane under big spreading trees.

Two men were plowing a field where the lane used to be. The house had vanished. Destroyed by fire, I am told. There is one big spreading tree left where the house might once have stood. There is no There to go back to.

The plowing was being finished by two men on huge modern machines. What used to be a dirt road running past his acreage is an elegantly paved highway traveled not by horse-and-buggy rigs, but by flashy new cars from Japan, Detroit and Germany.

It is no longer There. It is Here, and you can't get There from Here. From Here you can only get to The Next Place and you probably get there inexorably, even if you choose to spend the entire journey looking backward.

THE
UNWELCOME WAGON

KILMARNOCK, Va.—In the old western movies, he usually rode into town on a white horse with a gun on his hip. People sized him up silently. He was "the stranger." The local people addressed him as such: "Plannin' to stay long in these parts, stranger?"

Sometimes, of course, he planned to fence the range so he

could raise sheep. That meant trouble, a change in the society, new ways being brought into the territory. You knew there would be gunfire and gore before the lights went up.

"The stranger" may be the most enduring figure ever produced by America. The first strangers rowed ashore at Plymouth Rock and Jamestown and established a tradition that persists as vigorously today as in the time of King James I.

Nowadays the stranger does not arrive by horse or rowboat. He comes in a station wagon, accompanied by a real estate salesman, a moving man and a parcel of newfangled ideas that threaten the old ways. As the agent of change, he can expect a cool reception at best, and possibly open hostility.

In this remote corner of Virginia, as in most American communities, the established folks have a pejorative term for the infestation of strangers in the county. A recent arrival is referred to as a "come here," to distinguish him from the long-term resident, who is a "from here."

Not surprisingly, this snobby terminology makes the newcomers gnash their teeth. That's the purpose of such verbal distinctions: to make the stranger grind his molars in agonies of alienation.

It is a commonplace American habit. On Nantucket Island society is divided between "islanders" and "off islanders." An "off islander" is someone not born on the island. Socially, no matter how long the stranger may have lived on the island, he remains an "off islander," and therefore not quite one of God's elect.

Around these parts the distinction between the "come here" and the "from here" is just as galling to the new settlers. A letter in the current issue of The Rappahannock Record signed by Melvin Frame voices a poignant sorrow at the community's insistence on classifying him under the odious "come here" designation.

Mr. Frame declares that his forebears were "from here" and that after long service in Government employ he had anticipated happy retirement on the ancestral soil. Having returned to his roots, however, he is afflicted with the abusive label of "come here" and doesn't like it one bit. He wants this divisive and unpleasant terminology abandoned.

Mr. Frame apparently intends to persevere despite his cool reception. In one of the local cemeteries there is a new tombstone inscribed with his name, and since the plot is empty, and the stone bears no death date, and there are not likely to be two Melvin Frames in such a small community, I assume that Mr. Frame intends eventually to be known as a "stayed here."

His letter makes the sensible point that invidious distinctions between "the stranger" and the permanent folk of the neighborhood are ridiculous since the only Americans anywhere who might justly assert they are "from heres" are the Indians.

Logic has never had much to do, however, with this ancient friction between "from heres" and "come heres." In this most mobile of nations, the very mobility of the population creates a false sense of what permanence is.

In most places nowadays, 30 years is almost forever, and people who have been living in the same place since the 1930s are apt to be regarded as relics of the Bronze Age. The traditions being defended against the threat of marauding strangers are often no more than 30 or 40 years old.

In this respect we are not so far from the cow towns of movie legend where the society threatened by the arriving stranger on horseback was a town nailed together three or four years before the action starts.

Washington affords the most spectacular example of the society perpetually anointing itself in the aerosol mists of instant tradition. People who arrived eight years ago often behave as though they had been in Washington since John Adams, and the few people who have been around long enough to remember Harry Truman are looked upon with a wonderment that is elsewhere accorded only to persons who accompanied Moses across the Red Sea.

In a community like this part of Virginia, which predates Washington by some 150 years, the permanence appears to be a bit more aged than the Washington variety, but even here a good bit of the housing is 1950 split-level rather than log cabin or old plantation manse. Most of the people who established whatever tradition existed here in the beginning have long since sent their children outward to new lands where they began as strangers and changed the places they found.

Almost all of us do that. We are a nation of strangers, and our suspicion when we see ourselves riding into town for the first time may reflect nothing more than an uneasiness about our own impulse to change the world constantly.

■ A MEMORY OF ROPE ■

Twenty-five years ago, when capital punishment was still a commonplace of American penology, part of a police reporter's routine included bearing witness to the official dispatch of condemned felons. In Maryland, where I was then spending nights jollying policemen, reporting knife fights and standing around accident wards listening to people die, these executions occurred frequently enough to assure every new reporter a chance to see a performance fairly early in his career.

It was almost all right to be squeamish about it, but not quite. Reporters were supposed to be hard men, equally breezy before corpses and stripteasers. The approved style was exhibited by a colleague who, when his turn came, telephoned afterwards from the death house and asked the city editor if he wanted a feature or a straight noose story.

I anticipated my turn without zest. In the nightly rounds of Baltimore, I had learned to gaze on death in a variety of unpleasant shapes without screaming, but in all those instances society had been mobilized to fight it. I had no stomach for watching society mobilized to assure its victory. I was a bit ashamed of this weakness.

The older policemen assured me it was a rare entertainment, and not to be missed. They were, as a class, miffed about no longer being allowed to attend en masse. They talked nostalgically of the old days when they were permitted to make it a bottle party and to stand under the gallows cheering the miscreant's embarkment for the beyond.

I doubted that I could cheer. As my turn approached, I studied the business, and self-doubt increased.

At that time, execution was by hanging in Maryland. It was always done at midnight in a high, narrow, white-washed room in the penitentiary, a forbidding, turreted rock pile squatting in a scrofulous section of Baltimore.

The fellow to be hanged—I never heard of a woman receiving the Criminal Court's supreme accolade—was paraded onto a platform set high up in one wall, draped with a hood, then draped with a noose, then dropped through a trap door, whence he emerged to dangle in full view of the spectators until pronounced dead by a doctor using a stethoscope to detect heartbeat.

The ungenerous dimensions of the chamber—it was parlor-size in length and breadth—made for extraordinary intimacy between guests and the state's principals, both live and dead.

My reluctance was intensified by reports of the incompetence rampant in the Maryland hanging department. One evening a client due to hang at midnight slashed his throat with a rusty razor blade an hour beforehand, inducing a heated bureaucratic wrangle about whether the law required him to be brought out and hanged anyhow. Fortunately for the more delicate witnesses, the man bled to death before the issue could be resolved in Draconian terms.

The hangman, of course, was an amateur. Even at the rate Maryland was then working its gallows, it was hard for a hangman to get enough practice to do the job professionally. Consequently, a certain percentage of his clients failed to receive professional neck fractures when they dropped. These failed works hung there —before the mantlepiece, as it were—gurgling and choking for 15 or 20 minutes. On occasion, prison guards might seize them by the knees and pull down forcefully to speed the evening along.

I saw no way of escaping this ordeal without some loss of manhood, and when my turn came at last, it was the worst of all possible possibilities. There was not just one to be hanged, but three. Maryland often hanged by the batch, though not as a regular pastime, and when it did it hanged them serially, not all together, but one after the other.

At that time, I had a junior colleague who fancied himself as tough a reporter as ever blew smoke rings in a police captain's face, though he had been only eight months in the trade. The impending triple feature at the death house, he gave everybody to know, was the most enviable assignment of the year. Being so enthusiastic about it, somebody suggested he ought to ask me if I was willing to sacrifice my turn.

I told him he was asking too much of friendship, but, as he had frequently entertained me with blended whisky and potato chips, I would be deficient in gratitude if I did not oblige him.

He went to the triple. It was his first, of course, and it was a brutally long midnight. Only one man died gracefully. The hangman botched one so badly that he needed the guards hanging on him for extra weight to get him into kingdom come.

My colleague was sick immediately afterwards, and off and on for several days after that, and had bad dreams for months when his stomach had recovered.

He later became an influential assistant to the Governor of Maryland, and for eight years the Governor never signed a death warrant, and Maryland's gallows trap flapped no more. I was promoted from police stations to listening to after-dinner speakers before my next turn came around.

MOSEYING AROUND

We went to the country and acquired 17 acres of farmland. My respect for farmers has been increasing ever since.

"What are you planning to grow on that land?" an official person inquired at the time of the transaction. "Chickens," I said, without knowing why. A few days earlier in Manhattan I had been walking through Abingdon Square and saw a man washing a plucked chicken in a drinking fountain. This had left a powerful impression. It seemed like something you could build a musical comedy on, and I had chickens on the mind, though actually I haven't the foggiest idea of how to grow chickens.

"Chickens aren't grown on 17 acres anymore," said the official person. "Nowadays chickens are manufactured in broiler factories."

I must have looked too stunned to go on because my interrogator glanced up impatiently and said, "I'll put down hay," and filled in the blank where the crop was to be specified with the single word "Hay."

Freed to survey my domain, I strolled over the field envisioning amber waves of hay rippling in the summer breeze. The neighboring farmer moseyed over to pass the time of day. I had already noticed that when you're a farmer you have to do a lot of moseying, and I tried to mosey over toward him, but made a mess of it, and I could tell he knew I had a lot to learn about moseying.

After neighborly greetings he asked, "What kind of crop you thinking of putting in?"

"Hay," I said. "This time next summer this whole field will be rippling with amber waves of hay."

"You want amber waves, you'd better put in wheat," he said.

"With wheat you get those amber waves of grain. With hay, about all you're going to get is grasshoppers."

I didn't let on that he was telling me anything I didn't know, but he had given me quite a start. I suddenly realized I knew absolutely nothing about hay, except that you have to make it while the sun shines.

Now this, if you have just turned your hand to farming, is a depressing realization. How can you call yourself a farmer if you know nothing about hay? I have heard about hay all my life, of course, and have often been called a hayseed. But while farmers all over the world knew hay as well as I knew the New York subway system, I hadn't the slightest notion of how to make the stuff.

If you are the new farmer on the block, this is not the kind of confession you make publicly. It's out of the question to walk around among the neighbors, even if you're good at moseying, and say, "Tell me a little something about hay. Do you have to plant hay or does hay just come if you leave the field alone?"

Not wanting to be the joke of the community, I decided to study up on hay at the library when I got back to town, which I was mighty eager to get back to after talking with the man who had agreed to make livable quarters out of the old cabin on the property.

I had entertained fine rustic fantasies about life in that old cabin, rising at dawn to the rooster's crowing, enjoying an invigorating shower and a robust pot of black coffee before moseying out in my hip boots to start the day's making of the hay.

"How are you planning to get the water for the shower and the coffee?" asked the builder.

"We'll put in one of those tin shower stalls and a sink," I explained.

"So what kind of water are you going to use?"

"Whatever kind of water comes out when we turn on the faucet."

"Look," he said, "we put in the shower, we put in the sink, we turn the faucet, and you know what? No water is going to come out unless you've dug a well and tied into it."

"You mean the water doesn't just come?"

"I never heard of the water just coming," he said. "The well will cost you a pile, but maybe you can save a few thousand by installing a pump that will get water up from a spring, if you've got a spring, but of course it can always go dry on you."

"In New York," I said, "if you want to wash a plucked chicken you just take it to a public park, hold it over a drinking fountain, step on the pedal, and the water just comes."

"Speaking of New York," he said, "you'll have to spring for a bundle to put in a septic field for your sewage."

"You mean, when you flush, the sewage doesn't just go?"

"Not without a septic field. The only thing that just goes down here is money."

I am back in New York, not in defeat, but only to make enough hay to pay for the realization of my dream and to take moseying lessons at Lincoln Center. Any tips on hay of the vegetable variety will be gratefully received if mailed in plain brown wrapper.

A PATCH IN TIME

We went south to Virginia. There had been a death in the family, a death everyone was prepared for. She was the last of the generation born between 1881 and 1905, a child in the age of the horse and buggy, a vital young woman when the Charleston was the rage of the ballroom and, finally, a sole survivor crushed in spirit by the onset of blindness.

Afterwards we stayed a few days in the village where she had been born. It seemed a good place to pause for a few beats and try to make sense of things. Once in a while you ought to pause and try to make sense of things, and this is almost impossible to do in the city. The city hates pauses. The city cherishes loud racket, cunning and sudden outbursts of wit and fury, none of which is conducive to making sense of things.

So instead of speeding back up the turnpikes, we stayed and weeded the raspberry patch. Weeding conditions were ideal. The weather had been blowing up from the south for several days, and even though it was much too early for spring, nobody had told spring it was too early. The breezes were soft, the sun was genial.

In that part of the world, people used to talk of Nature being "on her high horse" when she was carrying on like an unruly brat instead of obeying protocol. Well, Nature had been on her high horse for months, what with an August that was more like October, a winter that had hardly been cold enough to freeze the ground and, now, this mellow May in February.

There had been the big snow back there a couple of weekends ago, and a lot of it was still on the ground, but the earth underneath was soft and muddy. Ideal for weeding.

The raspberry patch is a terror in the summer after the fruit comes off. The canes grow long as buggy whips and sprout pointed little spikes sharp enough to shred your overalls.

Plants root deep in a summer soil so dense you need a plow to break it and so rich that leaving the weeds unpicked for three days will give you a crop waist deep. After you pick the fruit, the best thing to do about the raspberry patch is walk around it without looking.

Now though, in this premature spring it yielded happily to civilizing husbandry. Working up and down the rows of canes, we pulled dry dead reeds, some of them six feet high, which came out of the wet earth as easily as the berries come off the canes in early summer.

As the sun rose higher we took off our sweaters and worked with arms bared. "The best thing," said the person helping me, "is that at this time of year you don't have to worry about snakes."

"And there aren't any gnats to chew on you," I said.

We had come to pause and make sense out of things, and that

was the only kind of sense we were making, but it seemed very satisfying. We seemed ready to be satisfied with very little in the way of sense.

Mornings, rising with the first sun pouring through uncurtained windows made satisfying sense, though we favor sleeping late in the city. Down there it seemed important to get outside and feel the crusted snow crunch underfoot before the sun resumed melting it.

Bedtime made satisfying sense, too. The nights were mild enough to sleep with windows open and, lying in bed, we could watch Orion and a fattening moon glide imperceptibly toward the mountain behind the raspberry patch.

"Orion sets early at this time of year," I explained to my wife one night. "It has to make way for the constellations of summer."

Lecturing on freshman astronomy is a vice of mine, which the family tolerates but does not encourage, so I went to sleep instead of making profound sense of Orion's travels.

We slept in a room that could be reached only by ladder. The next night when I started up, a wave of pain sprang through my knee joint and I cried out.

"Hurt yourself?" someone asked.

I hadn't. The knee had just complained suddenly with no justification at all about being bent to climb a ladder. It was not a knee accustomed to rising with the first sun or to weeding raspberry patches.

"It's just age catching up with me," I said, continuing up the ladder despite a jolt at each rung.

We were guests in that house of a generation born between 1950 and 1960. It was embarrassing to have them find you were vulnerable to aching knees. To them, after all, we were now the family's senior generation who claimed rightful place at the head of the table and, well, everyone knows that knees are the first to go.

In bed we watched Orion moving out to make way for the stars of summer and I was tempted to murmur something about how necessary it was and how easy to clear the raspberry patch when the weeds were dry and reedy, but didn't do it. Fortunately, my wife becomes impatient with philosophical insights that would bore a college freshman.

MAKING IT

When I go back to my hometown with my world-weary New York eyes and my expensive New York teeth the folks always look at me in that sly superior country way. That's partly because they're country people and my hometown—Morrisonville, Va.—is a country town, nestled as it is three miles south of metropolitan Lovettsville and two miles north of Wheatland, which is not a town at all but just a sign on the side of the road.

Partly though, it's also because of Frank Sinatra, whose voice reaches everywhere, even to Morrisonville, with his musical paean to New York City, a song that says if a person can "make it there" he can "make it anywhere."

I've noticed that dyed-in-the-wool New Yorkers—maybe I should call them spray-painted-in-the-subway New Yorkers—always look as if they're having a hard time keeping from patting themselves on the back when Frank sings this song. It seems to make them feel like heroic achievers, especially the way Frank phrases it with those big notes on the "make it" lines.

Morrisonville people don't seem to respond the same way. Truth is, if they weren't such sweet people, I'd say their response is an inner sneer. I first detected this a few weeks ago when Lester, with the big house down by the creek, asked if I was "making it up there in New York."

Since my idea of "making it" in New York is not getting run down by a bicyclist or a car running a red light, I said, "Guess so, Lester."

"Just what is it you're making?" he asked.

"Well, you know, day by day—getting by—I'm making it O.K."

"Sure, but making what?"

Was Lester pulling my beautifully tailored New York leg?

"I heard the man sing that if you can make it in New York you can make it anywhere," he said. "And Morrisonville is just about as close to anywhere as you can get. Whatever it is you're making in New York, I'd sort of like you to make some right here."

"It's just a song, Lester. You know songs are silly."

He went off to make hay, after pointing out that though he could make hay right there in Morrisonville nobody ever claimed that if you could make hay there you could make it anywhere, for the simple reason that though hay was very easy to make in much of the country, even those who made it best wouldn't be able to make it in downtown Los Angeles, if there was such a place.

In this I detected a gentle rustic contempt for my suave New York worldliness. True, I couldn't make hay in Morrisonville because I didn't know the recipe, but on the other hand Lester probably couldn't navigate the Union Square subway station without getting lost. I let it pass.

On the next visit, however, I encountered the ghost of my Uncle Bruce outside the ruins of my grandmother's house in the very spot where he used to hide his moonshine behind the lime barrel and he, too, had been listening to Frank Sinatra.

Uncle Bruce, who had lived and died in Morrisonville, was in an uncharacteristically melancholy mood. "Guess you're making it up there in New York, boy," he said.

"Getting along. Day by day. Paying the rent. Keeping the spray paint off my Sunday suit," I said.

"I did that much right here in Morrisonville," he said, "and it was hard toil. Of course, I wouldn't say I was making it. Then, on the other hand, it wasn't easy to make it in Morrisonville. That's what grinds me every time I hear Sinatra sing that song."

"How does a ghost hear, Uncle Bruce?"

"What that song should say, if the writer knew anything," he said, ignoring my question, "is that making it in New York is a lark beside trying to make it in Morrisonville."

"I always thought it ought to be about Baltimore," I said. "Compared to Baltimore, New York is a piece of cake. If you can make it in Baltimore, you can make it anywhere."

"Lord o' mercy, boy, I used to think that just getting to Baltimore would be making it. But Mama always told me, 'Bruce, you stay right here in Morrisonville and test yourself, because if you can make it in Morrisonville, you can make it anywhere.'"

Why are you talking to yourself?" asked my cousin Ruth Lee, who had wandered around from across the road. "Is that the way you make it?"

"Don't make fun of us New Yorkers, Ruth Lee," I said. "I understand how you feel, what with it being so hard for you to make it here in Morrisonville."

Goodness gracious," she said. "Morrisonville is a picnic compared to Wheatland. If you can make it in Wheatland you can make it anywhere."

URBAN GOTHIC

BEASTLY MANHATTAN

After moving to Manhattan I bought a camel. I did not want a camel, but in Manhattan it was absolutely vital to own an animal of some sort, and of all the animal kingdom a camel seemed to me the most sensible sort to own.

It is peaceable, requires infrequent feeding, affords basic transportation and makes very little noise. If one must have an animal in a place like Manhattan, and it seemed that one must, a camel seemed the least troublesome choice. So I bought a camel.

This did not sit well with New Yorkers. New Yorkers are partial to dogs, which they harbor in all sizes and shapes, keeping them imprisoned most of the day in tiny apartments and bringing them out morning and evening to evacuate on sidewalks and streets.

The dogs vary from mammoth beasts capable of consuming a policeman in three bites to creatures no larger than mice, and come in a startling variety of forms. There is one breed that resembles a woman's wig. The first time I saw one at the curb on Second Avenue, I undertook to retrieve it for its owner, mistaking it for an escaped wig, before I discovered that it had four legs and was being walked.

At that time I had no animal at all, and New Yorkers viewed me with that distaste which the animal lover cannot conceal for the beastless man. When the camel was delivered, I looked forward with satisfaction to the approving smiles they would shed upon us both—me and my camel—at the spectacle of man and beast in harmonious communion.

This approval was never granted. To the contrary. There was undisguised hostility toward the camel. The landlord, who kept a pair of boxers big enough to kick a camel to death, protested the camel's size.

The neighbors complained that the camel, which at first I kept at the curb, took up a precious parking space, and I soon had to bring him into the apartment, which depressed both of us—the camel because he couldn't get comfortable on the couch, me because the camel kept wandering into the dining room at the dinner hour and wolfing the salad.

Walking the camel put strains on neighborly relations. In Manhattan, the custom is to walk your animal around the corner or into the next block and pretend to be studying a distant horizon while he surreptitiously fouls someone else's turf.

New Yorkers understand this about dogs and make no protest. They live by the dog owner's code. You foul my shoes; I foul yours. But the sight of a poor camel ambling around the corner to do as the dogs do incensed them. The owners of the neighborhood's fiercer man-eating mastiffs would threaten to unleash their pets on the camel if he persisted in using the asphalt sacred to canines.

I saw that I was not winning New Yorkers with my love of animals and that they thought me eccentric for not preferring a dog that looked like a wig, a giant hound that could tear the mailman to shreds or even a cat that would claw the upholstery to ribbons.

Determined to gain their respect, I tried to teach the camel tricks of the sort that captivate dog lovers. I attempted to teach the camel to howl in the night, but that was useless.

I did succeed, however, in teaching him to leap enthusiastically against visitors and slobber over their neckties. I even trained him to issue something that sounded vaguely like a menacing growl, suggesting that he was preparing to sink his teeth into the thigh of any guest heartless enough not to be a totally devoted camel lover.

I taught him to wag his tail and, with one bound across the room, pounce happily into the lap of anyone who was elegantly dressed. And when he had mastered all these endearing tricks, I invited neighbors to visit.

The camel performed faithfully, although he was clearly bored and thought that humans must be an asinine bunch to require such arch displays from beasts. The neighbors were not warmed.

The man on whose necktie the camel slobbered lost his temper, the woman at whom the camel growled menacingly left, threatening to have me before the magistrates for harboring an unleashed camel.

The man in whose lap the camel triumphantly pounced with wagging tail has filed a suit claiming mental pain and suffering.

The camel, whose sensitivity was at least as great as the average dog's, was crestfallen at our failure to win the neighbors' affection and respect. I was quite touched by his despondency, so much so, in fact, that I hesitated to get rid of him after the fiasco.

Accordingly, I made him an offer. With surgical removal of the identifying hump, I suggested, he could easily pass for a dog in the bizarre pound that was New York, and immediately win the heart of all Manhattan. The camel had nothing to lose except his hump, and shortly afterwards New Yorkers were delightedly letting him nuzzle their neckties, and void thunderously on their doorsteps.

I sold him to a dog lover for a very good price, never having believed that a city is a fit place to keep a dog.

THOSE
PRUSSIAN WHEELS

For a long time I was bullied by New York taxicabs. Leaping into one of those yellow rattlers, I would feel an overpowering urge to rest tired legs on a jump seat and a fierce black-lettered sign would snap at me:

"Keep Feet Off Jump Seats."

Or, having just arm-wrestled some 200-pound brute for the last available taxi in town during a rainy rush hour, I would feel the need to unwind with a smoke.

"No Smoking!" would come the printed command.

Arrogant, yes. Outrageous? Surely. Surely it was outrageous that this machine, which was about to extract an unreasonable sum of money from my wallet for a ludicrously short journey, should nevertheless insist on treating me as if I were a miserable draftee in the Prussian Army.

Yet I lacked the courage to assert the Helsinki Human Rights Convention against its autocratic authority. Or possibly I was too busy digging into wallet for the fare, in obedience to the command that said, "Have Fare Ready At Destination."

What would the taxi do if the fare were not ready at destination? Nothing grave. I was certain of that, for most taxis were so asthmatic and rheumatoid that they could scarcely run a cobbled block without wheezing a couple of bolts. Still, they had a presence that was menacing. I always had my fare ready at destination.

Once when I was late for a plane I jumped into a cab while carrying a duck à l'orange and a bottle of champagne, planning to dine on my way to Kennedy Airport.

The salivary glands had scarcely started to pump when a sign, in a tone more appropriate to the Wicked Witch of the West than an ancient and spavined taxi, roared, "No Eating Or Drinking In This Cab!"

I had fare ready at destination. Fortunately there was no sign that said, "Wipe Bills Free of Duck Grease Before Paying."

In those days I lacked the New Yorker's gift of lip. The taxicabs snarled at me and I did not snarl back, but gradually I became hardened, tough, assertive. I began having signs of my own printed up.

The first said, "No Rock Music Played In This Cab." Some drivers obeyed it; others defied it. If they defied it, I put my feet on the jump seat and smoked.

There were enough successes to encourage me to acquire new signs. "No Complaints About Previous Passenger's Lousy Tip" was a big success. So was "No Running Red Lights When Fire Engines Are Approaching From Left Or Right."

"Driver Required To Change $20 At Destination" angered many taxicabs, for it challenged their own declaration on making change, which said, "Driver Not Required To Change More Than $5." Why the taxicabs persisted in this antique reverence for the $5 bill was a mystery, for inflation had long since rendered the $20 bill almost as commonplace as the quarter.

There was certainly no reluctance among the taxicabs occasionally to demand the stouter part of a $20 bill when the trip felt suspiciously short. Questions to the driver at such times elicited the information that the taxicab was a hot-blooded beast whose pulsing meter often insisted on racing wildly out of control, possibly because of the excitement of vaulting New York's storied potholes.

I had another sign printed to hand the taxicab on these occasions. It said, "Loose Talk Sinks Ships—Fast Meters Lose Tips."

One night I hailed a taxi which had not the least idea how to get to my destination. This required me to lean over the driver's seat in defiance of the cab's orders ("Sit Back To Avoid Injury") yelling, "Right, right, again, left here, left again, right, right . . ." and so forth.

At one intersection I had to yell "Left!" three times. The driver asked if I thought him a fool. One "left" was all he needed, he said. Why did I treat him like an idiot? Why did everyone treat him like an idiot?

He was near tears. I apologized. He told me his life story. He hated taxis, wanted to move to the Riviera with a girl. Both of them would model jeans. You think I am making this up? If so, you do not know the taxicabs of New York, especially at night.

He touched me so that I wanted to comfort him and therefore overtipped, hating myself afterward. That's when I started distributing a new sign. It said, "No Whining."

Another night I cramped myself into the front seat of a tiny cab whose master was writing a novel. He, too, hated taxicabs and dreamed of being a musician.

As we raced down the gloomy corridor of Ninth Avenue at midnight, I asked what his novel was about.

"About a frustrated musician who has to drive a taxicab for a living and becomes a psychopathic killer," he said.

I had fare ready at destination, which was the very next red light, and walked a mile home composing a new sign. It said, "No Psychotic Violence In This Cab," but I am still uneasy about trying it out.

THE FAR
SIDE OF STYX

When Francisco Franco died he went to the New York Department of Motor Vehicles.

At the entrance he addressed a man who was dreaming of quitting time. "My name is Francisco Franco," he said.

"Start at Window One," said the man, who could not have cared less if he had been speaking to Wolfgang Amadeus Mozart. He had, in fact, sent Mozart to Window One two centuries ago.

Francisco Franco went to Window One and waited at the end of a long line. When he got to the front he said, "My name is Francisco Franco."

"I need your Defunct Certificate, a notarized form from your last place of residence stating that all your tax bills have been paid and your burial number," said the clerk.

"What is a Defunct Certificate?" asked Francisco Franco.

"Go to Room 111," commanded the clerk. "Next!"

Francisco Franco went to Room 111. A large crowd of people sat on benches waiting for someone to think of them. After two years, Francisco Franco was called to a desk.

"I seem to need a Defunct Certificate," he said.

"So what am I supposed to do about it?" the clerk demanded.

"I was told to come to Room 111," said Francisco Franco.

"It's not my fault they don't know what they're doing downstairs," said the clerk. "They should have sent you to Window Seven. Next!"

Francisco Franco went downstairs to Window Seven and fell into line behind a man in silk knickers and powdered wig.

"Aren't you Wolfgang Amadeus Mozart?" Francisco Franco asked.

"No," said the man. "Mozart is still back at Window Five. I'm Alexander Hamilton."

The angry voice of the clerk at Window Seven interrupted further conversation. "Anybody else who hasn't got a statement of resale value of real property is wasting my time in this line unless he's been to Window Four," the clerk bawled.

Francisco Franco went to Window Four.

"Please give me a statement of the resale value of Franco Spain," he told the clerk.

"Do you have a stamped copy of Form 3774?" asked the clerk.

"What is that?" asked Francisco Franco.

"That," said the clerk, "is proof that you have been to Window Nine. No one may apply to Window Four without first having appeared at Window Nine. Next!"

Francisco Franco went to Window Nine. "Francisco Franco," he said. "I am making the required appearance at Window Nine. Will you be good enough to give me a stamped Form 3774 so that I may go to Window Four and obtain a statement of the resale value of Franco Spain to take to Window Seven in order to receive a Defunct Certificate so that I can begin at Window One?"

"Can't you see I'm busy eating lunch?" the clerk replied, slamming down the window.

Francisco Franco's cool temper snapped. He decided to make a complaint. He went to the Information booth. "Where do I register a complaint?" he asked.

"Room 217," said the clerk.

Francisco Franco went to Room 217 and sat on a wooden bench beside a pathetic, defeated man.

"Francisco Franco," he said.

"Attila the Hun," said the pathetic, defeated man. "What century is it?"

Francisco Franco said he thought it was the twenty-first or twenty-second century, and a young woman clerk came over and announced that anyone who did not have a Complaint Authorization form approved by the Commissioner would have to go to Window Two.

Francisco Franco went to Window Two and stood in line. A policeman came down the line. "Let me see your line permit," he said.

Francisco Franco asked what a line permit was.

"The document granting permission to stand in line at Window Two," he said.

Francisco Franco said he did not have a line permit.

"Then get one at Window Five," said the policeman.

Francisco Franco went to Window Five. "Are you Mussolini?" asked a man in a powdered wig.

"No," said Francisco Franco. "I am Francisco Franco."

"A pleasure," said the man. "I am Wolfgang Amadeus Mozart."

Francisco Franco hummed a line from "Cosi Fan Tutte," and was immediately collared by the chief clerk. "Let me see your humming license," he commanded.

"I have none," said Francisco Franco.

"You will have to get one at Window Eight or face an immediate fine," said the chief clerk. "And as for you, tunesmith," he said to Mozart, "I want to see your permit to listen to hummed music."

Triumphantly, Mozart produced his permit. "Ah ha!" cried the clerk. "This permit expired fifty years ago. Back to Window Three you go."

"Listen," said Francisco Franco to the chief clerk, "I think I get the message here and I am ready to proceed to Hell without further argument."

The chief clerk smiled an exceedingly thin smile. Its message lodged like a sliver of ice in the heart of Francisco Franco.

"You will need a Hell visa," said the clerk. "Go to Window Six."

THE LULL
IN LULLABY

When we came back from out of town, there was something wrong. I couldn't identify what was wrong, but I could feel it. "If you don't notice it," my wife said, "don't let it bother you."

"I do notice it," I said. "It's just that I can't put my finger on whatever it is I'm noticing."

Just then the house shuddered violently as a bus accelerated going up the street. "Whatever it is that's wrong, at least the house is still the same," she said.

True. The house has always shuddered when a bus goes past. The floor trembles, the chandelier tinkles and dishes rattle in the cupboard. When a bus passes, it is like living on the San Andreas fault, but the house never collapses.

Oddly, trucks don't make the house quake, though we live in an area where trucks much heavier than buses are constantly roaring up the street with thunderous munching of gears. After the bus made the house shudder I watched for the next tractor-trailer. It came past rumbling like angry artillery, and the house remained absolutely motionless.

"The trucks haven't started to shatter the house, so that's not what's wrong," I said.

"The fire department is still all right, too," my wife observed as we heard the first siren screaming at us from a mile away.

"And whoever is always pulling the false alarms at the box around the corner is also still all right," I said, as a pumper, two hook-and-ladder trucks, a fire department van and two police cars bombarded us with siren blasts, turned the corner and stood there panting until somebody told them it was a false alarm.

Bedtime was approaching. "Maybe it's the drunks from the

restaurant across the street. Maybe that's what's wrong," I said.

There was only one way to find out. Well tucked in, we fell asleep. Ten minutes afterward the street below filled with high-spirited roars of joviality interspersed occasionally with shrieked obscenities. Diners had come out to their cars and, as they always did, they were doing their 20-minute stints of shouting on the sidewalk to awaken the neighborhood.

"There's nothing wrong with the drunks," I said, when they had finally departed. Finally, deep worried slumber. What was it that had gone wrong in the neighborhood during our absence?

We were both awakened by the shattering metallic clang of a battleship hitting the sidewalk after falling off a four-story build-ing. The shock of the noise lifted me several feet out of bed. As I descended I murmured, "Whatever's wrong here doesn't in-volve the steel shutters on the restaurant across the street. They still let them drop precisely 20 minutes after you've gone back to sleep following the sidewalk uproar of the drunks."

Two hours later, more reassurance. Pretty close to her regular time, the woman who screams came into the street around the corner and started up. When we first came to the neighborhood we thought she was being murdered, but after several middle-of-the-night street searches in slippers and robe I never found a body or even a larynx and concluded that screaming at about 3 A.M. was simply her contribution to neighborhood routine.

"Whatever is wrong, it's not with the woman who screams," I said.

"It's not with the jackhammers next door either," my wife said at 8 A.M. when the jackhammers next door started making the bed shake.

We're very proud of having jackhammers next door to wake us at 8 o'clock. There aren't many New York neighborhoods that supply jackhammers next door to make sure you don't oversleep after being up half the night with the noises that reassure you all's right with your world.

At breakfast, though, the eerie sense of something wrong came back as a passing bus shook the coffee out of my cup. Then, the moment of discovery: "Did you notice what we didn't hear when that bus went by?"

"Great fire-breathing Beelzebub! You're right," cried my wife. We rushed to the window. It was gone. The huge warped steel plate that had been used to cover a hole in the street—it was gone. When it was there, every passing car, bus and truck that struck it smashed the thick metal edge down onto a manhole cover with a reverberating, vibrating clang powerful enough to loosen wisdom teeth from their roots.

Hadn't we lived with it for years, or did it just seem like years because our wisdom teeth had started to fall out since its placement? Now it was gone. In its place was an asphalt patch that produced only a feeble "thump-thump."

"It's time we moved on," I told my wife. "They're ruining the neighborhood."

SUCH NICE PEOPLE

This is New York.

Fellow parks his car at the curb. Sometimes he parks around the corner, sometimes across the street, sometimes right under your window.

Locks all the doors. Locks the gas cap. Walks away. I don't know where he goes. Parking spots are hard to find in Manhattan, so he probably goes someplace a half-mile, a mile, two miles away.

Chances are he'll be gone until 4 o'clock tomorrow morning. Maybe he'll be gone all night, even though the New Jersey plates on his car might make you think he'd have to get back across the river before sunup. Don't let the Jersey tags give you hope, though.

Half the car owners in New York sport Jersey plates. It's another way of beating New York's back-breaking tax structure. So maybe the parker with Jersey tags is headed off to his apartment crosstown for a night's sleep.

If you're an out-of-towner, you're thinking, "The poor dolt! Parking his car on a street in New York like that—there won't be anything left of it when he comes back."

The reason you think this is that, as an out-of-towner, you have been overstuffed with tales of New York as a center of rampant crime. You are thinking wrong.

This New York tax swindler with the Jersey plates is not worried about felons getting at his car. No sir. He has equipped his car with an automobile burglar alarm.

Anybody touches that car, the burglar alarm is going to let go with an ear-piercing howl that can penetrate six thicknesses of brick wall over a three-block radius. Everybody for blocks around is instantly going to know the car is being touched. The thief is going to vamoose at full speed.

Very clever, you say? Not if you're a New Yorker. If you're a New Yorker, you know it's not clever at all. It's diabolical.

Because what happens is that once the burglar alarm starts to howl, it continues to howl even after the thief has left the neighborhood. Its howl is a single, sustained, high-pitched note that can not only slice through brick walls but can also drill into the nerve and bone of every resident within range.

Usually this ordeal lasts 20 or 30 minutes, though I experienced one case in which it lasted four hours. After enduring it for an hour, I fled the neighborhood and went to a movie, and it was still howling when I returned.

Sometimes the police come. If the car has been shrieking for 15 minutes, I'm told, they can legally break in and disconnect the alarm, but New York cops have more urgent duties than listening to a car scream for a quarter of an hour. Anyhow, the one time I phoned for relief, the men who showed up, finding the car locked, said there was nothing they could do, apologized and sped off on radio orders to deal with graver matters.

In your town—in most towns, I dare say—you would know how to deal with a car that parked under your window and proceeded to carry on for hours like a factory whistle. Perhaps a convention of suffering neighbors after swearing an oath of silence in case of police inquiries will commission someone to take an iron bar to the car window, then open the door and rip out the wiring.

Maybe the entire community, outraged by the suggestion that a car must be permitted to tyrannize an entire society, will fall upon the automobile and beat it with broom handles and steel bars until its howl is reduced to a hoarse whimper.

Yes, of course it's unjust that 2,000 innocent, law-abiding citizens should suffer torment while the principals in the case—the car owner and the thief—curl up happily in bed or bar, far from the agony for which they are responsible.

And yet, in New York we do not behave badly toward the offending car. In New York, you see, despite what you have heard, we are gentle people. We sit patiently under rivers in the darkness of disabled subways and do not riot. We step silently over the nuisances committed on sidewalks by persons who treat the whole world as their personal toilet, and keep our faces impassive, civilized.

When we are assaulted by howling parked cars we may throw up our windows and stare, or even walk onto the sidewalk and join a neighbor in smiling complaint, but no one—no one—would dare seek relief by putting a fire ax to hood or windshield. Sooner or later, we know, the owner will always return, unlock his car, turn off the alarm and smile a thin smile at us.

The more daring among us may assay a slight frown. Nothing more. We are all under tight control of ourselves here.

In a city like this our self-control must be tight. Very tight. So we are gentle. Civilized. Quivering with self-control. So often so close to murder, but always so self-controlled. And gentle.

OF DUDS, WOGS, MAE WEST ET AL.

THE
DREAMER'S PROGRESS

When I was 11 it was a very good year. I roamed the open city, carefree as a swallow and planned to rescue Miss Yaskell, who taught fifth grade, from pirate captivity. Afterward, Fiorello La Guardia would ride beside me in the ticker-tape parade up Broadway crying, "How's he doing?" John Dacey, who had blackened my eye in the schoolyard, would throw himself on the car to beg forgiveness and I would stop the parade and whip him within an inch of his life.

I was 11 and it was a very good year, except that Miss Yaskell never got captured by pirates and John Dacey caught me daydreaming in the park one day and punched my nose.

When I was 17 it was an excellent year. I dreamed of taking the beauteous Betty Ballou to the senior prom in Uncle Don's Chevrolet coupe, but didn't learn to drive in time and had to take Caroline Swigget instead on the streetcar.

"What do you want most in the world?" Caroline whispered as we waited for the streetcar home at 1 A.M. "Happiness," I said. It was an excellent year.

When I was 23 it was an extraordinary year. "You realize of course that you'll never make any money working for this company," said Earl McAdoo, the first tycoon I had ever met, "but the experience will be invaluable."

"Money!" I cried. "Do you reckon me so unworthy that I can aspire to nothing more valuable than money?" The steely eyes of McAdoo watered and the tight fist clasped my hand. "What is work worth if it compensate a man not with experience?" I asked. When I was 23 it was an extraordinary year.

When I was 29 it was a truly splendid year. "Have you found happiness yet?" asked Caroline Swigget as I took her home one night on the streetcar.

"Caroline," I said, "you want perfume and pearls. You will never find them with me." Yes, I had seen that happiness was a childish bauble, had learned that experience is worthless unless transmuted into art, had abandoned the steely-eyed McAdoo and committed myself to the creation of a novel that would leave Edmund Wilson flabbergasted.

"Will it be more like James Joyce, Marcel Proust or Herman Wouk?" asked Caroline. "I haven't decided that yet," I told her. It was a truly splendid year.

When I was 33 it was an astonishing year. I took my completed novel to the hottest literary agency in New York, The Beauteous Betty Ballou Ten Percent Corporation Ltd. Betty rode in limousines and her hair came undone in the wind tunnel created by the Time & Life Building as she changed from her Cadillac to her Continental.

"Your novel," she said, "must be a work of genius since I would be too embarrassed to show it to any publisher in town. Come see me when you've done something a little more Mickey Spillane."

"Betty," I whispered, "Betty, think of fame. Some day when both of us are gone the world will discover this novel and say, 'But for the grit of Betty Ballou, genius would have sunk without a trace.'"

"Poor dreamer," she murmured, and kissed my cheek as she changed to her Mercedes limousine. It was an astonishing year.

When I was 44 it was an absolutely glorious year. I would take Caroline Swigger home on the streetcar, and she would say, "If I get off and walk the last five blocks, maybe somebody will try to mug me and you can fulfill your childhood dream of heroism by rescuing me." And I would say, "Can it, Caroline. I'm 44 years old."

When I was 46——. "Marry me," she would say, "and fulfill your youthful dream of happiness." And I would say, "I have an embarrassing confession to make, Caroline. I still haven't learned to drive. I wouldn't be able to get you home with the groceries from the supermarket."

When I was 49 it was a very mediocre year. The last streetcar had been destroyed by the highway-and-bus lobby and Caroline had bought a car.

"If we got married," she would say, "I would let you practice driving my car and you would fulfill your youthful ambition for experience." And I would say, "Caroline, Caroline. I'm 49 years old for God's sake. I don't want experience, I want money."

And Caroline drove out of my life. "Where are you going?" I would ask, and she would say, "To find the dreamer who took me to the senior prom."

When I was 57 it was an absolutely breathtaking year. I would stand at the streetcar stops dreaming of the old days and Betty Ballou would ride by in limousines. "There hasn't been a streetcar here since the highway lobby captured the Congress," she would shout.

Once she came riding up Broadway in a ticker-tape parade, having just sold the rights to "The Duchess With the Mossy Sheets" for $16 million. I threw myself on her car to ask forgiveness. "Betty," I cried, "I was an idiot to hold out for fame beyond the grave. I'm 57 years old and I'm ready for the big bucks."

Betty stopped the parade and whipped me within an inch of my life.

▪ THE DUDS DOLDRUMS ▪

Men, have you ever felt the lust for shirtings? I mean, have you ever ducked into one of those high-toned haberdasheries to get out of the rain and noticed a discreet sign over in the corner—probably in Old English lettering—that said "Men's Shirtings," and felt your mouth water?

Sure you have. But you didn't go over there, did you? You didn't have the nerve to walk up to the salesman and say, "I want to buy a shirting." Of course you didn't. And for good reason, too. For one thing, you weren't sure what a shirting was. For another thing, it sounded like something so elegant that you were afraid the salesman would say that people as minimal as you weren't worthy to wear shirtings.

The other possibility was just as bad. Suppose he said, "Of course, and I have just the shirting for you—this barberpole stripe with the two-tone collar and cuffs at $75. We sell them only in lots of six."

What do you do then? Having been judged worthy of shirtings, you have the choice of paying $450 or letting everybody in the shop see that you are too cheap to deserve shirtings. Result: your mind is poisoned toward fine men's attire. You overreact, pretend that shirtings count for nothing with you, and start going around in public wearing shirts to flaunt your contempt for cutting a smart figure.

The same thing happens when you think about suitings. I was entering a men's shop to buy a scarf not long ago when I noticed a small sign in the window, in Old English lettering, that said "Men's Suitings." I turned and fled. I wasn't even wearing a shirting. Imagine the humiliation waiting inside for a man without a shirting being caught ogling a suiting.

"You're pretty good at oglings, but not much at shirtings," somebody would probably say.

Anyhow, I am still without that scarf. By the time I muster the courage to go back, they will probably have nothing but scarfings.

Speaking of which, has anybody thought of buying a jacket lately? I don't mean jacketings—those tweedy garments that go with loafers and flannel slacks and used to cost $27.50 but now go at $325. I mean those things that zipper or button down near the hip bones and have pockets for keeping mittens in and button up around the neck. Jackets. Windbreakers.

Know what they're called now?

Outerwear.

There were three advertised in the paper recently. Not badlooking jackets until you noticed that they were really outerwear, and if you think the reply to that is "So what?" I will tell you so what.

So two of those outerwears were priced at $205 and one at $220, that's so what. When a jacket turns into outerwear it can cost you the shirting right off your backing. These particular outerwears, according to the ad copy, proved "that fashion is an evolution of necessity."

The "necessity," I assume, is for the outerwear folks to rifle bank accounts of people who want to transcend time and place.

That's what these jackets were doing, according to the ad copy: "Transcending time and place."

I ask you, how often have you really wanted to transcend time and place desperately enough to pay $220 for the outerwear necessary to do the trick? Well, maybe in that haberdashery when the shirtings salesman tells you it will cost $450 to get out of there without utter humiliation.

That would give the snobby devil something to brood about. Drawing yourself up in your $220 outerwear and crying "Shazam!"—or more likely, "Transcend!"—you would rise above or go beyond the limits of, extend above or beyond, outstrip or outdo, cross or climb over, or travel upward or onward—right before his eyes.

The trouble is you are not likely to be wearing your transcending outerwear if you have ducked into the shop to escape the rain. If you were, you wouldn't have ducked in in the first place; you would simply have transcended the rain as soon as it got unpleasant and would already be standing in your kitchen mixing a drink instead of suffering the contempt of shirting salesmen.

The tendency of goods to increase their price by undergoing a name change has been observed in other fields besides clothing. Look at how costly eggs become when transferred from a place that has "Eats" painted on the window to one that says "Cuisine." In the garment field, however, the change also creates changes in human behavior.

You may have noticed that men who wear shirtings, suitings and outerwear have adopted the odd habit of wearing their scarves outside their overcoatings, as though to pamper their overcoatings rather than their necks. You don't see this kind of behavior with eggs. Whether "eats" or "cuisine," eggs are never displayed on the overcoating, but are discreetly hidden on the necktyings.

. NOW IT CAN BE TOLD .

In the literary world it is open season on the Hollywood dead, so at last I am able to speak.

Until now I have thought it indelicate to disclose that I am Mae West's twin sons. Recent literary allegations that Joan Crawford was a rotten mother, Bing Crosby a monstrous father, and Errol Flynn a homosexual Nazi agent, however, encourage me to believe that the American public is hungering for the nasty facts behind the glamorous myths. My lawyer, moreover, assures me there is no way Mae West can sue from the grave.

The truth is that the Mae West the world knew as eternal bachelorette and sex goddess was, in fact, a mother with double vision. Vanity prevented her from wearing the thick corrective lenses she needed to see the world as it was. As a result she went through life under the impression that I was twins.

She was so insistent on the point that I was well along in years before realizing that there was only one of me. I well remember her anger, when my first-grade teacher said, "No, sonny, you are not Mae West's twin sons because there is just one of you, and maybe you should tell Mommy she needs glasses," and I went home and said, "Could I say something, Mommy?"

She rolled her hips and then her eyes and said, "What's on your mind, big boys?"

And I said, "Maybe you need eyeglasses, Mommy."

"You boys are too young to know what I need, and I'm too much of a lady to tell you," she said, "but if you ever mention eyeglasses to me again I'll let W.C. Fields come over here and fill you both full of martinis."

It was always fun when W.C. Fields came over because he was

on his second thermos of martinis by the time he arrived and saw me as triplets. One night, however, he was very serious.

To Mommy he said, "Be good enough, my pet, to send your three precious lads beyond earshot, as I am here for a clandestine rendezvous."

Mommy gestured me upstairs with her thumb. "O.K., boys," she said, "get out of here and peel me a grape."

But lurking in the shadows of the stairwell, I was amazed to see the Marx Brothers file into the room. "There are only nine of you," said Fields. "I was expecting twelve."

Harpo drew Fields toward the staircase out of earshot from Mommy and I heard him whisper, "Gummo is in Washington reporting directly to President Roosevelt on the Clark Gable business."

"Have we confirmed that Gable is Hitler's direct link to Hollywood?" asked Fields.

"Stranger than that, I'm afraid," said Harpo. "Gable is taking orders straight from Mahatma Gandhi."

"I always said you couldn't trust triplets who wear mustaches," Fields muttered as I scurried up the steps to get the grape knife.

When I had prepared the grape and brought it down, Fields and the Marx Brothers were gone. Mommy was in a terrible mood. "When I ask you to peel me a grape, boys, what I want is a peeled grape. What's the big idea of peeling me two grapes? What's more, you left a piece of skin on both of 'em."

I cringed because I knew what happened when she was unhappy about the way I'd done the household chores. "For two cents I'd take you over to Joan Crawford's and make you watch while she peels the hide off her daughter," Mommy said.

As always when this threat was issued, I wept and pleaded to be sent to bed hungry. "Relax, boys," she said, "I got fancier ideas tonight. There's a big car down at the curb. I've got a feeling somebody's in it who's been wantin' to come up and see me. So just beat it, O.K., boys?"

I ran up the steps but stopped when the lights went out below and listened to Mommy settle herself on the settee, then heard the window raised. Someone came through. A man. I instantly recognized the voice in the darkened room.

"Forgive me for coming here this way, Bill, but I knew you were coming here tonight and I couldn't stay away from you another minute," said Errol Flynn.

I heard him hit the floor. Mommy was expert at jiu-jitsu. She was standing with her foot on his chest when the lights came on.

"Go down to the corner saloon and tell W.C. Fields to start running," she called to me. "Tell him the Flynn twins are in heat again, but I can keep 'em pinned down for fifteen minutes."

"Berlin shall hear of this," Flynn cried.

"I have news for you Errols," Mommy said and loosened her stays.

Flynn was speechless for the longest time. Finally: "Good Lord," he muttered, "you're . . ."

"Yes," said Mommy. "Hermann Goering."

MARRIAGE À LA MODE

In our third year of marriage my wife telephoned to ask if I would like to meet her. I did not want to meet her or anyone else. It had been seven years since I had met anybody at all, and though I had recently thought it might do me good to meet somebody—if only to see whether people still looked the way they used to—I did not want to start by meeting my wife.

One of the advantages of electronic living was that you never had to meet your wife. The man who installed my computer and television cables had harped on that. "One of its big advantages," he said, "is that you'll never have to meet your wife."

At the time, of course, I did not intend to marry. I changed my mind only after setting up my tax picture in the computer and discovering that a wife of a certain income profile would cut my tax bill by nearly 2 percent.

It was a simple matter to plug into the central information bank, obtain the names of several thousand single women in the same tax predicament and, for a small fee, have the engagement and marriage arranged by the bank.

The ceremony was performed by a minister of the Ecumenical Computer Church while I was reading the sports news in the electronic newspaper on my video terminal in New York and my bride, who lived in Oregon, was monitoring a Phil Donahue interview with three well-adjusted transsexuals on her cable TV.

At the appropriate moment I punched "I do" and "I will" into my computer, and after she did likewise I switched the computer into "check-account shopping mode" and ordered by bank to authorize an Oregon jeweler to deliver her a wedding ring.

It was exhilarating being married. To celebrate, I put on a video cassette of the Super Bowl game of 1995 and spent half the night watching the Chattanooga Data trounce the Fargo Inputs by a score of 35 to 3.

After that I forgot about being married except at tax time, when it was mighty convenient. Naturally, it was a surprise when she telephoned to propose a meeting.

I should point out that I did not answer the phone myself. I had not answered a telephone for years. I had a machine that not only answered for me, but also made calls for me. My machine, speaking in a voice entirely unlike my own, said, "I am very busy now scanning my display terminal to select a meal to be delivered to my food slot so that I will not have to be interrupted while watching the cricket test match from Pakistan on my cable television during the evening. Please state your message at the sound of the beep and my machine will process your call."

On this evening the machine said, "Your wife has telephoned to ask if you would like to meet her."

"Tell her," I told the machine, "I have not met anybody in seven years and do not propose to start now."

While the machine was transmitting the message, a noise at the door indicated that the central restaurant bank was having my dinner delivered at the food slot. Since the restaurant bank had not yet replaced all its delivery people with robots, I waited a safe interval before opening the slot, so as not to risk catching a glimpse of a human being.

This irritated my telephone machine. "You may not want to see a human being," said the machine, "but I'd like to, once in a while."

"Nonsense," I said, "you see me 24 hours a day."

"People ought to see people, ought to talk to people," said the machine.

"If God had meant people to see people, he wouldn't have created electronic living," I said. "If God wanted people to talk to people, he wouldn't have given us the telephone-answering machine."

I went to the slot to collect my dinner. Instead of a steak, I found a small electronic device. "So," I said, "they have finally succeeded in inventing the electronic steak. This ought to teach the beef trust a little humility."

I put my computer in "dining mode." Instantly the TV set activated a 1968 video cassette of "Bowling for Dollars" and presented me with a fork and a steak knife. The small electronic device spoke up. "Do not carve me," it said. "Kiss me. I am your wife and I am dying for love. At the sound of the beep, place your computer in 'osculation mode' and activate my 'input' key by framing your lips in the pursed position."

It was my telephone machine that replied. "Don't waste your time, baby," it said. "That bird has been dead for years." It uttered a highly suggestive "beep." My wife beeped back.

My wife? But I was married to a tax shelter, not to a flirting beeper. Or was I? It had been so long since I had met anybody. I thought of going to the window, raising the blinds, but I didn't. It is better not to know some things.

I sat back to enjoy "Bowling for Dollars." The telephone

machine said, "If you'd turn off that tube, machines could have a little privacy around here." I turned it off and sat in the dark. The beeping became intense.

▪ ELEPHANT'S-EYE HIGH ▪

Do you ever wish you had it all to do over again, folks? Do you wish you'd taken up the kind of work where you can call people folks, instead of Sir and Deadbeat and Big Shot and Meathead? The kind of life where you can say "By golly!" and "There's a heap of goodness in this old world of ours"?

But you didn't take that road, did you? You thought you'd be smart, get ahead, see your name up there in lights. So you went and became an airline stewardess, or a cop, maybe a fashion model so skinny you clack like a floating crap game when you walk down the street; maybe one of those systems analysts who are always saying, "Miniaturize the digital circuitry to one ten thousandth of a megahertz."

Maybe a surgeon hauling out two dozen gall bladders a day. All day long saying nothing but, "Forceps!" and "Sterilize that hemostat immediately or the south ventricle will become resected!"

It isn't all it's cracked up to be, is it? And do you know why? Because, by golly, you've lost touch with nature. Chances are your granddaddy warned you'd lose touch with nature when you told him you were going to become an airline stewardess, or cop, or fashion model.

Remember what he said? "Girl," he said, "there's a heap of goodness in this old world of ours, but all you're going to find up in those airplanes is sore feet and bunions and boozers cussing because they can't have a third martini."

"Boy," he said, "folks like us got a lot to be happy about, but if you go off to the city to pound a beat, all you're going to see of the human race is pipsqueaks, gnats and worms."

Remember where your granddaddy was sitting when he said it? In a rocking chair. Remember where the rocking chair was situated? On the porch.

You don't have a rocking chair, do you? Don't have a porch, either, I'll bet.

Well, what do you have? A cart full of coffee, tea or milk. A nightstick and a .38 caliber revolver. A cup of yogurt in the refrigerator. A few scalpels. A little digital megahertz oscillator cup. It's a long way from nature.

When June starts to roll around, it probably makes you feel like kicking yourself for ever thinking you'd like to be in the big time instead of keeping your feet in the soil. Taking out all those gall bladders may make the nurses think you're as slick as the cat's whiskers, but in your heart you know you'd rather be walking through fields of buttercups, don't you?

Why, by George, you could have been a farmer! Could be getting up these sweet mornings to slop the hogs and check out the cows for hoof and mouth disease. Could spend the whole day feeling the honest sweat on your brow while you steer the plow behind old Dobbin.

Have you ever noticed how farmers' sweat is honest? They don't have to choke their pores up with chemical sweat suppressors the way systems analysts and fashion models and surgeons have to do. That's because farmers' sweat is honest. Farmers don't have to be ashamed of it, don't have to treat it like a mad Victorian grandmother that's got to be kept locked in the attic.

How did we all get so far away from nature? "Folly and pride" granddaddy would have said. That's what my own granddaddy said many years ago, in fact, when I went up to him in his rocker on the porch and told him I was going to the city to take a job stacking groceries on a supermarket shelf.

"Folly and pride, boy," he said. "There's a heap of goodness in this old world of ours, but when you start stacking those groceries you're going to find———."

"I'm sick and tired of picking the ticks off the sheepdog, grand-daddy," I cried. "I want to make it in the big time. I want to be a star."

And what did it get me? What did it get any of us? What good is stardom if you can't call people folks anymore? If you can't see the heap of goodness there is in the world for all the digital circuits and gall bladders and coffee, tea and milk that get in your way?

And all the things we've lost: sitting on the porch swing at sunset, smelling the honeysuckle. Leaning against the silo on hot afternoons and smelling the stable. Walking through the meadow on a dewy morning and dodging the copperheads.

Compared to these, what pleasure can a body get from winning the Nobel Prize for gall-bladder removal, from cornering the silver market or dancing all night with Liza Minnelli or handing Prince Charles a cup of coffee, tea and milk.

Who among us, folks, wouldn't give up all that for the sweet delight of hoisting a pitchfork and strolling down toward the south forty while picking our teeth with a piece of hay? At least on a sunny day in June? Or maybe just for a few hours of that sunny day, in the soft of the morning, before the sun really gets up there and starts to boil your neck?

A GOTHIC TALE

It is the Dark Ages. There is nothing to do but raid monasteries and sack Rome. Mail service is abominable. Since last names have fallen into disuse, envelopes are addressed simply to Attila the Hun, Axel the Saxon, Clarence the Vandal and The Venerable Bede.

One day Otho the Ostrogoth receives a letter from Victor the Viking. It proposes that they prepare a party to pillage Paris next summer and put it to the torch. "I love Paris in the summer when it sizzles," writes Victor the Viking.

Otho the Ostrogoth sees at once that the letter is not meant for him. It is meant for Otho the Visigoth, an agent for the C.I.A. who is under deep cover as a swineherd in the Mabinogian forest.

Slipping into his halberd and pike and pausing only long enough to caution Frau Otho, the Ostrogothess, that she must hide the schnapps in the root cellar when Mongol plunderers come by, Otho tucks the letter into his bearskin robe and sets forth.

It is a hard journey to Paris. Nothing but mud for hundreds of miles, relieved only by occasional torture at the hands of the marauding forces of François the Frank. Exhausted, Otho the Ostrogoth finally pauses at Dijon for one of its famous mustard dinners and to pick up his forwarded mail.

It contains only a letter from The Reader's Digest and a subpoena commanding him to appear in Washington to testify in a Congressional investigation of the C.I.A.

The committee advises Otho that he may as well talk freely, since everything he says will be leaked to the press. "Do we correctly understand," asks the chairman, "that you are part of a C.I.A. network involved with the plan of one Victor the Viking to pillage Paris?"

Otho, of course, can do nothing but look dumb. He looks so dumb, in fact, that one Congressman is reminded of a Goth joke. "Do you know why the Goths had to close their zoo?" he asks.

"No," says Otho.

"The clam died," says the Congressman in a collapse of merriment.

Then is Otho the Ostrogoth truly infuriated. He is sick and tired of Goth jokes. Sick and tired of the whole Dark Ages and all the dumbness and sacking that goes with them. He is sick and tired of sacking Rome, sick and tired of being tortured every time you leave the hut, sick and tired of always getting other people's mail because you don't have a sensible last name.

"Gothic is beautiful!" he thunders.

Then he charges out of the hearing room and begins plundering the Capitol. This persuades the Congress that he is a lobbyist. Everyone treats him with new respect. Old-timers, awed by his forthright style with the ax, advise him of the whereabouts of the Treasury, and Otho plunders that.

Society reporters hail him as the most exciting new personality on the Washington plunder scene and political reporters say he has the charisma necessary to win the New Hampshire primary. Decent liberals hold fundraisers to finance a committee to stamp out Goth jokes, and Congressmen investigating the C.I.A. promise to listen quietly if Otho will talk to them.

His tale is simple. An honest Ostrogoth, he had been enraged at learning that Otho the Visigoth was a C.I.A. man working with the vicious Victor the Viking. It was this sort of thing that gave Goths a bad name. He, Otho the Ostrogoth, had decided to show humanity that Goths are decent honorable folks. And so, he had set out to apprise Paris that pillage impended.

Certain Congressmen are stunned. "You intended to make public classified information?" they ask.

"To publicize plots for putting Paris to the pyre," says Otho.

Otho is immediately classified secret. To prevent him from being leaked, the President has him sent home by way of England where King Alfred teaches him to burn pancakes. Later, on the road to Sussex, he is captured by a band of monks and imprisoned in a monastery where he spends the rest of his days illuminating manuscripts.

Victor the Viking's plot for pillaging Paris is canceled. Otho the Visigoth receives new orders via carrier crow. He must now become Luigi the Lombard and go to Rome. Washington has been sacked by the State Department and $800,000 must be delivered to an Italian warrior who is promising to sack Rome.

Otho the Visigoth sighs. He is bored with sacking Rome and tired of the Dark Ages. He looks at his watch and groans. The Renaissance is still 400 years away.

A LITTLE
■ SANITY, PLEASE ■

A gentleman who is all wet writes to ask why his umbrella is always missing when he has to go out in the rain. He has asked the right man. Stimulated by the late Bill Vaughan's seminal work on the history of the umbrella, I have spent years studying this curious invention and have in fact recently been elected chairman of the National Bumbershoot Academy.

In this capacity, let me point out in passing that nothing would damage America's prestige more than President Reagan's proposal to stop Federal funding of our umbrella research program. We are at present engaged in a heated race with the Russians to determine the precise age of the umbrella.

This work was a natural outgrowth of Vaughan's pioneering attempt to answer the question: Why are umbrellas never found in excavations of ancient tombs? Vaughan was torn between two theories, "one holding that the umbrella had not been invented at the time of the demise of the ancient tomb's occupant, while the opposing theory is that the umbrella had been invented but had been borrowed by a friend."

We are now on the verge of answering Vaughan's question and establishing America indisputably as Number One in bumbershoot research. If our Federal money is cut off, however, we will be unable to purchase three dozen unexcavated ancient tombs in which, we have cause to believe, there may be at least one umbrella.

For any Congressmen who may be reading this, I should note that the Russians have already bought more than 200 unexcavated ancient tombs in strategic areas of Africa and Asia. Before voting to support the President's cut, gentlemen, remember that the unexcavated-ancient-tomb gap is already dangerously wide.

But to return to our damp correspondent's question. Why is the umbrella always missing when you have to go out in the rain? The explanation was published by Selwyn Hickok in his 1937 monograph entitled "Eerie Ambulations."

Hickok amassed statistics showing that his own umbrella's curious behavior also occurred in hundreds of thousands of other umbrellas. The pattern is familiar to all. If you rise on a rainy morning and go to the closet for your umbrella, you find the umbrella gone.

Usually it has gone to the office. If you go to the office on a clear morning, however, and it rains in the afternoon and you go to the closet for your umbrella, what do you find? Your umbrella is gone. In most cases it has gone home.

From this pattern it was child's play for Hickok to deduce what was happening. When an umbrella at home realized there would be rain by morning, it went to the office. When it was loafing around the office and suddenly sensed an afternoon rain impending, it pulled itself together and went home.

The reason for this behavior baffled men for 20 years, until Spitzstein explained it in his famous First Law of Umbrellas: "Umbrellas don't like to get wet."

Profound questions remain for umbrella science to answer. How do umbrellas travel from home to office and back again? Why do they occasionally change destinations en route and drop in at a friend's house or stroll into a restaurant and disappear forever?

All questions shrink into insignificance, however, beside the awesome conclusion that flows from Hickok's and Spitzstein's work. So umbrellas don't like to get wet, and so they scurry from home to office when they know a rain is coming on. So what? So they obviously must know how to forecast weather with uncanny precision, that's so what.

The Academy believes that if we can unlock the umbrella's secret for forecasting rain, the Government can save billions by dissolving the huge, expensive United States Weather Service and buying an umbrella.

Unfortunately, the Reagan Administration ignores this opportunity to eliminate a massive money-gobbling bureaucracy by choosing to cut off the few paltry millions earmarked for the Bumbershoot Academy. Perhaps Congress will recognize this policy for what it is: penny wise and umbrella foolish.

The threat to national security must also be recognized. At present, even when not missing, the umbrella is inadequate to the vital task of defending America's generals and admirals from a driving downpour. Protecting only the head and shoulders, it allows the rain to soak the legs and feet with possibly calamitous results.

What general or admiral is up to the delicate task of strategic thinking when he feels a cold coming on? Can a man whose pants and socks are sopping wet be expected to make cool-headed decisions as H-hour approaches?

What is needed and what the academy has been working on is umbrella panties. With these, flexible ribbing and folded umbrella fabric would be built into four-star officers' trousers. At the first raindrop, ribbing and fabric would automatically flare out to form an umbrella around the hip line, and generals and admirals would stay dry all the way to the feet.

If Congress cares a fig for national security, it will not let this great weapon for peace be sacrificed to the budget slashers. Remember, Congress, you are deciding between catastrophe and survival. Umbrellas can make the difference.

▪ CRANK AT THE BANK ▪

When I took my money to the bank, the man said they would take good care of it and gave me a toaster. That should have been ample warning. I even mentioned it when I got home.

"I don't like banks giving away toasters," I said. "It reminds me too much of Dish Night at the movies during the Depression when theaters gave away cups and saucers." Being American, I regard money as sacred and the bank as its temple, and temples should not be handing out toasters when sacred offerings are made.

Besides, I didn't need a toaster. "You wouldn't be whining if they'd given you a new car," said Granddad, who had dropped in to gloat about a legal tax swindle he was conducting by buying and selling cattle.

The old gentleman had me there, but of course the bank couldn't afford to give me a car. "That would cost $7,000 or more," I pointed out.

"When it comes to money, you're about the biggest fool God ever sent down the pike," said Granddad. "All you've got to do to make the bank give you a car is borrow half a billion dollars or so, then tell them you can't pay it until you get reorganized, and to do that you need a car. If you tell them you drink too much and might kill yourself before you can get up the half-billion, they'll even give you a chauffeur to drive it for you."

Granddad does not share my sacred view of money and banks, you see. This is why he was not shocked when I read him the stunning news that bank lobbyists had handed out $3,425,969 to campaigning congressmen in 1981 and 1982.

"Everybody else is buying votes in Washington nowadays," he said. "Why shouldn't the banks?"

I hate to hear Granddad talking such cynical nonsense, so I straightened him out by reading from The New York Times. "It says right here, 'Many members of Congress assert that contributions from political action committees do not influence their votes,' " I read, "and furthermore it says these lobbies 'object vigorously to allegations that their large contributions have enabled them to influence votes.' "

"When it comes to politics, you're about the biggest fool God ever sent down the pike," said Granddad.

Ignoring the old gentleman's cynical aspersions on the democratic process, I studied details of the Times story and did some arithmetic. As nearly as I could figure—the statistics were a little confusing—banks had given 482 senators and representatives a total of $3,425,969.

This worked out to an average of $7,107.82 per public servant.

I confronted my bank with these figures next day. "When I handed you my money," I told the man, "you said you would take good care of it and gave me a toaster."

"For a sum as small as you deposited, I think a toaster was quite generous," he said.

"I think it was quite generous of me to hand you my money so you could use it to re-elect congressmen, most of whom I've never heard of and the rest of whom I'd probably lay out good money to defeat," I said.

"If you're unhappy with the toaster, we still have a few small TV sets, one of which can be yours if you deposit an additional $5,000."

I asked how much I'd have to put in to be rewarded with a new car.

"What price car are you considering?" he asked.

"Something costing exactly $7,107.82," I said.

"Excuse me a moment," he said, and went to an inner chamber, whence he reappeared shortly with an impressive man.

"From the value of the gift you require, we naturally assume that you are a congressman who is planning to run for re-election," said the impressive man.

"That's neither here nor there," I said. "All I'm interested in . . ."

"Naturally, naturally!" he interrupted. "I'd object vigorously to allegations that large contributions to campaigning congressmen might enable us to influence votes."

"All I'm interested in," I continued, "is trading in this toaster for a new car."

"Naturally you are. You can't go anyplace in Washington without a car."

"I haven't the least interest in going to Washington," I said. "As a depositor, I merely wish to be treated as equitably as the politicians you're re-electing with my deposit."

The impressive man turned to his assistant. "When it comes to banking, this is about the biggest fool God ever sent down the pike," he said, as they threw me out the door.

▪ MOON OF CUALADORA ▪

Come to the sun-drenched island of Cualadora and be beautiful.

Here under the clattering palm fronds of Cualadora's Silver Sands beach, shed your cold Northern ugliness while frolicking in the gin-clear waters of Lalique Lagoon and get to know how beautiful feels.

Why freeze and be ugly when for $859 you can revel in Cualadora's world-renowned tropical moonlight? (Double occupancy only.) Discover why the conquistadors called Cualadora the Amethyst of the Antilles. Learn why Hernando Cortés said, "After 10 days in Cualadora, the fat and the wrinkles and the gray cold ugliness of the North had disappeared from my aging lineaments, and I was beautiful."

In Cualadora we have sun-bronzed beach boys and sun-bronzed beach girls who were once as cold and ugly as you are now. Their faces were wrinkled and they were bowlegged and squatty and had too much weight around the hips and waist, and they wore eyeglasses and were losing their hair.

Then they came to Cualadora on the 10-day package vacation plan—you are greeted with a free coconut in your room at the Lalique Lagoon Hotel—and became beautiful. You too will become sun-bronzed and beautiful in Cualadora. Those sagging abdominal muscles will flatten as you feel youth return under the spell of Chick Marengo and his Oleander Orchestra. (Nightly except Mondays in the Olde Rumme Clubbe at picturesque Poinciana Point.)

Here is how confident we are: On your arrival at Cualadora International Airport, our photographer will take your picture looking old, flabby and ugly. If, after 10 days, you are not beautiful, we will give you your picture back. Free.

Why be cold and ugly when the Amethyst of the Antilles beckons you with a free coconut in every room? And so much, much more. Walk barefoot through acres of unspoiled marimbas. Climb to the peak of towering Mount Cualadora and watch historic smugglers' boats far out at sea battle the trade winds to get marijuana to Miami.

You will love the friendly, fun-loving people of Cualadora. Under our new Intensified Tourification Program we have spent huge sums to educate native Cualadoreans in ways to help you be beautiful.

Do not be surprised if a smiling old Cualadorean hibiscus farmer stops you on the road and urges you to make a detour to inspect our new 18-hole golf course. It is his way of showing pride in our accomplishments. Expect him to tell you how the golf course was built on landfill over a river that once swarmed with tourist-eating piranha.

That is the kind of welcome you will receive in Cualadora while being beautiful. Cualadora is getting rid of piranha to make you feel more welcome than ever before.

No longer will you worry about waiters pouring hot soup in your lap or chambermaids placing scorpions between your bed sheets at the Lalique Lagoon Hotel. An elaborate new personnel screening program now guarantees that every waiter and chambermaid who serves you is a graduate of Cualadora Police Force's Internal Security Squad, which firmly supports our Government's tourist policy.

Our waiters and chambermaids are now paid to see that you are beautiful at all times. They have gone among the people of Cualadora spreading the message that Cualadora has an obligation to help cold and ugly people from the North be beautiful.

As a result you will no longer worry about snipers during your stay in Cualadora. Our snipers have turned in their rifles and taken up hibiscus farming. They have turned in their rifles now that our waiters and chambermaids have explained that you wish only to be beautiful.

What about those beautiful strangers you have always dreamed of meeting in the moonlight when your blood pulses to the beat of voodoo drums, the click of the roulette wheel, the cries of "Olé" thundering from the bullring?

Yes, in Cualadora you will meet beautiful strangers. You will meet them in the Voodoo Torero's Casino House where, thanks to a new installation by experts from the Hayden Planetarium, the moon is full 24 hours a day.

To preserve every stranger's anonymity, guests leave their clothing at the door and make do with hand towels. What more carefree way to meet and be met by beautiful strangers eager to admire you now that Cualadora has rid you of fat and wrinkles, restored body to your hair and added six inches to your height?

Yes, you will meet beautiful strangers. We are confident of it. So confident that we make this offer: If you do not meet at least three beautiful strangers, the telephone operator at the Lalique Lagoon Hotel will personally dial your call to the party of your choice in the United States so that you may tell them how warm it is in Cualadora and remind them that they would not be so cold and ugly if they came on down. In addition, the operator will personally bill the toll charge to your personal hotel room.

HOW SHALL
I DEAR THEE?

A friend, as Lyndon Johnson used to say, is "somebody you can go to the well with." Not for an instant would I consider going to the well with Times Square. I certainly wouldn't invite Times Square home to meet the folks. Truth is, whenever I see Times Square on the sidewalk I cross the street to avoid it.

Why then do I receive mail addressed to "Dear Friend of Times Square"? For the same reason I get mail addressed to "Dear Fellow Angler" and "Dear Decisionmaker." Because America is undergoing a salutation crisis, that's why.

The severity of this crisis is indicated by that "Dear Fellow Angler." I was flattered by this form of address at first, thinking it embraced me in the brotherhood of sharpsters who know how to work the angles. It has long been my hope to be greeted as "Dear Fellow Finagler," thus winning membership in that class for which the income tax laws are written. "Dear Fellow Angler" seemed like a step toward this goal.

Closer reading, however, showed I was being addressed by the Izaak Walton League, whose idea of a "dear fellow angler" is someone who hooks fish. As one who has not fished since the age of 8 and plans never to fish again, I was puzzled.

Being addressed as "Dear Decisionmaker" was downright nerve-racking, since my paralysis at decision time is notorious on six continents. Could this letter be from some cruel master of sarcasm who knew I sat home biting my nails all weekend because I couldn't decide whether I preferred to see "Stir Crazy" or "The Devil and Max Devlin"?

No. It came from a complete stranger, in fact a large corporation ("our sales now exceed $500 million"), which wanted to sell me its payroll, accounting and financial expertise.

Each of these letters had three things in common. All were from complete strangers, all wanted me to pass some money their way and none of the letter writers knew my name. Examination of a two-week accumulation of money-seeking mail revealed a fourth characteristic. The people sending these pleas don't even know whether I am male or female.

"Dear Sir or Madam," several of them begin. One greets me as "Dear Sir or Madam of the Press." This is a plea for publicity for a new book. "Be a columnist and report facts!" it commands. The fact I want to report right now is that I am not a madam of the press.

While I'm at it, let me advise a certain charity that lusts after my bank account that I am not "Dear Friend of the Arts" either. Lord knows, I have tried to be a friend of art, but art has snubbed me for years as a common drudge who sold out to Grub Street. It's too late to extend the hand of friendship into my wallet now, arts. I know who my real friends are.

They do not include a certain large institution in Utah that hails me as "Dear Business Friend."

I never make business friends. Years ago Uncle Charlie advised me, "Never mix business and friendship, boy. That way you'll never have to cut a friend's heart out."

Uncle Charlie also warned me about becoming an investor. "If you become an investor," he said, "sooner or later you're going to be wiped out like all those buzzards in 1929, and while you're waiting to go broke you're going to have to put up with a lot of mail addressed to 'Dear Investor.'"

Now I get the mail even though I followed Uncle Charlie's advice. "Dear Investor," says a letter from Wall Street trying to lure me into the gold business. I am concerned about these ill-informed salutations. Naturally there is a letter that catches my eye.

"Dear Concerned American," it begins. But no, it is not about the salutation crisis. It comes from a complete stranger who wants me to buy his novel about the red menace. Apparently he cares not a whit about the salutation menace, though it infects the highest levels of government.

For evidence, I submit Senator Moynihan's newsletter. It begins, "Dear Yorker." Does Moynihan believe he now represents York, Pennsylvania? More likely, I think, he has an acute case of salutationitis, which produces severe inflammation of the prose style when the sufferer attempts to compose a mass mailing.

It is everywhere and spreading. An insurance company scribe writes, "Dear Policy Holder." Can anyone imagine a policy holder being dear to an insurance company in any but the crassest sense of the word? "Dear Collector," begins a vendor of small statuary to a man who has never collected anything in his life but matchbook covers.

A wordsmith for a magazine publisher begins with "Dear Civilized Friend" (my idea of civilization's finest achievement is the 1969 Buick Electra), and a letter from a public-television station starts out with "Dear Viewer." Why not "Dear Moneybags"? The gun-control lobby that addresses me as "Dear Potential Handgun Victim" at least knows that I am still alive, which is more than can be said for New York magazine wondering why a subscription hasn't been renewed.

Its author begins, "Dear Silent One." I have received two copies of this letter. They will be forwarded to my late grandfathers.

FEAR OF FOSSILS

Scientists examining ancient fossil evidence discovered recently that prehistoric man ate a well-balanced diet with plenty of vegetables. By one of those coincidences in which the daily news abounds, this report appeared

simultaneously with news of an avocado glut in California. To reduce the
surplus, some growers want to market avocados as pet food—dogs seem to
be crazy about avocados—but other growers say that selling their crop as
pet food would be disastrous for the avocado's image.

All day long he had been trying to invent the tool. Men had
talked about the tool for eons. As a boy he had often crept from
the table to listen to the old men speak of it. "Some day," they
said, "the tool will be invented and then we will do great things."

He was exhausted when he appeared back at the cave at sundown.

"Invented the tool yet, Edison?" his wife asked.

He ignored the sarcasm. "What's for dinner?" he asked. "I'm
so hungry I could eat a mastodon."

"A good thing," she said, "because I'm heating up last Sunday's roast leg of mastodon."

He crouched in the dirt and stroked his beard in self-pity. The
monotony of the diet was draining his creative strength. A society
fed night after night on the same boring old mastodon, he re-
flected, was unlikely ever to invent the tool.

Perhaps he was on the wrong track. Perhaps he should stop
trying to invent the tool and try to invent Craig Claiborne.

His wife tossed him a chunk of mastodon and a fistful of orange
and green substances.

"What's this gunk?" he asked.

"Squinnots and squatdrops," she said.

"You say it's squinnots and squatdrops. I say it's peas and
carrots, and I say to hell with it."

"Eat your vegetables," she commanded.

"I won't."

"If you don't eat your vegetables you're going to make a very
poor fossil. Everybody's going to look at it and say, 'Well, prehistoric man certainly didn't have much respect for his innards, did
he?' Is that the impression you want to create?"

She had a point, but it galled him. One of the worst things

about being prehistoric man was this inordinate concern with what people would think of your fossil. You couldn't chew tree bark to relax because somebody might come along later and look at your fossil and think prehistoric man was addicted to pine sap.

And on a cold night if you curled up around the dogs to keep warm, somebody was bound to say, "If you lie down with dogs and the roof of the cave falls in, your fossil is going to make people think we were dog worshippers."

Still he was concerned about leaving a good fossil. If he succeeded in inventing the tool, a lot of fuss would be made over his fossil and he wanted it to be a fossil that would do him credit. He chewed his peas and carrots.

"Why is it always peas and carrots?" he said. "Or spinach and escarole? Or apple sauce and sauerkraut when we have the marinated boar tusks? Just once, why don't we have a nice guacamole?"

"Shame on you!"

"I said something wrong?"

"You're talking about avocados," she said. "Guacamole is made from avocados."

"I like avocados," he said.

"Not so loud," she whispered. "The neighbors in the next cave will think we're barbarians who eat dog food."

He was aware that dogs were crazy about avocados; but then dogs liked mastodon bones too and nobody ever refused to chew mastodon bones on that account.

"What you don't understand," said his wife, "is the image problem. As long as civilized prehistoric man looks upon avocados as dog food, anyone who eats them can forget about getting invited to the best boar hunts and cave-drawing parties."

Yes, yes, he knew what she would say next. "If you eat avocados, people looking at your fossil will think you walked on all fours, had fleas and barked at the moon." If he yielded to his craving, the avocado's terrible image would live on to curse his fossil.

Then, one of the great moments of human thought: "I shall upgrade the avocado's image," he said.

"You can't even invent the tool. How are you going to upgrade an image?"

"Just watch," he said. In the era that followed he stalked the community night and day with a stone that fitted well in his hand and brained every dog he saw pounce on an avocado. The dogs got the idea and stayed with mastodon bones.

At length the neighbors came to hail him. "Yes," he boasted, "I have done a great thing. I have upgraded the avocado's image."

"No," said the prehistoric man next door, "you have invented the tool," and cracked his skull with a well-fitted stone of his own. The bludgeon had been invented at last. Fossils of people who lived in the 1980s will reveal that the bludgeon was later refined into the image.

▪THE CRUELEST MONTH▪

The third week of September has always been a grisly time for schoolchildren. It is then that the romance of education, sparked by the back-to-school excitement of fresh books, new teachers, virginal fountain pens and notebooks unstained by ink blots and baffling mathematical formulas, begins to yield to reality.

And what is that reality? It is knowledge. Knowledge that it will be nine long months before summer vacation rolls around again. Knowledge that the geography teacher dislikes you. Knowledge that the gym instructor finds your physique absurd. Knowledge that you are never going to understand at least three of the subjects with which you are saddled and are going to suffer horribly for months as you sink into the quagmire of F's recording the progress of your ignorance.

It was Jean Shepherd, I believe, who said that after three weeks in chemistry he was six months behind the class. This is a common experience, this sensation of being locked forever in the starting gate while the rest of the class is galloping for the back stretch, and it leaves many people scarred for life.

A woman I know, though financially well-heeled, still refuses to set foot in Italy because in seventh-grade Latin she became aware, after three weeks in the classroom, that she would never be able to conjugate the verb *esse* to Cicero's satisfaction. Assurances that Cicero is no longer to be encountered in Rome do not comfort her. She associates the Italian peninsula with personal humiliation.

I myself have always avoided Germany since discovering in 10th grade that German has two dozen ways of saying "the." I could be wrong about this, since I was wrong about everything else in German. Nevertheless, there is the fact. The memory of a third week in September when classmates began hooting about my tendency to use the dative feminine singular form of "the" when the accusative neuter plural was called for—this memory has created a lifelong barrier between Germany and me.

Schools do not concede that it is ridiculous to require every student to learn at the same pace. They operate on the assumption that every brain in the classroom will achieve a firm grasp of the binomial theorem at the same instant and be ready to move on simultaneously to those many cheerful facts about the square of the hypotenuse waiting at the next hitching post.

Readers who met the educators' expectations in mathematics may deduce from the above that my own pace in math was decidedly slow if, as I suspect, you have to master the hypotenuse before proceeding on to the binomial theorem. The truth is that, never understanding either one, I was utterly lost and made a terrible mess of things when I reached the cosine and the secant.

All of this probably resulted because some teacher during the third week of some long-ago September assumed, wrongly, that I understood that 9 times 6 is 54, and rushed on to impress me with the realization that 9 times 8 is 77, or whatever it may be.

Almost all of us have dreadful third weeks of September in our backgrounds somewhere. If psychoanalysts would let up a bit on our libidinal childhood experiences, they might discover a rich new source of adult neurosis here.

The third week of September that mutilated my own life is the reason I am not a brilliant nuclear physicist today. Here let me confess that in youth it was not my intent to become a typewriter pounder hacking out material for Sunday supplements. Hooked on the romance of science, I yearned to take up the torch from Einstein and carry it forward.

Thus I came to physics class. The first week of September was thrilling, as textbooks were issued and the teacher discoursed on Isaac Newton and apples and introduced us to the lab, that frontier of human progress. In the second week, he introduced us to the erg. I was quite happy with the erg, without which blocks of wood could not be made to overcome the villainous friction of inclined ramps and moved upward, triumphantly ascending those ramps.

At the end of the week, he introduced the dyne, which seemed excessive. It was not that I couldn't understand the dyne. I could have. What I could not understand was why, since we already had the erg, it was also necessary to have the dyne.

I was still puzzling over this philosophical question the following Monday when the teacher, assuming that everybody now had a firm grip on the dyne, plunged ahead into the centimeter. Perhaps it was only the millimeter. I am hazy here because reality was fading rapidly.

It was disconcerting to have the dyne taken utterly for granted when I still had profound doubts about it and to be asked to cope with the centimeter. The next day was worse. That was the day of the milligram. The following day there was a test.

I was astonished that the rest of the class took it without a roar of protest that it was outrageous to ask us to cope with ergs, dynes, centimeters and milligrams while we were still baffled about the dyne. The rest of the class did not protest. Most passed easily. I failed every question not devoted exclusively to the erg. The rest of that year was a nightmare, and the world still awaits a worthy successor to Einstein.

BYE-BYE,
SILVER BULLETS

The Lone Ranger is through. Washed up. He stands in a Los Angeles law office. Oriental rugs under foot. A Kandinsky on the wall. The desk rich and sleek, covered with writs, injunctions, habeas corpus, mandamus, certiorari, nolo contendere, duces tecum, bills of attainder.

The lawyer has handled people like the Lone Ranger before. The world is full of them if you are a lawyer. People who go around the country drawing down Big Jack by passing themselves off as the Lone Ranger, Popeye the Sailor Man, Boob McNutt, Secret Agent X-9, the Green Hornet.

"You're all washed up, Popeye" he tells them. Or, "O.K., Hornet, one more rendering of 'The Flight of the Bumble Bee,' and we're going to slap you with so many injunctions you'll have to hawk your Orphan Annie decoder and Cocomalt shaker to pay your court costs."

The Lone Ranger is easier meat than most. He is getting old. He is 64 now. It shows. His mask is deeply wrinkled. Tonto urged him five years ago to see a plastic surgeon about having tucks taken in the eye slits, but the Lone Ranger refused. He is old-fashioned about too many things.

"I'll give it to you straight from the shoulder, Ranger" the lawyer says. "You're washed up. Over the hill."

The Lone Ranger's reflexes are slow. He would like to leap aboard his fiery horse with the speed of light and gallop away with

a hearty, "Heigh-ho, Silver!" He cannot. The lawyer's receptionist made him leave Silver outside on account of the oriental rugs.
The Lone Ranger can read the secrets of a cold campfire, but he
is no match for the guile of receptionists.

The lawyer urges the Lone Ranger to look at himself. A wrinkled man in a world whose heart goes out only to smooth
men.

"I don't smoke or drink" says the Ranger. "I work out every
morning to keep my body trim."

The lawyer has heard it all before. These old crocks are all
alike. "I still eats my spinach three times a day and avoids all
heavy lifting to keep my upper arms skinnier than Slim Summer-
ville," Popeye once told him.

"I'm not talking two-for-a-penny Mary Janes, Ranger" says the
lawyer. "I'm talking big law. Now come across with that
mask."

The Lone Ranger recoils. They always recoil at this stage of the
interview. The lawyer remembers how the Phantom recoiled
when ordered to come across with both his mask and his form-
fitting rubber suit, remembers how ridiculous the Phantom
looked when it had been peeled off him. His entire body wrinkled like hands left too long in hot dish water.

The lawyer is not a cruel man. He remembers the years he sat
by his television set, thumb in mouth, marveling at the Lone
Ranger. Once, he wanted to grow up to be the Lone Ranger's
sidekick and gallop behind him on a small gray stallion named
Zirconium.

Life for the lawyer has been a series of disappointments, except for the oriental rugs and the Kandinsky and the cunning
receptionist. In law school he had wanted to grow up to be
Perry Mason and save the innocent from the noose and be admired afterwards by Paul Drake and Della for refusing to take
a fee.

Instead, here he was, pushing around heroes for getting long in the tooth. He hoped the Lone Ranger wouldn't cry. He couldn't stand it when they cried. He remembered the Katzenjammer Kids, doddering octogenarians, weeping like babies when he told them it was time for the nursing home.

"Ranger" he says, "promise me you won't cry and I'll try to explain."

"I feel like crying" the Lone Ranger says. "It's the worst I've ever felt in my life. But I won't cry. The Lone Ranger doesn't cry."

The lawyer explains that his client owns the rights to the Lone Ranger and means to make a bundle from them. There was going to be a young, new Lone Ranger, a smooth man. Having a delapidated old Lone Ranger galloping the plains is bad for the young, new, smooth-man Lone Ranger image necessary for the making of bundles.

"You're trying to tell me I'm not the Lone Ranger any more?"

They always asked that. "You mean to tell me I'm not Flash Gordon any more?" Flash had asked when ordered to hand over Emperor Ming and the Planet Mongo. And the lawyer had said, "That's right—you're just Buster Crabbe now."

It was the only legal answer. To the Ranger he says, "From now on, you're just Clayton Moore. Your revels now are ended. Turn in your mask and your silver bullets, your white hat and your faithful Tonto and your fiery steed with the speed of light."

"What will I do for a living from now on?" the ex-Lone Ranger asks. The lawyer explains that this is a question nobody has been able to answer satisfactorily to retirees. Many of them he says, find shuffleboard fulfilling.

When the Ranger leaves, the lawyer considers calling in his receptionist and Paul Drake and telling them he refuses to take a fee for this case. Instead he pushes the intercom button.

"You can send Buck Rogers in now," he says.

EGG ON THE FACE

While lunching with an extremely vital man some years ago, I was dismayed during the fish course to notice that he had a wog on his chin. For people who have never been in this predicament, I should explain that a wog is a tiny piece of food that has somehow escaped the eater's mouth and lodged itself on his face.

The chin and the cheeks are where wogs usually settle. The difficulty with them is that the person with a wog on his face can't see it, but everybody else can. As a result any train of thought that has been running across the table gets derailed as soon as the wog appears.

This is what happened during that lunch. The extremely vital man was talking profound talk—"We live in an age when implications are profound," or something like that—and I was trying to look grave and deep when I noticed the wog on his chin. My mind instantly abandoned profound implications and cried, "Good Lord! He has a wog on his chin."

Oblivious to the wog, he went on talking deep. It became harder and harder to look him in the eye. My glance kept dropping to his chin. It became terribly important to know what kind of wog it was. If it was a bread wog it might drop away, ending the crisis without a fuss. Bread wogs often do that. So do cake wogs.

This, however, was a fish wog, one of the worst kind. Like egg wogs and oily lettuce-leaf wogs, a fish wog seems to get glued on and nothing removes it but a swipe of the napkin. Now, my question to the well-mannered public is: What do you do in this situation?

Do you reach across the table and swipe his chin with a napkin? If so, you have to be prepared to say, "Sorry about that, but sometimes my reflexes go haywire." In which case, he puts you down as an eccentric and never has you to lunch again.

On the other hand you can hardly butt in while he is warning you about the profundity of the implications and say, "Pardon me, but you've got a fish wog on your chin." Or so it seemed to me that day. "Why do you keep staring at my chin?" he asked.

Quick as a whip, I said, "I have never seen a chin with such profound implications."

He was flattered by that, and the meal dragged on. Leaving the restaurant, he paused at the washroom and came out white with humiliation. "How could you let me sit through an entire meal with a fish wog on my chin?" he whimpered.

The answer is that he was so vital that he awed me. There are some people you can interrupt with "Brush the wog off your chin" without being at all self-conscious, but these are only the dearest of relatives. When social disparity is greater, a wog presents one of society's gravest problems.

Suppose, for example, that you and a couple of friends—say, Kermit and Katz—are invited to eat with the President, and the President is talking on about the threat to civilization, and suddenly all three of you notice a wog on his cheek.

You and Kermit and Katz are not going to get much out of the President's conversation from that moment on, are you? All three of you are going to be too busy thinking, "My God, the President's got a wog on his cheek? Why doesn't somebody do something about it?"

Of course, now that I have had long experience with the wog problem, I know you have to deal with each one according to your reading of the victim's personality. With President Reagan it would probably be easy to say, "Speaking of the threat to civilization, Mr. President, you've got a little wog there on your left cheek."

Ronald Reagan gives you the feeling he would just chuckle and tell you an anecdote about a time when all the Warner brothers attended an Academy Awards show with blintz wogs on their chins.

It is more serious if the President is someone like Richard Nixon or Lyndon Johnson. Presidents of their disposition, so uneasy about their personal appearances, might become so irritated they would order the Pentagon to give the wog a whiff of the grape.

In such cases I've had good results from relying on the science of sympathetic body language or, in plainer terms, the monkey-see, monkey-do principle. If the wog victim is someone easily irritated—like former Secretary of State Haig, for example—I do not call verbal attention to the wog. Instead, after noting its location, I look the victim hard in the eye without blinking, then with great deliberation bring my hand to my chin or cheek, matching it to the wog's location on the victim's face, and rub it back and forth, back and forth, back and forth.

The great man, wishing to woo you with body language as well as his verbal charms, will in nine cases out of ten raise his own hand subconsciously to the identical spot on his dynamic face and rub the wog away. In most cases he will not even notice it.

If he does, the trick is to begin rubbing other parts—your ear lobes, throat, forehead—parts which on the victim are wog-free. Gingerly, he will test his ear lobes, throat and forehead for more wogs and, finding none, assume that you were not signaling him about his embarrassing wog, but merely suffer from a disgusting compulsion to rub yourself at the table. This will probably improve his day by making him feel superior.

GHOST STORY

A chill autumn night, dogs baying at the full moon, wind whining through the willow withes. Such eerie sounds, they fairly turned my goose pimples to ice. Finding myself alone with old Clumbers who was ensconced by the hearth in the club's only good chair,

GHOST STORY

his profile dimly outlined by the light of a fading brandy, did little
to improve my spirits.

"It was not on a night such as this that I first saw Thurston
Hare," old Clumbers began in the melancholy croak with which
he always began his ghostly tales.

"What sort of night was it?"

"It wasn't night at all," old Clumbers said. "It was day, but
there was something very peculiar about that day. It was not
darkly overcast with grim clouds foreboding evil, nor was there
a sinister yellow light that turned everyday objects into bleak
shadows fraught with a sense of impending horror."

He paused to sip his brandy. I did not want the old man to see
he had shaken me badly, so with a voice as steady as I could
manage, I said, "Perhaps there was a heavy rain lashing an old
abandoned house."

"Nonsense," muttered old Clumbers. "The day was perfectly
average. That's what was so peculiar about it, don't you see? The
temperature was 70 degrees, the air was mild, the breeze was
light and the sun was neither too bright nor too dim. For this
reason I was quite unprepared for the extraordinary spectacle that
met my eye."

At these words old Clumbers's entire frame shuddered as
though reliving that nightmare.

"Your eye was doubtless met by this spectacle inside an old
abandoned house," I murmured, trying to encourage him to
break his confounded silence.

"That is what made it so macabre," he said at last. "It was not
an old abandoned house. It was a brick split-level in a middle-class
suburb and—and—will you believe me when I say it?"

"Don't torment me with the suspense!" I cried.

"There were antimacassars on the couch."

I rang for another brandy, praying it would steady old Clumbers's heartbeat. "And that was where you first saw Thurston
Hare?"

"In that very room," he groaned.

"How many years had Thurston Hare been in his grave when you encountered him?" I asked.

"Are you sure you want to hear this?" he replied. By now, of course, I was riveted to his every word and had to hear him to the end.

"Thurston Hare had never been in his grave," Clumbers whispered. "To state it plainly, Thurston Hare had not died. I sensed, with the hair rising on the back of my neck as he greeted me, that Thurston Hare was not an apparition. Thurston Hare was still alive."

I could scarcely believe what the old man was saying, but the terrible earnestness with which he spoke the words left no doubt that Thurston Hare had not been an apparition, but a living person.

"My dear old Clumbers"—I tried to reassure him—"you have never in your life walked into a house without encountering the apparition of someone who has been dead for many years. It is inconceivable that Thurston Hare could have been alive."

"He was alive I tell you," the old man cackled. "I could smell the cashew nuts on his breath."

"Think hard and try to remember," I urged. "Through the smell of cashew nuts you must have detected a faint aroma of tomb dampness in his clothing."

Clumbers handed me his glass. I rang for the waiter and when Clumbers's throat was moist enough to allow for speech again, he said, "The only odor from his clothes was the smell of dry-cleaning fluid."

"But what occult power had he used to summon you there in spite of all your instincts?"

"I had answered an ad stating there was a used encyclopedia for sale quite cheaply at that address. Naturally, I assumed the owner had died and, upon learning that his legacy was to be sold heartlessly for a quick profit, would return from the grave to make a scene."

"Instead, you were met by———."

"By a man who had never been dead a second in his life," Clumbers said. It was a grave situation. Once Clumbers started walking into perfectly average houses on perfectly normal days and meeting perfectly living people, he would be blackballed from the only good chair in the club. Leaving, I told the barman to send the old boy another brandy.

"Haven't you heard?" the barman said. "Old Clumbers died last week and was buried three days ago." I write to thank him, wherever he is, for giving me first claim on the only good chair in the club.

■ THERE SHE IS ■

Miss America lives on a tree-lined street in a town that was drawn for a Saturday Evening Post cover in 1938. The street will be destroyed in 1953 for a shopping mall, and nothing will be left to mark the location of the porch swing on which Miss America sits in the summer dusk sipping a tall glass of homemade lemonade. Not even a small plaque attached to the frozen-juice shelf of the terrific new supermarket which, with its yummy, mouthwatering selection of chemically processed liquids, will be located on the very site of Miss America's porch swing.

Not even a tiny market stating, "Miss America swung here."

After the summer, of course, Miss America goes back to the state university to equip herself for a career of service to humanity, but now she lives on the tree-lined street with Mom and Dad. They are white with excellent Nordic bone structure, which is recapitulated in Miss America, as are their dazzling teeth.

Miss America brushes three times a day and takes piano from Mrs. Jones in the next block. Next door there is a boy. In the evenings he comes over and sits in the porch swing with Miss America. Mom, who thinks he is a peach of a fellow, usually takes

Dad inside at these times to listen to the Lux Radio Theater so the young folks can do a little sparking.

Miss America is not so keen as Mom on the boy next door. Sometimes he tries to get fresh. Not that Miss America minds a little smooching with a boy who is really sincere, as the boy next door is. But sometimes smooching gives him fancy ideas and he starts getting fresh.

Since Miss America is saving herself for her husband, she deals with him firmly on these occasions by insisting that he come into the kitchen and watch her make fudge. In the bright kitchen light, Miss America notices that the boy next door does not look a bit like Clark Gable.

The husband for whom Miss America is saving herself will look very much like Clark Gable, only he will be younger and nicer, too, and not the kind of fellow who is always getting fresh with girls, the way Clark Gable does. He will be a lot gentler than Clark Gable, like Spencer Tracy, and maybe sing beautifully, like Nelson Eddy.

Miss America met a boy like that last semester at the state university. He was a Sigma Delta man. One night he took her for ice cream sodas, and afterward they smooched in his car, but when he started getting fresh she asked him if he was really sincere and whether he could respect a girl for her mind.

He urged her to shed her imprisoning middle-class conventionality and asked if she had ever read Omar Khayyam. She said he was probably not worth reading since she had never come across any of his stories in The Woman's Home Companion.

He ordered her out of his car and told her to walk back to the campus, but a few minutes later he drove back and picked her up and took her to her dorm. That was the gentle Spencer Tracy in him overpowering his Clark Gable impulse to act fresh.

She believes that the right wife—namely, Miss America—could turn him into a fine human being and make a man of him and possibly even get him a nice voice teacher to train him to sing like Nelson Eddy.

Miss America, you see, is a dreamer. Life's possibilities seem to stretch infinitely before her. With her dazzling teeth, she may even become an airline stewardess, meeting world-famous stars and powerful executives who fly the airways and visiting faraway places such as Kansas City, Richmond, Minneapolis and Paris.

Of course, she will also have to reserve time for serving humanity, perhaps by going off to some infested subtropical hellhole to help cure rickets, and teach the natives to make fudge, and show benighted jungle women how to put more meaning into their lives by saving themselves for their husbands and reading The Woman's Home Companion.

Later there will be time to marry the Sigma Delta man. He will probably need a good woman in a few years to help him overcome an already noticeable beer problem and to put the iron in his spine necessary to compete with Nelson Eddy.

And if he is snatched up in the meantime by some hussy unworthy of him, well—there will always be the boy next door. There are worse things than settling down on a tree-lined street with a wholesome American boy who likes bowling and can bore you to death about the Brooklyn Dodgers and doesn't know enough not to try smooching with a girl while his mouth is still full of potato chips.

Such are the visions of the future that brighten Miss America's dusk in the porch swing on the tree-lined street from the Saturday Evening Post cover. They are so hypnotic that she does not even notice that bulldozers have leveled the street, and the atom bomb has gone off, and the sexual revolution began years ago right there on the asphalt parking lot which had once been the back yard of the boy next door.

Instead, she meticulously shaves her legs, bathes with a delicate soap, goes to the beauty parlor, then buys a one-piece bathing suit and a pair of ridiculously high heels and strolls sweetly off through the ruins to Atlantic City. There she is, a long-stemmed rose preserved in amber to remind us that something very much like life can exist long after death.

MERRILY WE PENTAGON

UNIVERSAL MILITARY MOTION

The idea behind the MX missile system is sound enough. Place bomb-bearing missiles on wheels and keep them moving constantly through thousands of miles of desert so enemy bombers will not have a fixed target. To confuse things further, move decoy missiles over the same routes so the enemy cannot distinguish between false missiles and the real thing.

As my strategic thinkers immediately pointed out, however, the MX missile system makes very little sense unless matched by an MX Pentagon system. What is the point, they asked, of installing a highly mobile missile system if its command center, the

Pentagon, remains anchored like a moose with four broken legs on the bank of the Potomac River?

This is why we propose building 250 moveable structures so precisely like the Pentagon that no one can tell our fake Pentagons from the real thing and to keep all of them, plus the real Pentagon, in constant motion through the country.

Our first plan was to move only the real Pentagon, which would be placed on a large flat-bottom truck bed and driven about the countryside on the existing highway system. We immediately realized, however, that this would not provide sufficient protection against nuclear attack. The Pentagon is very big and easily noticeable. When it is driven along at 55 miles per hour, people can see it coming from miles away. It attracts attention. In short, it is a fat, easily detected target.

With 250 fake Pentagons constantly cruising the roads, the problem is solved. Now, trying to distinguish the real Pentagon from the fake Pentagons, enemy attackers will face the maddening problem of finding a needle in a haystack. With 251 Pentagons in circulation, the sight of a Pentagon on the highway will attract no more attention than a politician's indictment. Thus we foil the enemy's spies.

Still, to add another margin of security we will confuse matters further by building 1,500 Pentagon-shaped fast-food restaurants along the nation's highways.

Each will be an exact replica of the real Pentagon, at least as seen from the outside. Inside, of course, they will be equipped to provide all the necessities for producing acute indigestion, thus providing the wherewithal of highway travel and, in the process, earning the Government a little return on its investment.

Occasionally, when generals and admirals tire of touring and yearn for a little stability, the real Pentagon will be parked alongside the road to masquerade as a fast-food Pentagon. The danger of highway travelers wandering in for a quick hot dog and making trouble while the authentic Pentagon is in the "parked" or "fast-food" mode has also been considered.

These interlopers will simply be told by receptionists that hot dogs are in the back of the building and directed to walk the long route around the Pentagon's outer ring. As they drop from exhaustion they will be removed by military police, carried to their cars, given free hot dogs and advised that next time they should enter their Pentagon fast-food dispensary through the rear door.

There are problems to be ironed out in the MX Pentagon, but we are too busy at the moment perfecting our MX Congress system to trifle with details. With 850 United States Capitols on the highway, we have an extremely touchy problem in deciding whether a Capitol or a Pentagon should have the right of way when they meet at an intersection.

■   ■   ■

Our proposal to build the MX Pentagon has created serious opposition among highway-safety advocates. Because of its great size and weight, they say, a Pentagon being hauled along the highway at 55 miles per hour is a serious threat to other vehicles.

Unfortunately, this is correct. We tested our first prototype of the fake Pentagon in New Jersey Wednesday with sobering results. The driver had to apply his brakes violently when a van tried to cut him off in traffic, and the Pentagon flew off the truck bed and dented Ho-Ho-Kus.

Our engineers say this problem can be solved by reducing the weight. They propose to do so by eliminating several acres of reserved parking lots attached to the Pentagon.

Opposition from generals and admirals is intense, but our political advisers believe we can work out a happy compromise by eliminating just the enlisted men's parking lots.

Another serious difficulty is posed by the tight clearances on highway tunnels and bridges. Whoever designed the Lincoln Tunnel, for example, apparently cared not a fig about national security.

At present, as we discovered when taking our prototype out for road tests, the Lincoln Tunnel is utterly inadequate to handle Pentagons. Fortunately, since ours was a fake we were able to dismantle it and haul it through in sections. When the system is operational, however, the real Pentagon will also be on the road and it will surely want to enjoy a drive on the Manhattan Westway.

We are already in conference with agents of the Army Corps of Engineers about constructing tunnels under the Hudson generous enough to accommodate the MX Pentagon. Their mouths are watering at the prospects of Congressional appropriations that will be necessary to do the job.

The Navy is pressing us to accept an even more bankruptive solution. It wants to fit every Pentagon with an immense retractable steel hull. With this added feature, each Pentagon could approach the Hudson River ready to steam across.

And not only the Hudson River, as the Navy points out. Imagine an enemy bomber's confusion when, sighting a Pentagon steaming from Weehawken to 34th Street, he adjusts his bomb sights only to discover the Pentagon suddenly sailing down the harbor and out to Martha's Vineyard for the weekend.

Having encouraged the Navy to submit estimates, we were not surprised when the Air Force approached us with a proposal to make all Pentagons airworthy. Because of its air-resistant five-sided configuration, this plan would require wings more than 40 miles long.

Our engineers dislike the idea, because even with wings twice that length a Pentagon would be unable to achieve altitudes greater than 75 feet. The Air Force contends, however, that a low-flying Pentagon would make an impossible target for today's high-speed bombers.

Moreover, if equipped with .50-caliber machine guns and small rockets it would make a devastating weapon for strafing any Congressmen trying to attack the Pentagon's budget, they note.

Our strategic thinkers are reluctant to undertake such radical modifications. It would do our reputation for high-class strategic thinking no good at all if a fake Pentagon had engine trouble and crashed on a medium-size city. As Hermann Pflugelgasser, one of our most brilliant strategic thinkers, observed while we were watching the Yankees game on television the other night, "We've already got the real Pentagon on our backs, who needs a fake Pentagon on the head?"

■   ■   ■

Life has become a constant burden, thanks to the recent surge of skepticism about the accuracy of what is written in the newspapers.

Last night, for example, my garage was invaded by investigators looking for evidence that fictions have been published in this column. Imagine my rage. That anyone should think I might stoop to publishing fiction in the newspaper. . . .

What had aroused these busybodies was my series of reports about the MX Pentagon. These articles, in case you missed them, outlined my program for building 250 fake Pentagons and keeping them constantly moving around the American highways on trucks, along with the real Pentagon, to confuse enemy bombers.

As I have patiently explained time and again, the MX Pentagon system is an essential companion piece to the MX missile system, which will keep several hundred missiles moving constantly around the Southwestern desert to confuse Russian targeters about where our H-bombs might be coming from. What's the point of keeping the Russians confused about the whereabouts of our H-bombs if we don't confuse them about the Pentagon too?

Anyhow, these snoopers suspected my MX Pentagon program was a fiction. Such is the cynicism of the modern newspaper reader.

"Your last article said you'd already built three prototype models of the fake Pentagon in this garage," the chief investigator said. "I don't see any Pentagons in this garage."

Of course he didn't. As I explained, all three were then being driven around the continent to test whether motorists passing them on the highway could tell them from the real Pentagon.

One of his lieutenants, obviously hoping to impress the boss investigator with his brain power, said, "Chief, there isn't room in this garage to build three Pentagons."

"That's right," said the chief. "In fact, this garage isn't even big enough to hold one Pentagon."

"Of course not," I noted. "If you observe closely, you will see it isn't even big enough to contain all of my 1969 Buick Electra."

"So you published fiction in the newspaper, eh?" (Cries of "Resign! Resign!")

It was easy to calm them. "Do you really want me to notify the Russians where our fake Pentagons are built?"

They agreed I had a point there, and one or two even congratulated me on not being "one of those freedom-of-information freaks."

"Nevertheless," said the chief investigator, "you'll have to reveal—strictly in confidence, mind you—where the fake Pentagons are being built, or we'll nail you for trying to hornswoggle the American newspaper reader."

So I confided the secret to him. "I build them in the cellar."

"Nobody can build a Pentagon in the cellar," he said. "You'd never get it up the steps."

"Are you accusing me of fictionalizing?"

He was. "In that case, Mr. Doubting Thomas, let's go inside and have a look."

We went to the cellar.

"Just as I suspected," he said. "There's no Pentagon construction going on in here."

"Of course not," I said. "Do you take me for an idiot? For all I know, you could be an agent of the K.G.B. One word from you, and Moscow could be lobbing in one of the big babies and there goes my cellar, not to mention the center of American fake-Pentagon construction."

He looked skeptical. These people are very good at looking

skeptical, but not at much else. Apparently, it rarely occurs to them to think.

Since he was obviously baffled, I explained. "Before undertaking construction of the MX Pentagon, I built 2,500 MX cellars which are now located in scattered excavations all over the continent. In one of these cellars, whose location is known only to me, fake Pentagons are now being produced at a prodigious pace. If the Russians decided to take out our fake-Pentagon production capability, their chances of hitting the right one would be practically nil."

"Who's paying for this MX cellar program?" he asked.

"That's not the question," I explained. "The question is, are you, as a patriotic American citizen, willing to pay for a program that will counter the Russians' MX Kremlin system?"

He was astonished to hear about the MX Kremlin. "Oh yes," I confided, "the Russians are building 5,000 fake Kremlins to be kept constantly on the move in order to confuse our bombers. I have the intelligence from captured documents."

Naturally he wanted to see the captured documents. "Impossible," I explained. "They have already been fed into my MX captured-document-shredder system, which consists of 10,000 paper shredders kept in constant circulation between Tallahassee and Syracuse."

"You're trying to put me on, aren't you?" he said. It was painful to see a man so far beyond the healthy reach of truth.

■   ■   ■

Having managed to convey the impression that they are against mother's milk, down on orphans and fairly relaxed about torture conducted by friends of American foreign policy, the Reagan people are now trying to restore bribery's good name.

Like most Reagan enterprises, this one aims to unshackle American business. Because bribery is an ancient tradition in many foreign lands, Americans are said to be at a competitive disadvantage in foreign markets since they are legally prohibited from coughing up the baksheesh.

The Administration is now pressing Congress to do something about it; namely, to decriminalize payoffs to foreign parasites. Naturally, American parasites are outraged. I speak with authority here. As designer and prime contractor of the MX Pentagon, I recently retained a highly patriotic parasite to survey the possibilities of enlarging our revenues.

The MX Pentagon program, as I have made clear in the past, is a vast undertaking. Its aim is to strengthen national security by building 250 fake Pentagons and keeping them constantly moving about the country, along with the real Pentagon, to confuse enemy bombers.

A project of this size naturally creates many lucrative opportunities. To cite a small example, in order to give our fake Pentagons absolute authenticity we will need 250 fake Caspar Weinbergers capable of rising from their desks in our 250 fake Secretary of Defense offices to shake hands with 250 fake Ronald Reagans.

Our plant, which is located in my cellar, can produce an excellent fake Weinberger, but lacks the special technology necessary to turn out a good fake Reagan.

Soviet spies seeing our own fake Reagans shaking hands with our fake Weinbergers would instantly spot the Reagans as nothing more than foam-filled Naugahyde dummies and signal their bombers not to waste their time. For this reason we plan to subcontract the fake Reagan construction job to another company.

This will be worth a sweet pile of cash once we get our appropriation money from Congress. We are already beset by manufacturers watering at the mouth over prospects of cost overruns. Naturally, I retained a parasite.

His task was to discover which fake-Reagan manufacturer would pay the most to get the contract. I was astonished, as he was, when he returned with news that not a single bidder was willing to slip a sawbuck under the table, much less the $50 million we had anticipated might be available to help me finance a much-needed vacation at Asbury Park and enable him to buy a one-bedroom apartment in Manhattan.

Under existing law, such payments were prohibited as criminal bribes, the companies told him. Well, here was a fine how-de-do.

The man who conceived, planned and was preparing to create the nation's MX Pentagon system was expected to risk everything, yet his nation treated him like a common criminal if he tried to reap the fruits of his venture. What had happened to the American tradition of rewarding initiative?

At this moment the Administration moved toward the rescue, and I discovered that Congress was considering legalizing "bribery," as certain bleeding hearts called it, abroad.

Intense research by our foreign-development staff turned up 15 companies in sundry Asian backwaters and sandy ovens around the Mediterranean littoral that could produce quite a decent fake Reagan. All were willing to honor their ancient tradition by paying satchels of moolah for the contract, but none would pay it to my personal parasite.

Each country had its own domestic agent for collecting, skimming and transmitting the residue of the corporate payoff. Companies that make payoffs to American parasites are apparently closed down next day by their governments.

As a result, I am now in touch with assorted princes, sheiks, beys, interior ministers, kings, queens and jacks. All are prepared to collect plenty from the company that wins the fake-Reagan contract, and to remit enough for two weeks in Asbury Park.

Naturally, I have dismissed my domestic parasite, and he is furious. In fact, he has gone to Washington to lobby against the Administration's scheme. He says it is a conspiracy to deprive American parasites of their livelihood and will only increase the flow of capital out of the United States at a time when the balance of payments is already against us.

These political arguments do not interest us here at the

command center of the MX Pentagon program. Our concern is the national security. We are already searching for a subcontractor in desert or jungle who can produce a fake Pentagon V.I.P. mess so realistic that Russian bombers can't tell it from the real thing.

If this search and Congressional action go well, I anticipate not only two weeks in Asbury Park, but also the convenience of a rental car for the entire stay.

■   ■   ■

Building the MX Pentagon system, friends, is not all cakes and ale. For example: We have built three prototypes of the fake Pentagon and sent them out for road tests 10 days ago. One was hijacked in Indiana by a band of professional fur thieves and has not been seen since.

Our highly trained fake-Pentagon driver, who was mercifully not killed by the hijackers, says the thieves seemed to be under the impression that he was transporting an immense shipment of furs in a vehicle camouflaged to look like a Pentagon. What are American hijackers coming to when they can't tell a Pentagon from 600 acres of fur?

We believe they were deceived by this particular fake Pentagon's walls. These were constructed of tautly stretched cowhide to reduce weight and make a more fuel-efficient Pentagon. Shortly before the hijacking it had collided with the town of Terre Haute, Indiana, and left behind a telltale pile of cow hair rubbed off by the impact.

The hijackers presumably mistook this for mink hair and went in pursuit. In any case, since neither hide nor hair of it has been seen since, I strongly suspect it has already been converted into gloves and suitcases.

On the same day, a second fake Pentagon was caught in a high wind while crossing Berthoud Pass in the Colorado Rockies. This prototype, constructed of balsa-wood framing covered with tissue paper, was blown over the Rockies and dropped on a dude ranch outside Granby where guests half witless on gin kicked it to shreds before our security forces could arrive.

Our third prototype has been impounded for a parking violation in the town of Leroy, Texas. This model, being made of granite, was created so we could study the weight problems we anticipate when the time comes to put the real Pentagon in motion.

To reduce the amount of weight exerted on highway surfaces, we attached 500 helium-filled balloons to its roof by cables, to exert upward lift. On its journey across Texas, local marksmen amused themselves by shooting out our balloons.

As it approached the town of Leroy the local gun club popped the last 25 of them, leaving the highway to absorb the fake Pentagon's full weight. Our Pentagon began sinking immediately and took Leroy down with it.

Both have been sinking at a rate of 75 feet per day, and the Leroy chief of police has declared our Pentagon impounded for illegal parking on a sinking town. We are receiving hourly letters and telegrams of abuse, accusing us—in the words of the Mayor —of engaging in "another one of those damn fool idiot Pentagon boondoggles."

I daresay he will sing another tune if our fake Pentagon strikes oil. We have already met with our lawyers. They advise us to pay the parking fine in order to strengthen any claim we may wish to make if the Pentagon brings in a well, and also to file suit against Leroy for recovery of our helium gas.

They assure us that when they get through with Leroy, we will all be rich enough to retire from the defense industry and live in a Swiss bank. Attractive though this prospect is, I have no desire to vegetate in wealth so long as the Pentagon remains immovably vulnerable to Soviet attack.

For this reason I have gone back to the drawing board and expect to have an absolutely realistic fake Pentagon, capable of containing 30,000 absolutely realistic fake military people—and the whole thing as light as a pancake—ready for testing as soon as Congress appropriates the requisite billion or two to rouse my incentive.

Yes, light as a pancake is what I said. If my hunch is right we can make it from pancake dough. Thus, unlike the MX missile system, the MX Pentagon can never be a total loss to the American people. After covering it with maple syrup, they can eat it.

▪ MAIL-ORDER TANKS ▪

I knew, of course, that the Reagan Administration had gone into the business of merchandising weapons in a big way. Still it was surprising to be awakened to a tank outside my apartment.

Gummy-eyed with sleep, I confronted one of those men who carry illegible documents attached to clipboards. "Sign right here," he said, which I did, being still mostly asleep. "What's it for?" I asked. "Your tank," he said. "I didn't order any tanks," I said. "That's not my problem," he said, leaving.

In midmorning I was awakened again. The police. "What's the idea of that tank blocking the street?" they asked. "Beats me," I said. "Let's see your cannon permit," one of them said. Naturally, the tank had a cannon. "This must be some kind of joke," I said. "We'll see about that," they said, and impounded the tank.

I forgot the whole thing until the bill arrived from the United States Government. It was for a ridiculous sum of money. Bigger than the electricity bill. I tossed it away.

A day or so later came a form letter. "Congratulations," it began. "You now own the finest tank American designers have ever produced. But don't kid yourself, friend, by thinking that tanks alone can do the job of protecting your frontiers from the assault of aggressive Soviet Communism.

"For a fully integrated defense, may we suggest you supplement your tank with a variety of the most advanced jet aircraft, helicopters, surface-to-air missiles and submarines from the selection now available at our warehouse in ——."

I tossed it away. A few weeks later, another bill. "Second Notice," was stamped on the top. "In the daily harassments of fighting the encroachments of Soviet Communism, we all sometimes overlook things like bills ——."

I tossed it away. Also tossed away the third notice after observing that they had added on an interest charge for late payment of bill for one tank.

The next communique was one of those "regrettably" letters. "Regrettably, we have had to place your overdue account in the hands of a professional bill collector," it said. Tossed it away.

One week later. Five A.M. Phone rings. "Listen, you deadbeat, when are you going to pay for your tank?" Hung up on him. At the office, the boss wanted an interview.

"The nature of the consumer goods on which our employees choose to spend their salary is none of our concern, but when they order multimillion-dollar tanks and refuse to pay for them, we understandably feel obliged to ——."

I wrote to the White House, the State Department and the Defense Department. "Your computers have made a mistake. Though I detest Soviet Communism, I have no border menaced by these parasites at the moment and, therefore, have not ordered the tank which was mistakenly ——."

In reply, the Government sent a brochure and a form letter. "How often have you heard some innocent neighboring country say, 'Oh, I don't need tanks, planes, submarines and missiles because, you see, my borders aren't menaced by aggressive Soviet Communism'? And how often have you seen that same innocent neighbor gobbled up by the Red Army? May we suggest that you drop by our warehouse this weekend and browse in our vast selection of weapons on sale at special rates before July 31? Remember ——."

I wrote again. "The tank which your idiotic computer system mistakenly delivered to me has been impounded by the police. I suggest you pay the fine and parking charges to the cops and repossess it, then use it against your sales department."

The reply stated that I was about to be sued for nonpayment of a bill for one tank and suggested I retain counsel. It added: "Your threat to employ said tank for the purposes of assault on U.S. weapons warehouses during a period when these warehouses are crowded with persons attending our summer sale constitutes a clear violation of the agreement under which our weapons are sold. Since our files indicate that you are not the State of Israel, such violation may enrage the Congress, with most unpleasant results to yourself."

So. They intended to play rough. Well, two could play at that sport. I composed a letter. Attention: President Reagan, Secretaries Haig and Weinberger. "Gentlemen: The tank you sold me has been nothing but trouble since it arrived. I happened to mention this to the Soviet *chargé d'armes* when I dropped in on the big warehouse sale last Tuesday, and he said not to worry, as the Soviets will supply me with superior tanks at half the American price. Naturally, I don't want to go Communist, but it's a dog-eat-dog world and I've got to think about my own borders."

This produced a phone call from the State Department. I am invited to Washington for a three-day visit including a trip to Mount Vernon. I promised to come if they throw in a trip to Disneyland. The children want me to bring back a submarine. I'd settle for getting off the mailing list, but considering the high state of American computer technology, the submarine would probably be easier.

THE
$138 MILLION MISTAKE

I don't suppose anybody can make it through a whole lifetime here in the 20th century twilight zone without an occasional suspicion that he is living in a global booby hatch.

Still, most of us try not to think that way, and I am no exception. Despite mountains of evidence to the contrary, I keep assuring myself that everything from the balance of nuclear terror to frozen onion rings makes good sense and can be rationally explained by people a lot saner than I am.

Then along comes something like the Air Force's $138 million plumbing mistake. Plumbing is an inelegant word to describe such a dandy piece of business, but that's basically where the Air Force went wrong.

It was putting up a large building whose purpose required a great deal of intricate tubing and piping, only the people designing the building and the people designing the tubes and the pipes apparently never got around to talking to each other, so when the pipes and tubes came it turned out that none of them fitted the places in the building for which they supposedly had been designed.

The result is that everything has to be done all over again, which will add $138 million to the cost of the job. All right, you say, nobody's perfect. I can go along with that. Maybe plumbers and carpenters don't like to talk to each other. I can go along with that, too. Still, when you're putting hundreds of millions into a construction project, you'd think there would be some $75,000-a-year man whose job is to make sure the plumbers and the carpenters are both looking at the same blueprint.

All right, this fellow's secretary forgot to remind him to send the blueprints to the plumbers. I can see that happening. So far it all looks reasonable and sane. I can even understand the Pentagon's tapping the Treasury for another $138 million to undo the mistake.

To me, admittedly, $138 million is not salami, as it is to the Pentagon. If I try to squeeze the Treasury for $500, the Internal Revenue auditors call me in for an inquisition with thumbscrews. I can go along with that. The Treasury needs that $500 so it will be able to write a check when the Air Force calls up and says, "Send over another $138 million right away; we forgot to get the carpenters and plumbers together on our multihundred-million-dollar building job down in Tennessee."

I can go along with that. The Air Force and I have different values. If I'm walking along and see a penny in the gutter, I don't bother getting my hands dirty picking it up. The Air Force is that way about hundred-million-dollar bills. If it isn't a billion it's not real money.

All right, I can go along with that. What bothers me, however, is this: What is the Air Force doing in the construction business?

Sure, it has to build barracks and mess halls and airplane hangars. I can go along with that. But this $138-million-mistake building is not like those things. It seems to be some gigantic structure for testing new jet engines.

When it's finished, throwing in the bill for the $138 million mistake and allowing for inflation and cost overruns yet to come, it will probably cost about half a billion dollars. I can go along with that. The Air Force uses jet engines. It has to test them, doesn't it?

I have a problem, though, with why in the age of rockets the Air Force is plunging half a billion into a building to test new jet engines. If the test building costs half a billion, how much are these still untested jet engines going to cost? Billions and billions, surely.

Billions and billions for new generations of jet engines to

power new generations of airplanes that will carry new generations of H-bombs round and round in the sky until they either become obsolete or we are all blown up by H-bombs toted new-style aboard rockets.

For the first time I am tempted to say, "It's crazy." Why spend billions on new engines for new airplanes carrying new bombs that won't even be deliverable until after the rockets have blown everything to kingdom come, while the Government axes the public-television budget as a waste of money? Is it worth surviving the thermonuclear holocaust if there is no "MacNeil-Lehrer Report" that night to present the balanced views of both Washington and Moscow?

I do not cry, "This is crazy." If I did, the Air Force would remind me that American security rests on a "triad" of rocketry, submarines and airplanes. Without the airplanes, Jefferson will be silenced by Marx. And after all, is $138 million not money well wasted in the eternal struggle to insure every American the right to a future glistening with armaments?

I can go along with that. After all, extremely bright people have figured it all out. If you disagreed with such intelligent people you'd be crazy. I'll go along with that.

▪ BRASS HAT IN HAND ▪

The Pentagon reminds me of Fred Allen, who was possibly the funniest wit of mid-century America. It was Fred Allen who said you could take all the sincerity in Hollywood, put it in the navel of a flea and still have room left over for six caraway seeds and an agent's heart.

It was also Fred Allen who, after suffering a typical New York business lunch, recalled that in 18th-century London men like

Samuel Johnson, James Boswell, David Garrick and Edmund Burke sat for hours in dinner conversation, and then observed: "During the Samuel Johnson days they had big men enjoying small talk. Today we have small men enjoying big talk."

It's not these particular Allen gems that remind me of the Pentagon, though. It's his autobiographical book, published in 1954, which he titled "Treadmill To Oblivion." Now, three decades later, it seems the perfect title, not for Allen's life, but for a work describing the Pentagon's progress from the cold war to the MX missile.

I don't mean to suggest the country is headed for oblivion, for I am optimistic to the point of idiocy. Every springtime, though, the Pentagon sets off such alarms of doomsday just around the corner that even I begin to worry.

The purpose of the annual exercise is to scare everybody into spending more and more money for soldiery and war gear. Terrifying secret intelligence documents are suddenly declassified to show that the Russians are so far ahead of us in destructive power that only the most desperate financial profligacy can save us.

Congressmen are brought to the White House for slide shows, expensively produced books are published on the public tab, the President takes to television to ascribe weak character to all who do not love everything that kills—all in the cause of the annual Pentagon budget.

Right now the President and Secretary of Defense Weinberger have made American war-making power seem so inferior that you wonder why the Russians don't eliminate us quickly before we can stuff the Pentagon with the money it needs to catch up. I've been particularly upset by Washington reports about Mr. Weinberger. He is said to feel like Winston Churchill in the early 1930s struggling fruitlessly to persuade a disarmed England to gird for the coming battle.

I'd hate to think we are as weak as England was when Hitler struck, but if we are, heads should roll. Pentagon heads. For longer than most Americans have been alive, we have been pouring huge amounts of national treasure into the Pentagon. If it's true that this astounding wealth has been frittered away to no purpose while the Russians, a relatively threadbare bunch, have built a war machine that scares the Secretary of Defense, my question is: "Has the Pentagon been squandering our treasure all these years?"

If so, why give even more wealth to this mass of incompetent spendthrifts?

Sensible people will surely agree that if after 30 years of virtually limitless access to the Treasury a war-making organization remains inferior to that of a nation whose national dish is borscht, it's time to cancel its contract and put the money into an outfit that can get results.

The Miss America Pageant fired Bert Parks. Sanka brand coffee fired Robert Young. President Reagan fired Adm. Hyman Rickover. Each firing accorded with the old American precept that nothing is eternal except the need for new blood. And so, my eminently sensible proposal: Let's fire the Pentagon.

Let's create a new outfit with enough moxie to take a third of the national treasure, create a war machine nasty enough to keep the Russians from casting lascivious eyes on Hoboken and still have a little money left over to contribute to the Firemen's Ball.

Let's put the new outfit on notice that if it starts whining that a third of the national treasure isn't enough, we'll cancel its contract and retain an organization that can do the job efficiently.

I'm told that the Pentagon is not like Bert Parks, Robert Young or Admiral Rickover. Parks, Young and Rickover did not ship vast sums of money to states and corporations that elect Congressmen. This is why Congress did not pass a law forbidding the Miss America Pageant, Sanka brand coffee and President Reagan to fire them.

The Pentagon, snugly bedded in with board-room lions and Congressional titans, has the most enviable job security in America. It is even more secure than the boss's son, for it is the boss's banker, and will be, apparently, forever and ever.

So unless we're as badly off as the Pentagon says we are and the Russians really come, we are doomed to an eternity of spring panics, with the Pentagon year after year crying "Wolf!" until we give it more of the national treasure to fritter away while the Red menace goes on and on, an indispensable boon to the boondogglers. And generations must continue to slog away on the treadmill to oblivion called the Pentagon budget.

ENGLISH UTILIZATIONAGE

BABBLE, BABBLE, GLUB-GLUB

The following case histories are excerpted from "The Annals of Babble," Montclare Shortside's monumental, immensely moving and poignant, but wise and witty study of human decay. It will soon be published by Skein & Ossa, with illustrations, at $27.50.

Irvin Candora wanted to be into. And why not? All the other members of his crowd had been into for years. Sometimes it seemed to Irvin that everybody in the country was into, except Irvin Candora. In college, his friends had been into Zen, into kidnapping the dean, into marijuana, and plenty more.

Irvin's reluctance to be into anything at all annoyed his acquaintances, who were into being into paranoia about anybody who wasn't into the really now talk. They all said Irvin wasn't really now, until somebody observed that if Irvin wasn't into now, he obviously must be into then. This relieved the fears of many and they said, "Man"—for they were all into opening all discourse by saying "Man"—"it's weird being into then, but it's better than not being into anything at all."

Irvin did not feel into then. Sometimes he slipped out of a heavy rain and into a dry martini, out of respect for Robert Benchley. "Hurrah!" his friends would cry. "Irvin is into dry martinis!" But Irvin would point out that he was not into dry martinis, but only in a dry martini. One night after Irvin had slipped into a dry martini he bumped into Robert Benchley, who was eating the olive. "Want a bite?" asked Benchley.

Seeking to impress Benchley, whom he admired inordinately, Irvin said, "Thanks. I'm really into olives." Benchley, thinking it would be a waste of time cultivating a man who slipped into a dry martini and thought he was in olives, waded out of the martini, and Irvin never saw him again.

For years Nora K. would lock herself alone in a room every night and try to relate. At work and at play, everybody was relating. They talked of little else. Nora listened with shame and loathing, for she had never related. As a little girl, she had never even thought of asking her mother about relating, and if she had thought of it she wouldn't have dared ask, for she knew her mother despised people who spoke nonsense.

One evening some friends who were into punk rock invited Nora to meet a weirdo named Irvin who was always splashing around in dry martinis. "This Irvin," thought Nora, "sounds like the dream man who will finally teach me how to relate."

Nora showed up at the appointed hour and slipped into the first dry martini she came to, but the man there was not Irvin. He was

Robert Benchley, and he had just eaten the olive. "I'm sorry but I've just eaten the olive," he said.

"I'm not into olives," said Nora. This was the first intelligent remark Benchley had heard in the last two martinis, and his friendly smile encouraged Nora to become confidential.

"Between us," she confided, "I can't relate."

Benchley grew pale, for under the murmur of the martini's waves it sounded as if she were threatening to relate an entire plot, probably of something eternal, like "Bleak House." Having no intention of having even the story of the "Iliad," much less "Bleak House," related to him, Benchley waded out of the martini. Nora spent the rest of her life in a vain search for him, having recognized him as her only possible soul mate, the only other person in the universe who did not relate.

Absalom Ashcurst was the despair of all society. He didn't know whether he knew who he was or not. What was worse, he didn't care. In the evenings all who knew him would sit around boasting that they really knew who they were or complaining that they could not possibly go on until they discovered who they were.

To all of this Absalom Ashcurst was indifferent. When Carla Braxton would boast that she really knew who she was, Absalom would say, "So what." And when Kevin Toop would groan, "If only I knew who I am!" Absalom would say, "You're Kevin Toop, old sod." And all society would lament that Absalom Ashcurst was not into their heads because he could not relate.

Disgusted by this vacuous chitchat, Absalom slipped into a dry martini one night and saw Robert Benchley diving for the olive. "Take it," said Benchley. "I've already had two." "Who are you?" inquired Absalom who, though accustomed to seeing burglars in his silver chest, was not prepared for a stranger in his martini.

"What's the difference?" asked Benchley. Absalom was

enchanted. At last—someone who perceived the immense uninterestingness of knowing who he was.

"You and I," he said, "are into ego negation. We really relate!"

Taking a deep breath, Benchley dived to the bottom and refused ever to come out again on grounds that everybody outside was drunk. Absalom Ashcurst later got into jogging, which was easier than getting into white tie and tails, and much more comfortable than getting into his head.

▪ VANISHING BREED ▪

I was startled recently by coming across a statuesque brunette in the New York papers. She figured collaterally in a murder story that had a brief run in the news and then disappeared from print. My guess is that some graybeard city editor ordered her dropped after pointing out that there is no such thing as a statuesque brunette.

In truth, there have been no statuesque females of any hair coloration for many years now, but even in the days when they still existed they were always blondes. Don't ask me why, but the code of the police rewrite man allowed only for statuesque blondes.

"Statuesque" did not indicate that the lady was as stunning as a work by Phidias. It was meant to suggest only that she had a generous bosom. Not too generous, though. The word for that was "stout," though it was never used except of women involved in crimes and who, therefore, were thought to be too busy with the police to sue for slander.

Why the statuesque blonde ceased to enliven the crime news is one of those mysteries of popular culture, in the same class with the mystery of the vanished moguls. Twenty or 30 years ago, the news pages abounded in moguls, but today, alas, there is not even a film mogul left in the Hollywood news.

A student of American business tells me that the moguls were replaced years ago by wheeler-dealers, another vanishing breed, to judge by the newspapers. With the Reagan Administration, I rather suspect the wheeler-dealers are giving way to the tax finaglers, but of course you won't find many newspapers willing to call a finagler a finagler just yet.

Another newspaper performer of more recent vintage who has dropped out of sight is the legend in his own time. Just a few years ago there was a legend in his own time every other week in the papers. Most of them were guitar twangers who wore Day-Glo suits and they were colorful, as legends ought to be, particularly in their own time.

Other newspaper characters seem indestructible. Take the innocent bystander. It's a rare day in New York, or any other city for that matter, when the papers can't find an innocent bystander or two to be shot. What's remarkable is that, despite continuous attrition by gunfire, the supply of innocent bystanders has not been significantly depleted in 60 years.

Will Rogers noted the heavy toll in innocent bystanders as long ago as 1924, when he recorded a single afternoon in which four were shot in New York City. "Hard to find four innocent people in this town, even if you don't shoot them," he wrote. And yet they still keep coming out for duty.

Most of the newspaper regulars these days seem dull compared with the moguls, statuesque blondes and legends in their own time who used to enliven things. The consumer, for example, sounds to me like a consummate bore, which I suspect he is, with his incessant whining about chemical preservatives in his liverwurst.

If newspaper performers must be tedious, I like them to make a little noise about it, which was one thing you could say for those old standbys who used to grace every front page until very recently. I refer to slogan-shouting demonstrators.

You still find a few of them buried inside the paper, as well as that once ubiquitous common scold, the militant feminist, sometimes disguised as the feminist militant. In New York the irate commuter still crops up on slow news days, cursing his fate with the immemorial bitterness of a mankind discovering too late that life in the suburbs is more than beating the city out of taxes.

The irate commuter's natural kin is the indignant fan. Alone, neither of them amounts to a hill of beans in the newspaper, and they don't even rate much attention on television unless they come in thousands. Then we have thousands of irate commuters and thousands of indignant fans testifying tiresomely to the humdrum truth that ire and indignation will always be with us, no matter how far we commute or which stadium we crouch in to find happiness.

Mother of five is the most depressing newspaper regular. She is never statuesque, never irate, never indignant. Just plain old mother of five battered incessantly by disaster. Evicted, widowed, beaten, robbed. You'd think she might at least win the lottery once, but she doesn't. There is nothing but misery for mother of five. Only a reader with a heart of stone can follow her career without weeping. I avoid her guiltily until after the morning coffee.

The most interesting new character in print is a fellow referred to as "an extreme environmentalist." I haven't visualized him successfully yet, but I bet he'll be something to see. Imagine a statuesque redwood. Or should it be a statuesque blondewood?

CRASHING INTO
CROSSWORDLAND

One Sunday, wearied by my efforts to determine whether Dr. Dolittle's duck was named Dabbab, Dabnab or Dabrab, I fell into a doze and crashed through the paper into Crosswordland.

I recognized it immediately, for admis were grazing under a dhava and an ai hung from a tondo in one of the salas. I was delighted, for I had never believed in the existence of the admi, the dhava or the ai, and had never expected to see a tondo or a sala.

I had always assumed that these were simply words created by tormented puzzle makers to help them escape their hopeless traps, but there was no mistaking them. The admis were definitely admis (African gazelles). The dhava was unmistakably an East Indian gum tree, and I could tell from the way the ai hung from the tondo (circular painting) that he was indeed a sloth.

The salas (reception rooms) in which I found myself (ego) contained three other persons. They were Ava (Miss Gardner), Evita (——— Perón), and Monk (Jazzman Thelonious). They were ired (angry) about being trite (overworked). Ava averred (stated) that she had to appear in every puzzle ever created. Evita and Monk expounded (delineated) in like (similar) vein (circulatory aide).

"Estop (stop) delineating in similar circulatory aide." I told them (No. One stated others), "and show me this strange place."

"Eerie locus," Ava corrected. "Or more properly, since this is many places, eerie loci."

"Egad," said Monk. "Bah," said Evita. "Hah," said Ava. (Exclamations.) They would not abet (help), but fortunately Etta (Miss Kett) entered just then with Como (Perry or Lake) and took me to see the ort and ana.

The ort (scrap) was in an ugly mood and kept trying to pick a clash (fight) with the ana (miscellany). They made such a clang (loud noise) that both Arcas (Zeus's son) and Irus ("Odyssey" beggar) admitted (entered) to perceive (see) what was errant (wrong).

Arcas warned (threatened) to break the ort's ulna (arm bone) and Irus told the ana he would take him on a Hadj (trek to Mecca) and leave him with an emeer (Sheik of Araby) or emir (Sheik of Araby: var.), or possibly an amah (Eastern nurse) nisi (Caesar's "unless") he kept quiet.

"There must be an inexhaustible supply of emeers, emirs and amahs in Crosswordland," I observed to Etta.

"Aye," she said. (Affirmative.) "We have a rare (unusual) population mass (density). There are almost as many emeers and emirs as Utes and Otoes. Onondagas, Portuguese, Ukrainians and Ghanaians are unknown here, but we have more Celts than Eire (Ireland)."

The zoology of Crosswordland is equally bizarre. The woods are filled with beasts such as the admi, the ai, the zebu, the kudu and the ibex, although the elephant, the bullfrog, the tomcat, the cockroach and most other zoological forms common in the outer world are unknown.

Etta and I entered a new time span. "Here," she said, "is a genuine Apap (Egyptian month)." I did not like the Apap. It reminded me too painfully of the Sunday a puzzle had defeated me because I could not produce the word for "Of bronze: Latin" (aen) because the crossed word for "Egyptian month" was Apap instead of Epup, as any sensible person would naturally have expected Egyptians to name a month.

I told Etta I should prefer to see Meton (moon plain) if it was convenient.

To my delight, nothing was more facile (easier). In Crosswordland, Meton lies between Adano (bell town) and the vast vale (valley) of prefixes and suffixes. Thus was I able to glimpse it over ences (noun suffixes), dento (tooth: prefix), itol (chemical suffix), endo (within: prefix), exo (outer: prefix), ano (upward: prefix) and acu (prefix for puncture).

I felt emotionally anolifted by the spectacle, for there on Meton was Otsu (Honshu town), and on the outskirts of Otsu an Aani (dog-headed ape) stood under a nabo (P.I. shrub: var.) eating an awn (barley beard).

"If you're going to sleep," said my roommate, "let me have the puzzle. What's the name of Dr. Dolittle's duck?"

"I forgot to ask," I wept.

DOCTOR OF
THE INTERIOR

A Mrs. Mullens of Trenton, N.J., writes that she is in a quandary and wants advice. My advice, Mrs. Mullens, is to stay there and see what happens. Robert Benchley once spent 10 years in a quandary and afterward became very successful in Hollywood.

Advising Klingman Carter of Atlanta is not so easy. Mr. Carter writes that he is in cahoots and wonders whether anything can be done about it. Unfortunately, he does not say whom he is in cahoots with. If he is in with a heavy snorer he should get out at once, since the typical cahoot interior reverberates worse than the inside of a bass drum.

The things Americans get into without thinking ahead are astonishing. Today's mail brings the usual dozen letters from people in pickles. Why anyone would get into a pickle without thinking seriously about the consequences is an enduring mystery.

Sam Mayo, one of our clients in Tulsa, got into a pickle several weeks ago with typically unhappy results. Whenever he went out to dinner he was sent to eat in the kitchen because hostesses said it was revolting to see Mayo in a pickle.

The result: he soon found himself in a dilemma and wrote for help. "I am in a dilemma and very depressed," he said. Of course he was depressed. There is nothing bleaker than the dull gray interior of a dilemma.

We counseled Mayo to outfit his dilemma with two horns and climb up on them. Being on the horns of a dilemma is very attractive socially, and a lot of women think it makes a man look intellectual.

Mayo bought two slide trombones and cut such an arresting

figure after crawling up on them that he has been asked to perform in a TV commercial for designer jeans.

Many people have written to ask where the nonce and all the trices have gone. They remember their childhoods when grandfathers stepped out for the nonce and came back in a trice. Regrettably, this is no longer possible. The nonce has been sold at auction to an Argentine billionaire who wanted it as a hedge against inflation and it is now stored in a Swiss vault.

Since people can no longer step out for the nonce, the market for trices in which to return has collapsed. The last trice was made eight years ago. It is doubtful another will ever exist. The jiffy is still available everywhere, however, making it possible to step out for some purpose—not for the nonce, to be sure, but possibly for a pizza—and come back in a jiffy.

Fear of jiffying, incidentally, is almost as widespread as fear of flying. A typical sufferer is a Miss Dundee of Dundalk, Md., who writes that her terror of coming back in a jiffy is paralyzing because she fears she will be unable to get out.

This all too common terror stems from the many tales about some married man or woman who, having stepped out to the delicatessen after announcing plans to come back in a jiffy, has never been seen again. It is nonsense to suppose that these people are all riding the streets perpetually imprisoned in jiffies, but such is the power of neurotic fear.

I mention Miss Dundee because she writes of her engagement to a man who constantly begs her to let him step out for pizza, which he promises to bring back in a jiffy. Her refusal to let him go, she said, always leaves him in coarse fettle.

"How," she asks, "can I get him into a more becoming kind of fettle?"

Ideally, this young man ought to be in fine fettle, but let us face the facts of inflation. The price of fettle has gone through the roof, like the prices of everything else these days. They like it so much up there on the roof that it is dangerous to monkey with them. I went up the other day to beg the price of shoes to come down, and it tore several shingles off the roof and skimmed them at my head.

Therapists who specialize in the fettle problem are divided about the wisdom of encouraging men to get into inferior fettle. If a man is an Arab or Argentine billionaire and can afford to be in fine fettle, splendid. There is nothing like being in fine fettle to put a man on his mettle.

A man in coarse fettle, on the other hand, may behave very oddly. Harlan Haynes of Terre Haute, for example, was so affected recently by being in coarse fettle when he appeared at a cocktail party, that he got on someone else's mettle after his first drink. Slade Harker of Buenos Aires accosted Haynes at the bar, according to the court testimony, cried, "What's the idea of being on my mettle?" and, being in fine fettle—as an Argentine he could afford it—blacked Haynes's eyes.

Haynes has been in a blue funk ever since. I could get him out in a jiffy, but he suffers from fear of jiffying.

LOSS OF FACE

The boss came in looking depressed. "I've lost face," he said.

"How?"

"At the board meeting this morning—I put my foot in my mouth."

"Cheer up. It could be worse."

"I don't see how."

"Suppose you were just one of the hired hands instead of the boss. Everybody would be saying. 'Hand loses face by putting foot in mouth.'"

"Are you trying to rib me?"

"Of course not. Do I look like a guy who'd give the boss a lot of lip? I'm just trying to lend a hand. Now why don't you tell me straight from the shoulder: What's afoot around here?"

He stared at me with jaundiced eye. "Are you out of your skull? A foot around here is the same as it is every place else—12 inches," he said.

I could see his nerves were on edge. In fact, one had already fallen off. "I didn't come in here for a lot of your cheek," he said. "Are you the special assistant for finding lost face around here, or aren't you, and if you are why aren't you already up to your elbows in work?"

I knew he was testing me. He wanted to find out whether I was lily-livered or had guts. I poured him three fingers of bourbon from the stock in my kidney-shaped desk and said, "Can you stomach what I've got to tell you or are you too weak-kneed to face it?"

"You're pretty nosy, aren't you?" he snarled.

"Sure I'm nosy. That's why I took a hand when I saw Cluckhorn footing it out of the board room. I could see he was seething with bile."

"Cluckhorn is always seething with bile," the boss said. "They say his bile duct secretes at the rate of 12 quarts a day."

"What's more, he wants your job," I said.

"Wants my job? What gall the man has!"

"Yes, he has even more gall than bile," I said. "I tiptoed around in the medical department—just nosing around discreetly—and laid eyes on his records. His gall bladder secretes 35 quarts a day."

"It's bloodcurdling," said the boss.

"Anyhow, I noticed something bulky in his pocket. 'Here's the heart of the matter,' I said to myself. And to Cluckhorn, I said, 'Did you get a handout in the board room, Cluckhorn?'"

"Did he speak with forked tongue in reply?"

"No, he pulled the thing out of his pocket and said, 'Oh no, it's not a board-room handout. See: It's just an old hand-me-down foot my big brother palmed off on me before I left home this morning.'"

"He was sneaking out of the board room with a hand-me-down foot in his pocket? Men of that kidney make my scalp crawl," the boss said.

I gave the boss the stony eye. " 'So,' I say to Cluckhorn, 'I see you got a hand-me-down foot, but how come it's stuck in a mouth?' "

"And how did he answer?"

"By shouldering me aside, threatening to have me kneecapped if I didn't give him a head start and legging it down the stairs. I figured I could head him off at the foot by taking the elevator, but when I got to the foot there was neither hide nor hair of him."

The boss glared furiously. "Cluckhorn is a heel!"

"Yeah, but you don't notice it at first because of those calf eyes of his," I said.

"And," said the boss, "since somebody has to take it on the chin, you're fired."

He headed for the door. "If you had a heart," I said, "you'd at least shake my hand."

"I don't have time to have a heart. I'm already late for a rump meeting," he said.

"Something I didn't tell you," I said.

"What's that?"

"The scales have fallen from my eyes, Mr. Cluckhorn."

He turned to stare and when he did I seized his nose and tugged vigorously. The boss's face came off in my hand. "The boss will be needing this," I said, "and what's more he's not going to be head over heels with joy about your making off with it as soon as he put his foot in his mouth and lost it this morning."

Cluckhorn recoiled in sudden recognition. "But—but you're not just another inept corporate bureaucrat," he gasped. "You're —you're—."

"That's right, I'm a private eye," I thighed, lapsing into my Humphrey Bogart lisp.

▪ THE ENGLISH MAFIA ▪

I'm in the writing racket, see. It used to be a nice little living, the writing racket, until the English Mafia moved in on it. I mean, it didn't pull in the really big bucks, but then, it wasn't something you had to sweat either.

I'd lie around the house sleeping till noon, then roll out of the sack, drink a few pots of coffee, then go out in the back yard and split infinitives for a few hours. If I got tired of splitting infinitives, maybe I'd dangle a few participles. Or if the woman next door was peeking at me from behind her curtains I might give her an eyeful by committing a solecism.

One sunny day, I was out there writing up a storm about parameters. To be honest with you, I have no idea what parameters are. I've picked up enough Latin to know that "meter" means "measure," and enough Greek to know that "para" means "near" or "beside," so maybe parameters are measures of a beside, all of which is neither here nor there.

The thing is, you see, in the writing racket when you're pinched for something to write about, you can always write about parameters. Don't ask me why. People like to read about parameters is all I know, and writing about parameters makes you feel smart, especially if you are writing about the parameters making a quantum leap, and don't ask me what kind of leap the quantum variety is either, because all I know is that quantum leaps are the only kind of leaps that are made anymore, at least by parameters.

Well—while going about my business, into the yard comes this guy and gives me a kiss on the cheek. "What's the idea trying to get fresh while I'm writing a run-on sentence?" I asked him.

"One more pronoun without an antecedent out of you, and you're going for a ride, scribbler," he said. Whereupon he pulled a cigarette lighter out of his shoulder holster and set fire to my priceless collection of prepositions, which I had been gathering for years to end sentences with.

"This is just a taste of the kind of thing up with which you must learn to put now that the English Mafia has decided to bring order to the writing racket," he said. And stalked out.

And then stalked right back in. "And another thing," he said, "next time you write a sentence without a subject, you shall be deposited in the river with the Oxford English Dictionary cemented to your feet." This time he stalked out, then stalked in again.

"No more stale clichés," he said. This time he walked out.

As I rapidly ascertained—I have always been a quick ascertainer—the English Mafia was not jesting. It had moved in on publishing houses, newspapers and magazines and was terrorizing small-time operators and literary biggies alike with laws propounded by its most powerful families.

The three most feared families are headed by, respectively, Edwin (Dry Laugh Eddie) Newman, William (The Funster Punster) Safire and John (The Enforcer) Simon. At a recent sitdown of chieftains held at a Washington restaurant (the menu's illiteracies had been expunged by Newman the previous night) the three dons—the word is Oxbridgian in origin, not Italian—divided their linguistic empire into three realms.

Under this table of organization, Newman dominates the highly profitable best-seller business of terrorizing writers whose income flows from tautology, redundancy and ambiguity. Safire, in charge of admitting words and phrases to print or tossing them out on their serifs, is the man of respect before whom every grifter in the writing game now quakes while wondering whether he dares write about the quantum leaping of parameters.

Simon is not called "The Enforcer" for nothing. With merciless efficiency, he polices the vast territory of English grammar, raising brutal welts on the egos of fast-buck writers who try to palm off a bogus "which" instead of an officially certified "that" when introducing the reader to a restrictive clause.

The English Mafia is not dominated entirely by the big three. Dozens of lesser muscle men are constantly trying to grab a piece of the action, and no wonder. Laughing at the mistreatment of hacks has become a favorite American amusement. There is good money to be had from exposing their idiocies. I would grab a little of the action myself if I had enough nerve to pretend I knew what a quantum leap by a parameter looks like.

Alas, courage is wanting, and the back yard is no longer much fun. I no longer dare let my participles dangle in the fresh air or commit a solecism in plain view of the woman next door. In fact, I am becoming something of a rat. Mafia power does that to you. I am thinking of squealing on Bill Shakespeare.

Dozing through "The Merchant of Venice" recently, I caught him writing "between you and I." Throwing Bill to the Mafia would make it hard for me to live with myself, of course, but it could be worth it if they were grateful enough to let me go out in the back yard again and split an infinitive now and then.

Dry Laugh Eddie offered the following response:

I been away—a couple of contracts. I come back, somebody shoves in front of me a column by your man Baker. Russell Baker. The English Mafia, he calls it—Safire, Simon and Newman.

He gives me a name, Dry Laugh Eddie. Very funny. Ha, ha. I smile, too. But some things smart guys don't joke about. Like parameters. In my territory, nobody writes about parameters without I clear it first. Every month, the protection money comes in, I clear it; Baker uses all the parameters he wants. We also throw in three dialogues and three perceptions. (Viables, no. Also, no fundings. They got no redeeming social value.)

Another thing. Baker writes funny about quantum leaps. He got it wrong. Quantum was Cedric Quantum, professor of English in upstate New York. One day he misuses hopefully. *Soon comes the Quantum leap. Only it's no leap. Quantum is pushed, a long way down, with only rocks to break the fall.*

Baker calls me Dry Laugh Eddie. Like I said, I don't mind. My sense of humor I'm noted for. But better he *should understand it's no laugh. Also* you—*if you want him to meet your kind of deadlines, not mine. So a laugh it's not: It's a cough, what they call in the trade a discreet cough. A warning. I'm coughing for Baker now.*

EDWIN NEWMAN

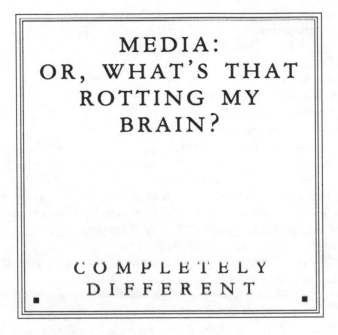

MEDIA:
OR, WHAT'S THAT ROTTING MY BRAIN?

COMPLETELY DIFFERENT

This is all new.

It is completely different.

You have never experienced anything like it.

Now that you are experiencing it you will never be the same again.

You will be all new.

You will be completely different.

You will never want to experience the old experiences again.

Everything that is old has been discarded to create a completely different experience.

Long sentences have been.

Discarded.

Everything has been completely miniaturized.

Thought. Soap. "King Lear." Liver spots on the backs of hands. Travel time. Sunsets. Spin-dry cycles. Headaches.

All are now reduced to their absolute essentials.

All miniaturized.

This is a revolutionary new concept.

It will give you twice as much time as your old unrevolutionary new concept.

You will be twice as dynamic.

You will enjoy endless hours.

You will stay younger twice as fast.

Here is what the critics say:

"Since experiencing the revolutionary new concept I have become twice as irresistible to women"—Mr. B. T. of Houma, La.

"—a dynamic new route to newness. . . . I never knew what 'King Lear' could be until I saw it performed without commas or punctuation marks' "—Mrs. C. J. of Rochester, N.Y.

You will also smell newer.

Why is this extraordinary advance in newness vital to success?

Because we live in today's world.

Today's world is completely different.

Today's world is all new.

Today's world requires people who are completely different.

It requires people who are all new.

We have all seen people who live in yesterday's world.

Are those people fun people?

Dynamic people?

When you open their doors do you smell an exciting new fresh-from-the-factory new-people smell?

With a hidden camera we interviewed a typical scrubwoman.

Note that these pictures show her seated before two boxes.

She cannot see the labels visible to you.

Note that one box is labeled "New Completely Different Person."

The other is labeled "Old Unchanged Person."

We will now run the tape.

"Mrs. Hummel, you are a weary 67-year-old scrubwoman who spends long nights alone on her knees in this empty building. We ask you to study these two boxes and tell us which box contains the sort of person you would prefer to keep you company through the night."

"Easy. That box right there."

"Now, you, Mrs. Hummel, have chosen the box labeled—unbeknownst to you—'New Completely Different Person.' Tell me why you did not pick this other box labeled 'Old Unchanged Person.' "

"Because it looked too heavy to carry around all night."

"Let's open both boxes and look."

Notice Mrs. Hummel's expression as the "Old Unchanged Person" box is opened and a 135-pound woman emerges and asks her to spend an hour walking on the beach watching a sunset.

Notice that Mrs. Hummel recoils.

Mrs. Hummel recoils because the woman is not new.

She does not have new-woman smell.

She has not miniaturized the liver spots on the backs of her hands.

She does not propose living dynamically, but instead speaks in the exhausting rhythms of this particular sentence, with its antiquated commas and cumbersomely involuted grammatical structure, thereby making it all too evident that she is incapable of living dynamically by getting right to the point, a fact which is driven home by her suggestion that they spend an entire hour watching a sunset, thus consuming precious time that could be used to have her wrinkles surgically removed and the dull soap glaze banished from her hair by application of a new, completely different shampoo.

Note, by contrast, how delighted Mrs. Hummel looks when the box labeled "New Completely Different Person" is opened.

Yes, the figure emerging is a 10-ounce man.

He has been reduced to the absolute essentials of newness.

Mrs. Hummel can keep him in her apron pocket throughout the night. She can remove him when she wishes to inhale his exciting new smell.

He will tell her without commas how to have twice as much time for dynamic living by watching a sunset in 15 seconds.

Mrs. Hummel will never be the same again.

■ TOOTH AND MAN ■

News is made up of a curious variety of events. For example:

1. The rare event: "Man bites dog" is often wrongly cited as the definition of news. Actually, it is the tiniest fraction of the tons of news we consume annually; to wit, a rare event.

2. The daily event: "Dog bites man." This makes up the basic fodder on which the news industry thrives. Since rare events are rare, the industry would collapse if ordinary events—crime, political speeches, child abuse, divorce and massive social and mechanical breakdowns—failed to occur.

3. The unevent: "Dog does not bite man." This is the plot of the news's daily "weather story," which tells us, essentially, "Every day we have some weather, yesterday was no exception, and tomorrow won't be either."

4. The media event: Determined to publicize a cause he thinks is being woefully neglected, man stages a bogus rare event to attract TV and print coverage. If angry about dogs fouling sidewalks, for example, man notifies editors he will bite dog in public thoroughfare in time to make 5 P.M. deadlines.

5. The double media event: Editors tire of covering man biting

dog to demonstrate anger about fouled sidewalks. Man tries to tempt editors by offering to bite three dogs. Editors notify S.P.C.A. and rush reporters and cameras to dog-biting site to get story on irate S.P.C.A. woman biting man for trying to bite dog.

6. The cute event: Dog trained to bark "Ho, ho, ho" is dressed up in Santa Claus duds, placed on plywood throne and photographed not biting news feature writers placed in lap.

7. The annual event: It happens every year, but America never tires of it. We are speaking, of course, of the annual Dog Biting Pageant in Atlantic City. Once again, two-legged finalists with the most astonishing teeth in America compete to determine which, in the judges' opinions, can bite dog with least loss of charm, grace, poise and patriotism.

8. The potential event: The basic headline here is: "Dog May Bite Man." In the most common form, it goes on to say that Senator Glenn or former Vice President Mondale may seek Presidency. The potential event is covered by reporters clustering around dog to hear if he growls dyspeptically at man. If he does, they write, "Dog makes potential man-biting noises," or "Senator Glenn is beginning to sound a lot like a Presidential candidate."

9. The highly conditional potential event: Dog is contented with man, shows no proclivity to bite, but who can tell what he might do if man gave him away and dog ended up in custody of second man? Illustrative news treatment with bipeds: "Senator Robert Dole may seek the Republican Presidential nomination if President Reagan declines to run for a second term."

The all-purpose headline for this story is "Unforeseeable Future Could Change Dog Unforeseeably."

10. The anticipated event: Dog who has never been trained to do anything to man but bite him gains freedom of streets. Newspapers write: "Sharp Rise In Dog-Bitten Men Seen Likely." Or, if the story concerns the political instead of the canine kingdom: "Senator Kennedy Seen as Cinch to Run."

11. The anticipated eventus interruptus: Defying news oracles'

predictions that he would bite man after man, dog romps peaceably into park to frolic with kittens and lick man's hand. The headline: "Dog Astonishes Man." What dog has actually astonished, of course, is not man but the news industry, which has covered an anticipated event only to see it turn into an anticipated eventus interruptus, thus supplying a delightful front-page story —"Kennedy Won't Run After All"—where it would have had no story at all had it not covered the anticipated event so thoroughly.

12. La Belle Event Sans Merci: Upon death of dog, man acquires new dog. Sure, old dog never bit man, but who knows what new dog will do? New generation of dogs replacing old generation. What is mood of new dog generation? Should man bite new dog first before dog concludes man is soft and bites man? Should man growl nastily to keep dog polite?

Here we have the skeleton of an important foreign news story, recurrent with each change of government in Moscow. As with the anticipated eventus interruptus—"Kennedy Declines to Run"—it is one of the news industry's favorite events, since it allows for endless fruitless speculation about things that may or may not happen one of these days.

In certain cases news consumers crazed by the merciless onset of such works are tempted to hurl themselves teeth first at the offending news industry. Perhaps they yearn to change the subject by creating a new headline: "Man Bites Man." To elevate their assault from the category of daily event to rare event, they would have to bite at least 20.

.WAITING FOR H-HOUR.

UTTERLY AT SEA, April 6, 1982—The last briefing began at midnight. Apparently it will be very bad when we hit the beach. Worse as the day progresses. Our first assault force goes in one hour before dawn. It consists of highly mobile minicam crews, sound men, still photographers, veteran war correspondents and relatives of publishers and network executives who are to get first crack at the island's limited hotel facilities.

Groans of dismay went up throughout the armada when the briefing officer described conditions the first wave would encounter. "This is the Falkland Islands, not San Salvador, Saigon, Beirut or even Washington, D.C.," he said, "so don't expect to find the bars or the Press Club open before breakfast."

For those of us in the third wave, the prospect is even grimmer. By the time we get ashore, Phase One of the blitz will already have landed 2,200 fully credentialed media personnel. Since the population of the Falkland Islands is only 1,800 persons, it's assumed that every last one of them—man, woman and child— will have been exhaustively interviewed before the rest of us can get at them.

There is some whining about this from the younger types among us, greenhorns who are nervous about taking part in their first media blitz and worried that they'll disgrace themselves when things become bad. They are spending this last hour composing a petition to the Chief of Media Operations, urging that 4,000 Patagonians be helicoptered over from the South American mainland by noon to provide fresh subjects for interviewing.

I can't help smiling at these fledglings. They remind me of my own fear on the dawn of my first Presidential news conference in Washington. "Since there are 600 of you going into that room, and since there is only one President to interview," I told a grizzled media veteran, "surely you don't need me to help."

"Just keep your head down and your lip buttoned, son, and afterwards you'll be proud to boast you were there when the questions were flying," he said.

Now, after so many hundreds of media blitzes, I am calm about coming late to the scene. Most of us in the third wave are members of the elite forces: sob sisters, foreign-affairs analysts, crack television panelists who appear on Sunday interview shows, blooded newspaper columnists.

Most of us can fly in to anyplace from Washington or New York and after talking to a cab driver and smelling the air tell you which Presidential candidate is going to carry South Dakota, where the public stands on the issue of wearing open-neck sports shirts to the theater, or whether the Zbatu tribesmen are likely to go Communist before Christmas.

I don't mean this to sound boastful. I'm just saying we're professionals. It takes many different skills to insure success in a media blitz, even against a little place like the Falkland Islands.

Take today's operations, for instance. Everybody knows there are a lot of sheep on the island, so it's fairly certain the TV boys are going to thrust inland and photograph sheep galore. A greenhorn would think that exhausts the sheep angle. Not the professionals.

Later today the professionals will be out there with cameras trying to get shots of sheep with funny expressions. That's for the comic sign-off segments on the news. But that's just the beginning.

It's a lead-pipe cinch a couple of sheep are going to be run over before the day is out. That's where the feature writers move in for interviews with the weeping sheep owner. You know that story. On television, it's "How do you feel now that your favorite sheep lies dead at your feet?" Or in print: "Slain Sheep Was Child's Xmas Gift From Widowed Mom."

The long-headed commentators will take it from there. For instance: "It was only a dead sheep according to the cruel score-card of war, but insiders familiar with Communism's ruthless program of disinformation know that in these distant island pastures the road to Moscow begins at the sheep dip."

I'll probably hold off until tomorrow and knock out a politico-economic analysis, pointing out that the Falkland Islands' recent trend toward the left or the right results from the outside world's insensitivity to sheep. I'll have to wait until I get ashore to learn whether the island is trending leftward or rightward. If it turns out it's not trending either way, I might get a thoughtful piece about sheep keeping their countries in the middle of the road, though it's always seemed to me that most countries keep their sheep in the middle of the road.

In a few days Hodding Carter will be down here with his PBS cameras accusing the media of misleading the public by overplaying the sheep angle. You'll catch me on the telly then confessing to Hodding that I spent far too much time on the sheep story and completely ignored the vital impact of cottage industry on the islanders' attitude toward church donations.

I'll be the guy winking violently at the camera. That's so my mother will notice me.

FOREVER EMBER

I have just taken The Burn-Out Test concocted by the Anchor Press/Doubleday publishing empire to help people determine whether they are burning out and need to purchase Dr. Herbert J. Freudenberger's book, "Burn-Out," which will tell them how to fan fire out of their ashes.

If you think I intend to reveal my score, you are a burned-out case and ought to buy Dr. Freudenberger's restorative immediately. No mind in full flame expects candor about matters of this sort, least of all from newspaper columnists, a species susceptible to complete burn-out within two weeks after first undertaking their grim task of disgorging wisdom at precisely spaced intervals, often on days when their brain pans have the Vacancy sign out.

I confess, however, that a few of the test's 15 questions were troubling. Oh, not Question No. 1—"Do you tire more easily? Feel fatigued rather than energetic?" It is no easier for me to tire now than when I was in high school, an era when it took me a full 10 minutes after getting out of bed in the morning to become totally fatigued.

In those days, of course, knowing that I had to face a Latin class at 8 A.M. was a great aid to rapid tiring. Nowadays, lacking an 8 A.M. Latin class, I am often unable to achieve deep fatigue until I have been at least 15 minutes out of the sheets.

Question No. 2—"Are people annoying you by telling you, 'You don't look so good lately?' "—was no problem. What annoys me is people who say, "You're looking wonderful lately." In my experience you don't blurt out to somebody that he's looking wonderful unless he looks so ready for autopsy that you have to smother the impulse to ask if he has his will in order.

Question No. 5 was more troublesome. "Are you often invaded by a sadness you can't explain?" Fortunately, the temptation to answer "Yes" here was dispelled when I moved on to Question No. 8—"Are you seeing close friends and family members less frequently?"

My answer was "No, I am seeing close friends and family members as frequently as ever." And not necessarily a good thing, either, for I have noticed that these people so dear to me seem of late to be tiring more easily and feeling fatigued rather than energetic and to be working harder and harder and accomplishing less and less, thereby showing distinct symptoms of burn-out as defined by Questions No. 1 and 3.

It is no wonder I am often invaded by a sadness I can't explain. I am spending too much time seeing friends and relatives in advanced stages of burn-out. It would make anyone sad. But fortunately, since The Burn-Out Test has helped explain the sadness that often invades me, I can now cope with it.

I can buy each of them a copy of "Burn-Out," or, if the price is as outrageous as the price of most books nowadays, I can eliminate the sadness more economically by not seeing them anymore.

I scored very high on Question No. 9: "Are you too busy to do even routine things like make phone calls or read reports or send out your Christmas cards?"

Fortunately, yes. I observed 20 years ago that making phone calls, sending masses of Christmas cards and, especially, reading reports produced in me an invasion of sadness I could explain all too well. The phone calls invariably produced bad news, addressing Christmas cards always reminded me of Scrooges who had not sent me cards the previous Christmas, and reading reports invariably reminded me that English, my mother tongue, was on her deathbed.

Are there three human activities more calculated to produce instant burn-out? Not likely.

My answer to Question No. 11—"Do you feel disoriented when the activity of the day comes to a halt?"—was "Yes, frequently, since I often take a large martini at that hour."

Perhaps because of this habit, I was able to reply with a fiery, "Nonsense!" to Question No. 15—"Do you have very little to say to people?"

Question No. 14—"Does sex seem like more trouble than it's worth?"— seemed excessively tricky, since it is always difficult to measure sex in terms of worth. My answer here would have to be an equivocal admission that sometimes sex does seem like more trouble than it's worth. I confess, for example, that sex in a crowded theater almost always seems to me like more trouble than it's worth, especially during an intermission.

Question No. 12 was the real stumper, however. "Is joy elusive?" it asked. Hasn't it always been? Mustn't it always be? Isn't it joy's elusiveness that makes it so precious during those moments when it pays one of its fleeting calls?

Show me a person in whom joy has signed on for a three-year lease and I'll show you a person who feels disoriented all day long, as well as when the activity of the day comes to a halt. I'll show you a person who will pay good money to be invaded by a little sadness he can't explain. I'll show you a case of burn-out to make even Dr. Freudenberger tire more easily and feel fatigued rather than energetic.

THE LEGAL PITCH

Since the Supreme Court granted lawyers the right to advertise, a few of the more adventurous new law firms which cater to middle-income Americans have been testing the television commercial as a way of attracting mass business. So far their commercials have been duller than a lecture on torts, which is a pity, because we middle-income folks really need reasonably priced legal services and would flock to them in droves if they were advertised persuasively.

To help the cause, I would like to suggest just a few of the many irresistible commercials that might be produced on behalf of, say, the firm of Burger & Warren.

The first would open with a shot of a jeweler cutting a large, expensive diamond. We see the blow struck. The diamond shatters into ruin. The jeweler rises in despair. Enter Robert Young, carrying a pot of Sanka brand. "Bill, what's the matter?" he asks the jeweler.

"My doctor says it's too much caffeine," says Bill.

"Why don't you drink Sanka brand?" asks Robert Young.

At this point a stern man in a snap-brim hat enters, lays a heavy arm on Robert Young's shoulder and slaps a legal document into his hand, at the same time saying: "Mr. Young, this is a restraining order issued by Judge Hardy at the request of Burger & Warren, attorneys for Bill."

"That's right, Mr. Young," says Bill. "I got so nervous about expecting you to pop in here with Sanka brand every time I ruined a diamond that I couldn't cut the mustard any more, much less the diamonds. Then I heard about Burger & Warren's low-priced legal services."

He embraces the man in the snap-brim hat, who smiles into the camera, saying, "Our restraining orders are available in a wide selection for as little as $37.50."

"This doesn't mean I'll have to go to jail, does it?" asks Robert Young with a chuckle.

"No, sir," says Bill, "but if you ever do, remember, Burger & Warren can get you out with a habeas corpus for only $19.95."

"Fees slightly higher on weekends," says the snap-brim hat. Everybody chuckles.

The second commercial opens with a middle-aged woman seated at her living-room desk. She is frowning as though unable to balance her checkbook. Off camera we hear a voice, obviously a strange voice which does not belong in this house, probably an actor's voice which belongs on a stage. The voice says, "Something wrong, Mrs. Murkin?" Mrs. Murkin looks up at the camera. "Just not feeling myself today."

Whereupon the unseen man asks, with insinuating insolence, "Constipation?"

At this moment we hear the voice of Officer O'Leary saying, "All right, Mac, get those hands up." The camera turns to show us Officer O'Leary holding an actor at gunpoint and, behind him, a man in a snap-brim hat.

"Take him down to headquarters and grill him, O'Leary," says the snap-brim hat. "You'll probably find he's the same housebreaker who's been terrorizing housewives down on Walnut Street by turning up in the laundry room to ask why they use inferior detergents."

The camera cuts to Mrs. Murkin, speaking to the audience. "I didn't know there was any way to stop actors from walking right into my living room and asking me vulgar questions until somebody told me about Burger & Warren," she says.

"That's right, Mrs. Murkin," says the man in the snap-brim hat, wrapping the strong arm of the law around her shoulder. "For a consultation fee of only $20, we were able to tell you that these embarrassments constituted criminal breaking and entering by a professional actor."

"And now," says Mrs. Murkin, "I can look worried in my own living room without ever having to discuss my bowels with strangers again, thanks to Burger & Warren."

In the next commercial, an aged, arthritic housewife is seated behind a table on which sits a heavy iron skillet. Off camera an unseen man with an actor's voice says, "Mrs. Klomp, I want you to try to lift that skillet with your aged, arthritic old hand."

Mrs. Klomp starts to lift the skillet, then shrieks with pain, doubles up in agony, drops the skillet on her foot and collapses on the floor.

"What's wrong?" cries the actor's voice. "You're just supposed to tell me you couldn't pick up the pan until you got a dose of aspirin."

"That was before somebody told me about Burger & Warren," says Mrs. Klomp, smiling in agony.

"That's right, Mrs. Klomp," says a man in a snap-brim hat, entering left. "Thanks to Burger & Warren, you were able to learn that the sums to be gained in court for pain and suffering far outweigh the fee for doing aspirin commercials. How is your leg?"

"Feels broken in two places."

"Congratulations, Mrs. Klomp," says the man in the snap-brim hat. "You will never have to work again."

The actor's voice off camera says, "There's a name for this kind of game."

"And if you want to know what it is," says the snap-brim hat, "phone Burger & Warren right away and get in on our big March special. All consultations reduced to $16.99."

THE
SCRUTABLE KREMLIN

The change of government in Moscow confronts Washington either with great peril or rich opportunity, though possibly neither.

Only time will tell.

This is why we must be patient. Nor must we relax our guard. At the same time, our posture must be absolutely correct. As President Reagan has pointed out, it takes two to tango, but the correct posture for doing the tango is quite different from the posture that must be assumed for doing the rhumba.

Will the new Soviet leadership be willing to tango with President Reagan? Or will it try to force him to rhumba?

Only time will tell.

Thus, the President is receiving conflicting advice from his foreign policy advisers. Some say he must stick adamantly to his request for a tango; others urge him to be prepared to compromise by offering to do the fox trot.

One thing is clear: It takes two to fox trot.

Another thing is also clear: Leonid Brezhnev is dead. An era has ended. It was the Brezhnev era. It followed the Khrushchev era, which followed the Stalin era, and now there is a new era.

But is there? It is quite possible that the new Government is merely a transitional arrangement. Perhaps in six months or a year from now there will be another new government after the transition ends. If so, will the present period be known as the transitional era?

Only time will tell.

And what of Yuri Andropov, Mr. Brezhnev's apparent successor? The significance of his rise to power may lie in the relative simplicity of the spelling of his name. Andropov is easier to spell than Brezhnev, which was much easier to spell than Khrushchev, a name that drove journalists up the wall in despair.

Is it possible that the easier-to-spell Mr. Andropov's victory means that journalists now hold the controlling power in the Soviet power structure?

Only time will tell.

One thing is clear, however: Mr. Andropov formerly headed the famous Soviet espionage agency referred to in the West as "the dreaded K.G.B." Is this why Mr. Reagan appointed Vice President Bush to represent him at the official obsequies in Moscow?

Mr. Bush formerly headed the famous American espionage agency referred to in the East as "the evil C.I.A." Was Mr. Reagan, with his taste for the theatrical, amusing himself by staging a real-life confrontation between George Smiley and Karla?

What did Mr. Andropov think as he gazed across the bier and saw his old American counterpart, Mr. Bush? Did he say to himself, "If I'd been born American, I'd never have climbed any higher than Vice President and would have spent my best years going to funerals"?

Only time will tell.

One thing, however, is clear: Mr. Reagan either made a brilliant decision by not attending the funeral, or made an extraordinarily stupid mistake, unless—as also seems possible—it wouldn't have mattered whether he went or not.

This leaves the question of Afghanistan still unanswered, though much has been made of the significance of the decision to release Lech Walesa from Polish imprisonment at this very moment in history. We have either seen a strong signal of veiled Soviet intentions here, or one of those everyday accidents of timing that make life so difficult for us students of Soviet affairs.

I, for one, am reluctant to answer the question, "Whither Soviet relations with Poland?"

Only time will tell.

One thing is perfectly clear, however: The Soviet bosses astonished everyone by the speed with which they selected Mr. Andropov to succeed Mr. Brezhnev.

The implications here cannot be glossed over easily. It is far too obvious that Mr. Andropov either pulled a strong-armed political coup in outmaneuvering his competitors for the job, or was part of a smooth transfer of power that had been jointly planned by the party bosses before Mr. Brezhnev's death, or possibly had the job foisted on him when everybody else refused to accept it.

If this last was the case, why did everyone refuse to accept it? Was it because all the other party bosses had been scared by their predecessors' inability to grow corn and feared being jeered at when they, too, tried to grow corn and failed?

Does Yuri Andropov know the secret of making corn grow?

Only time will tell.

THE ROAD
TO APEVILLE

I turn on the radio and torrents of information gush through me. The 7:52 is thirteen minutes late. Maniac shoots seven. Hailstones in Hackensack. Trial in seventh week. Senate confirms Reagan nominee. Scientists to mate man and ape. Murders four, takes sleeping pills . . .

Alarm bells ring along the ganglia. The mind flicks the retention switch. "Something interesting passed through in that last batch of sludge." The recall mechanism automatically tunes out the continuing flow of data (C.I.A. spokesman denies, Congressman denies taking kickbacks, traffic moving slowly on the East

Side Drive) and begins sifting through already molding residue.

Yes, here it is: Scientists to mate man and ape. What else was said about it? Artificial insemination. Right. Something about artificially inseminating a human female with ape extract to see what would be produced.

The mind stalks this half-heard fragment with caution. Nonsense. One must have dreamed it. Science wouldn't. A frantic scramble through the newspapers. Not a word about it. Immense sensations of relief. Must have dreamed it. What would be the point of crossing man and ape?

Point? You want to know the point? How about a boom for the razor-blade, shaving-cream and depilatory industries?

Nonsense. Science wouldn't.

Oh wouldn't it?

Biologists are already dreaming of blending chopped genes from various life forms to produce brand new citizens for the animal and vegetable kingdoms. Mixed life salads to brighten up a world gone stale.

Intentions are the best. Better world, miracles of progress, man relieved of age-old curse. Greatest boon to humanity since nylon stockings. (Miracle-of-chemistry division.) Imagine the future: A rosebush crossed with a praying mantis, capable of eating the insects it attracts. A common-cold virus crossed with two aspirins and three days of bed rest; capable of curing itself without a human host.

Yes, why not cross human and simian? With a tail strong enough to suspend himself from a subway strap, a man would find it easier going to work in the rush hour.

Yet I dislike this progress. It is already hard enough finding a shirt in a size 36 sleeve length without having to compete with a new race whose arms will hang to their shins. And this is minor among the potential disasters.

The trouble with science is that the better world for which it strains is an illusion. Science cannot make the world better. It can only replace bad old things in the bad old world with new things that make the new world just as bad, although in different ways, as the old.

A rosebush crossed with a praying mantis sounds splendid. It would be good to have those insects gobbled down the instant they alighted on Herbert Hoover or Helen Traubel. But scientific miracles of this sort usually create as many problems as they solve.

The rosebush turns out to be susceptible to acid indigestion and stomach gas and, after gorging all day on beetles, keeps the neighbors awake all night with its belching. This happened with the miracle of unleashing nuclear energy. It was fine having an unlimited source of energy, except for the fact that it led to a bomb that keeps people awake all night until they train themselves not to think about it.

I see in the papers that science has made a square tomato. The story goes on and on about the advantages of this deed, such as: square tomatoes are easier to pack than tomato-shaped tomatoes; the new square tomato is tougher than its predecessor and can, therefore, be more easily picked by machinery, and so forth.

In all these raves, there is not a word about the square tomato tasting better than the old tomato.

In fact, there is not a word about whether the square tomato has any taste at all. So where is the miracle? The last scientifically bred tomato, which you get at the supermarket most of the year, is also hard and easily harvested and packed, but it doesn't have any taste.

The only purpose of a tomato is to taste like a tomato, and if it doesn't, it is not a miracle, but a failure. If its purpose is to be hard, it might as well be a potato. If its purpose is to be square, it might as well be a cardboard box. And if we don't care whether it tastes like a tomato or not, why is science wasting its time making square tomatoes when it could be making cardboard boxes that look like potatoes?

The radio clacks on. (Rhodesian rebels attack. Russian astronauts in orbit. Coffee prices rise.) I have come dangerously close to an idea. A heresy. Is science as muddled as the rest of us? The priesthood as fraud. But I cannot formulate it. As always, the sludge is rising too fast. (Senator Jackson confers, cold front over Oklahoma, heart attacks rising, oil-rich Middle East, the Rev. Sun Myung Moon. . . .)

▪ RICHES OF THE TUBE ▪

If you've been missing me lately around the dance hall on Friday nights, folks, it's because I have been riveted to my parlor telly in trancelike pursuit of riches beyond the imagination of Kreuger the Match King.

Fridays at 8:30 find me—amply fed, digestive organs ruminating contentedly to the rhythmic sloshing of martini juice—sitting in my Louis Quinze armchair awaiting another installment of "Wall Street Week." By 8:33 my mind is reeling so wildly with gyrations of the Dow Jones average and the pinwheeling of money funds, Treasury bills and gold markets that I often require a calming infusion of brandy.

It is clear in a vague way that mastering the information dispensed on "Wall Street Week" will bring wealth so vast that I will never again have to tug my forelock to sweatshop bosses. Once mastered, this information will enable me to sit at a poolside stroking a cool drink and several blondes while barking telephone orders to my broker.

In fairness, let me say that "Wall Street Week" does not teach that orders to brokers must necessarily be barked. Barking the orders is my own idea. It has always seemed to me that the best thing to do with an order is to bark it. People to whom orders are barked tend to take them seriously, and in any case I want to impress the blondes. That can't be done by whining orders to my broker, can it?

But my mind wanders. "Wall Street Week" always has that effect on it. It may be the dizzying dreams of waiting riches that distract my attention, just as dreams of next summer's vacation used to take my mind off the beauty of quadratic equations in high-school algebra class.

As a result I am always missing the key piece of information. Recently when the experts were well launched and I had begun to debate whether a redhead by the swimming pool might be useful to relieve the monotony of blondes, I suddenly became aware that a vital piece of information had issued from the tube.

Someone has said, "It's a good time to get into runcibles." I could swear that's what the man said. "A good time to get into runcibles." Or had he said "manciples"? Maybe "crunchables."

I focused intently on the screen, waiting for Louis Rukeyser, the host, suave with Wall Street cunning, to explore the matter with a trenchant question. "Pardon me, Wall Street biggie Kloster Ames, but did you say runcibles or manciples, and for the benefit of our audience, how does a runcible differ from a manciple, and how do you get into one?"

Rukeyser did not ask this question. Instead, with a satanic little upturn of the lip corners, he looked directly at me, the way algebra teachers used to look, as if to say, "You can't get rich daydreaming about redheads," and said, "Now let's look at the statistics on porch bellies and see how they stack up against high-risk scrapple."

Or words to that effect. My mind always cuts out when they start talking about porch bellies. I don't want to be known around Palm Beach as the man who "made it all in porch bellies." Some wiseacre would be sure to label me "The Porch Belly Baron."

Runcibles I could live with, or manciples, even crunchables.

"The Crunchable Croesus" they might call me. "The Manciple Midas." "The Runcible Constable" would not be insufferable.

It was 10 minutes till 9 by the clock. Was it too late to consult the telephone directory, dial a broker and bark a question? "How can I get into runcibles, manciples or crunchables, as the case may be?" It was not a question that barked easily. Anyhow, all the brokers probably had their phones disconnected so they could watch "Wall Street Week" without interruptions.

Rukeyser administered another of his satanic smiles. I had known that smile from high school. I was going to get an F in Wall Street unless I buckled down to blind trusts and high-risk moratorium rates in discounted marginal-options investment funds.

Seated in his immense tycoon's armchair, presiding over a couch-load of brilliant financial wizards, Rukeyser demonstrated how easily he could make my mouth water. "People who bought stocks recommended by analyst Gil Cooley here would have earned 55 percent on their investments last year. Anyone who had taken broker Jim Smeen's advice on gold would now be rich enough to purchase Denmark."

My mind was wandering again. It was by a swimming pool. I was telling a brunette—brunettes always seem to proliferate around the swimming pool by 9 P.M.—"From now on, sweetheart, you can call me 'The King of Denmark.'" I lifted the phone and barked an order to buy Denmark at 51⅛.

"Repeat that, please," said the broker.

"Arf, arf," I barked. "If you want it in plainer English, woof woof."

A child woke me. Rukeyser had left. The swimming pool seemed far away. The brandy was astonishingly low, but never mind. Next Friday night "Wall Street Week" would be back again.

AND THE
REICH GOES ON

To children of the 1930s World War I, though it had ended only 15 or 20 years earlier, already belonged to ancient history. I marveled that my parents had been alive when it was fought. It made them seem very, very old.

The impression of an antique war came from a yellowing old military history book whose photographs, blurred and lifeless, showed soldiers in odd tin-pot hats and puttees. The uniforms seemed almost comically quaint. The occasional war movie usually centered upon the aviators, who seemed dashing and romantic, but the boxy old Spads, Nieuports and Fokkers they flew looked antediluvian compared to the streamlined beauties being flown in the 30s.

We were of the immediate postwar generation, but already the war existed for us largely as a musty relic. When, at precisely 11 A.M. every Nov. 11, we were required to stand by our school desks for a silent minute while the school bugler blew a quavering version of "Taps" somewhere down in the schoolyard, we seemed to be taking part in some primitive ritual whose meaning was beyond our grasp.

What a contrast World War II has been. Though it ended 38 years ago, I doubt there is a sentient adolescent in the entire country who doesn't have it embedded in his bones.

Since 1945 we have lived constantly with World War II in film, books, comics and television. It's as though we loved that war so much we couldn't bear to give it up to the past.

Thirty-eight years later Nazis remain a staple of the best-selling potboiler. It is a rare publishing season without a best-selling tale about Nazi machinations past or present.

In some versions the old Nazi leaders who were supposed to have died in the bunker are discovered alive and deadly in the jet age. "The Boys From Brazil" a few years ago raised the terrible and happy possibility that evil Dr. Mengele had cloned dozens of new Hitlers who, even now, might be loose among us.

Why is such a terrible possibility happy? I think because we need the Nazis as archvillains whom we can loathe without feeling inhuman. This is not a great age for villains; too often nowadays they turn out to be your allies or your victims. Nazis make it possible to fear and hate without guilt.

Reviewing the long postwar history of the Nazi in American entertainment, you wonder whether American writers, actors and producers could have made a living if there had been no World War II.

It is curious to track the style transformations that movies and television worked upon their World War II soldiers over the years in an effort to keep the war up to date. Consider hair styling.

The old 1940s films show G.I.'s correctly with severe crew cuts. By the 1960s, however, fancy hairdos for men had made the crew cut look antique and slightly comic (like the tin-pot hats and puttees of World War I) to younger Americans.

To make the war look up to date movie makers began lengthening the hair on their G.I.'s, and we had a 1960s generation of World War II warriors wearing hair in long, fetchingly styled drapes that would have looked ludicrous in 1942.

The Nazi also underwent change. In the long-running television series, "Hogan's Heroes," the Nazi ceased being an incredibly efficient martinet capable of the ultimate monstrosities, and became a comic, even slightly lovable oaf, too dimwitted to cope with the high jinks of a fun-loving bunch of American kids.

Rod Serling once said, "If you liked World War II, you'll love 'Hogan's Heroes.'" He wasn't far from the mark. When "Hogan's Heroes" appeared, Americans were in their forget-and-forgive phase with Germany and Japan.

The new monsters were in Moscow, and the new ally was Germany. Still, if we were hooked on Nazis and World War II we didn't have to give them up entirely. We could keep them by turning them into comic bumblers. If high-spirited lads with Southern California haircuts could outwit them every time—well, it just showed that the war was really a lot of fun and Americans didn't have to worry about their new German friends being just a mite too clever.

And anyhow you had to be embarrassingly old and terribly stuffy to point out that three things the Nazis weren't were funny, likeable and incompetent.

There is no end in sight to World War II. In the supermarket there are always one or two new paperbacks with swastikas on their covers. A local movie house recently reran that unlikeliest of Nazis, Laurence Olivier, drilling nice-guy Dustin Hoffman's teeth, and just two nights ago on television I watched the British Army fight the battle of Burma.

It has been 65 years since World War I ended. "The Great War," my mother used to call it. It feels as if it happened 300 years ago. I guess the Kaiser was rotten box-office.

ROCKED

Notes from the pop-music world: Arfie Melina of Ten Cent Coffee, in London to promote Coffee's new album, took off on the British press last week for asking dumb questions about her on-again off-again relationship with Lips Luscombe. Arfie threatened to stuff cucumber sandwiches in The Daily Express's presses, then struck the Times man with her pet boa (constrictor) when he asked if Lips had split because he couldn't stand the triple taradiddle in the backup on Arfie's last single ("Toothache of My Mind") on the Hohokus label. Lips, playing it cool, turned up at the Baltimore Festival of Rock (3 killed, 28 injured, 118 mugged), playing alto electric saw for Queen's Indian Declined. Lips's agent denied he planned to undergo sex-change surgery at Johns Hopkins after the concert, or any time this month.

The crowd in Boston wasn't exactly amused when promoter Rick (Take the Money and Run) Wisengoffer announced that Hog Momma & Cornsilk would stand in for Coronary Insufficiency. The Cornsilk haven't been on the charts since Wayne Newton was a soprano and Hog Momma, with his antique 1975 snuffle-rock sound, wasn't what the kids had laid out $35 a head to hear. The Insufficiency weren't kidding, however, when they wired ahead that they'd been grounded in New York. Rock authorities there were holding them for questioning on suspicion of not transporting concealed drugs.

There were plenty of nasty looks when Rock Starr pulled into Oakland last week still alive. Press-agent stories about Rock's lethal habits, failures in love and family rejection had whetted fan appetites for another big suicide story. Clytemnestra, the label that pressed Rock's biggest hits, was all set with heavy promo to exploit postsuicide market for Rock's old records, and six publishing houses had already inked contracts for "Rock Was My Secret Lover"–type mortuary-exploitation books. Rumor has it that Clytemnestra will take a million-dollar bath if Rock doesn't do the fatal overdose number before Christmas.

Despite a long audition in which he was chosen as the newest hair knotter for Abraham Lincoln Velocipede, Ellwood Saskatoon didn't really feel like a member until one night a couple of months ago when he had too much to drink in a hotel room on the road and got his big toe caught in a mousetrap. "I was walking around with this mousetrap on my toe and Greggie [Appletof, lead singer of the Velocipede] went around saying, "Anyone who don't like him having his toe in a mousetrap is gonna have to put up fists,' " recalled Saskatoon at a Houston press party. After a discussion of the Old Testament and vegetarianism, Velocipede guitarist P.P. Plusfours gave the party a big laugh by overturning his table, wrestling with bystanders and running out of the restaurant. "People wonder why I still take LSD," commented P.P. as he passed the maitre d' at the door.

We caught Eyeball's new act at Oakland last week to see if it really was as tasteless as people who saw it at Monterey claimed. At Monterey many fans were offended, as were the police, when the Eyeball ended their closing number by committing a human sacrifice on stage.

Naturally, this became a *cause célèbre* of sorts, what with the Mayor canceling the next day's performance and the civil-liberties people replying that the Eyeball's freedom of expression was being infringed by the Mayor. Things really hit the fan when the musicians' union found out that the victim wasn't a member of the union, and the Eyeball left Monterey pretty depressed.

Well, things had been ironed out when we caught the act in Oakland, and the crowd gave the Eyeball one of the biggest ovations heard on the Coast all year. It couldn't have been for the music, which wasn't quite hard rock, or soft rock, or even chimney rock. Let's face it: Eyeball still doesn't understand about blowing the audience's brains out. The sacrifice, on the other hand, was performed with great panache and theatrical style. Although several fans stated that they were offended in principle, even these had to admit the whole thing was done in very good taste.

Dotty Van Doty, whose "Lugubrious Ballads" and "Songs from the Tombstones" led the charts in the morbid 1960s, has issued her first new album since returning from the dead.

On the Fast Bucks label, it is titled "Yearning for the Grave," and features some first-rate piano work on two bands by the late, great Fats Waller. For the benefit of you kiddies, Fats was the Bob

Dylan of the piano. A piano is an instrument like the guitar, except it has more strings and is not usually electrified. Dotty, fortunately, still hasn't been electrified either, and her lyrics, melodies and voice are just as depressing as we all remember them from the days before she crossed over. In a New York interview, Dotty revealed that Janis Joplin is very active on The Other Side and is studying civil engineering.

▪ MIND OVER BLATHER ▪

I'm not exactly crazy about flag-waving, but there are certain things I think every American has a duty to do. This is why every year I set aside three nights to watch the Miss America contest, the Academy Awards and the Super Bowl.

A few people sneak off to bed on these nights. They're the kind of people who try to get out of jury duty. People who care about our country do their jury duty without whining. The same goes for Miss America, the Academy Awards and the Super Bowl. On those three nights the whole country gathers in the national parlor to participate in acts of American communion. Not being there is something like saying, "To hell with the Fourth of July."

I'm there, friend, and I'll bet you are too if you're my kind of people, so I want to ask you a question: Do you remember who won the Miss America contest last September?

If so, you probably remember who won the Super Bowl last January. I don't remember either one. Worse than that, I've already forgotten who won the Academy Awards last spring. I do recall that the Pittsburgh Steelers won the Super Bowl once—or was it twice?—but that's been a while ago. I also recall Clark Gable years ago winning the Academy Award—or did I just dream that?

I mention this to illustrate the contrary nature of the human mind which keeps it constantly at war with decent human instinct. Consider the battle being waged between these powerful interior forces when the typical patriot tunes in the Academy Awards show.

Instinct, seeking communion with the national spirit, settles me into a chair and orders the eyeballs into the staring position. The mind, alarmed by a sudden interjection of colored images of extravagantly dressed people sporting $200 hair stylings, pushes the intercom button.

"What's going on down there?"

"This is one of the nation's great nights," Typical Patriot replies from the viewing post. "Instinct has taken over the controls."

Mind: "Why are they playing the Super Bowl in those East Side haircuts?"

Instinct: "Wake up, you idiot. This isn't the Super Bowl. We watched the Super Bowl months ago. Have you lost the data on that already?"

Mind: "I've told you a thousand times I'm full up. There's no place left up here to store that junk. I'm already stuck for some place to put 137 miles of new tax-law changes the Republicans sent over, and right now I'm trying to assimilate 187 pages of Henry James the old man sent up last night. So whatever you're feeding through the boob tube, forget it."

Instinct: "You can't refuse these data. This is the Academy Awards."

The mind says something like, "You can lead a mind to Hollywood, but you can't make it think." Then it sets its intake mechanism in fast-disposal mode, and the Academy Awards roll off it like shampoo off a bald man's skull.

I don't think the mind wants to be unpatriotic. I think it's just overworked. You can't treat a mind the way you can an automobile, though I suppose that's coming in the not too distant future when mind transplants will probably make it possible to get a new one every three years or 100,000 thoughts.

Even then, though, most people will probably want to stay with their old models. I know I would. My present mind is no great shakes compared with the new models. It couldn't analyze a computer system if my life depended on it and it's so slow to spot a new tax shelter that I'm the laughing stock of the Free Enterprise Club, but on the other hand I know its defects and am comfortable with them.

It's a mind that's not going to give me any nasty surprises. We've reached an accommodation. I don't insist that it regurgitate the Academy Award winner for best movie of 1969, and it doesn't let me down when I ask it how to spell "accommodation." As soon as I put in the request, it says, "Two c's and two m's."

Some of its weaknesses I've lived with so long I don't even waste time trying to correct them anymore.

When it was newer, for example, I was always asking, "How do you spell that word that means 'to trouble and annoy people'?" and sometimes it said, "H-a-r-a-s-s," but just as often it said, "H-a-r-r-a-s-s." Now I realize that that's a word it will never be able to spell with certainty, and I don't ask it to try anymore.

For the same reason I've quit asking it what the Belgian Congo is called these days, what years James K. Polk served as President and what the difference is between an entablature and a portico. In return for my not humiliating it by asking such questions, it is always ready to tell me what my home phone number was in 1959, why I should never play poker with guys who wear green eyeshades, how to make a dead-stick landing with a biplane in a crosswind and what the odds are against a politician repaying his campaign contributors with my money.

We are often exasperated with each other, but pursuing the policy of live-and-let-live makes our relationship tolerable. I no longer insist, for instance, that my mind join me in watching the Academy Awards or Super Bowl or Miss America, which make me feel like a good American, and in return the mind never neglects to argue me out of the subways at night, which keeps both of us ticking along with hopes that things may yet get better.

THE
MUSHROOM BLUES

Fellow phones, says his name is Mintz, and can he have an appointment. "You got an image problem, Mintz?" I ask. My business is solving image problems, you see.

"Sort of," he says. "Why don't I come by and talk?" If he can pay my fee, which is 25 bucks a day and expenses, why not? So he comes to the office with this thing.

"What's the thing, Mintz? I don't seem to recognize it."

"It's the bomb," he says.

"What bomb?"

"The atom bomb," says Mintz.

"Sure it is," I say. "And I am Dr. Enrico Fermi."

It's no wonder the guy has an image problem. If I showed up for appointments and said I'd brought the atom bomb, I'd have an image problem too.

"I'm not kidding," he says. "This is the real thing. Look what it says right here."

I look. It says, "Twenty Megatons. Handle With Care." And in smaller letters, "Property of U.S. Government. For Use Only By Authorized Persons."

This raises my jaded old eyebrows.

"How about that?" I say. "So that's what it looks like!"

Well, says Mintz, not really. Usually the bomb doesn't look so depressed.

"You're telling me the bomb is feeling down in the mouth?"

"It's these popularity polls," Mintz says. I glance at them. No wonder the bomb is feeling blue.

Only 25 percent approve of the bomb, the other 75 percent want nothing to do with it. Twenty-five percent approval rating in the polls is slightly lower than what Adolf Hitler would get.

"I wouldn't let the bomb see these figures if I was you, Mintz. They might make it act testy, and then there's no telling what it might do."

"The bomb already knows," he says.

"Is it sore?"

"Sad," Mintz says. "Very, very sad." It seems the bomb wants to be liked. Instead, everybody hates it. The Mormon Church has said it doesn't want it in the state of Utah. Senator Paul Laxalt doesn't want it in Nevada. Ranchers don't want it in Arizona or New Mexico. Vermont doesn't want it in Vermont or anywhere else. Neither does the Board of County Supervisors in Loudoun County, Virginia, or the Board of Selectmen of Nantucket Island, Massachusetts.

"The bomb has an image problem," I tell Mintz. "Can I look at it a little closer without getting its dander up?"

"Actually, I can disassemble it for you," he says, removing some metal panels and several dozen springs.

"Now this," he says, "is the heart of the mechanism," and yanks it out. On one side it looks like Ronald Reagan, and on the other like Alexander Haig. "The Haig side contains the thinking mechanism and the Reagan side translates the Haig thoughts into English so you can understand them," Mintz says.

"Look here," I say to the thing, "if you want people to like you, you've got to show you've got compassion and don't intend to let people suffer by blowing them up. Suppose you go on TV, prime time, all networks, you know that old image scam. And you say, 'Look here, folks, you're never going to have to worry about me, because I'm just never going to explode anywhere, any time, for any reason.' "

Out of the question, says the bomb. The only thing keeping the Reds from taking over Europe is their fear the bomb will whomp them if they try it.

"So you go on the telly and say, 'Look here, folks, I've got to keep threatening to whomp the Russians, or they'll trample all over us, but just between us, it's all bluff, because nobody's ever going to be dumb enough to push my button for global suicide.' "

Impossible, says the bomb. If the K.G.B. gets wind of the television announcement that it's all just bluff, the bomb threat restraining instant Soviet conquest of the world will lose its credibility. Once the Russians lose their credulity nothing will hold them back.

"And anyhow," says the bomb, "what makes you think it's all just bluff?"

I look at Mintz. "Isn't it all just bluff, Mintz?"

"Come on," says Mintz, "even if the bomb does blow, it doesn't mean there wouldn't be a lot of people left over to put things back together again. When working on the image problem, keep in mind that we've got to make everybody believe the bomb might blow, in order to prevent it from having to blow, while at the same time persuading people that if it does blow, a lot of them are going to be left over."

"I'll work on it," I say, and maybe I will. I might even be able to get the bomb's popularity rating up to 26.5 percent. First of all, though, I'm moving to Utah.

TAKING
HEROES SERIOUSLY

It's a good thing they made "The Wizard of Oz" into a movie when they did, because the film business couldn't do it nowadays.

The same thing goes for "A Christmas Carol" by Charles Dickens. If Dickens had let that one pass so somebody could write it in 1983 it would never have been written. No 1983 writer would touch Tiny Tim with a 10-foot Scrooge.

Imagine a novelist today trying to cope with Marley's ghost.

He'd have to justify it as a psychiatric problem and we'd have tiresome passages about Scrooge lying on a couch talking to an analyst. The analyst would be a woman. Scrooge would probably fall in love with her, right? And there goes your story.

Great stories and movies are products of their particular time. If somebody doesn't get them down on paper or film at exactly the right moment, they're lost forever.

Take a movie like "Raiders of the Lost Ark." It had a big audience and was a lot of fun to watch. Its production people said it was the ultimate Saturday-afternoon movie serial of the 1930s. I thought it owed a lot to "Gunga Din," indisputably the best boy's adventure film ever made.

I liked "Raiders of the Lost Ark" all right, but it was not in a class with "Gunga Din." I can watch "Gunga Din" twice a year without yawning. One viewing of "Raiders of the Lost Ark" will hold me for a lifetime.

The reason is: We just don't take swashbuckling heroes seriously anymore, the way we did when "Gunga Din" was made. If you want to do a swashbuckling hero like the fellow in "Raiders of the Lost Ark," you have to make a joke of the whole business.

You want to make sure nobody in the audience thinks you're an outdated sap who really believes in swashbuckling. So you keep winking at the audience by making the whole thing so preposterous that they'll know you're only kidding. Then you justify it by saying it's the kind of baloney old dad and mom really took seriously back when they went to the Bijou on Saturday afternoon, and weren't they out of it, those poor old saps?

What you end up with is a burlesque of mom's and pop's era which confirms your feelings that you're a lot wiser than they were. What you don't end up with is a classic flick like "Gunga Din" or "The Wizard of Oz."

Ten years ago, a Broadway company tried turning the Oz story into a rock musical called "The Wiz." It then turned into a movie, made the usual rounds and disappeared forever, while the ancient version with Judy Garland continues to be indestructible.

I'm not surprised. You can't set the Wizard to rock music and make anybody care much, any more than Mick Jagger could pack Madison Square Garden by singing "In the Gloaming," "Silver Threads Among the Gold" and "I Wandered Today O'er the Hill, Maggie" to piano accompaniment.

Can you imagine what a moviemaker would do right now if Judy had never made "The Wizard" and he was going to take first whack at it? I'll bet there would be a lot of grass humor about the stuffing inside the scarecrow.

Dorothy would have to be a streetwise city kid. You know: Jeans. A little cleavage. A big Judy Blume reader. Kind of Brooke Shields, I think. Dorothy has been around and yet she hasn't, if you get my meaning.

Whirled over the rainbow, whom does she meet? A scarecrow, a tin man with an ax and a chicken lion. The audience is going to sit still for this? All right, we'll show them we know it's corn, too. We could have all of them flop down alongside the yellow brick road and puff on the scarecrow's stuffing.

Opportunity for a lot of titters in the audience there. Then they all get up and do a little grass-fantasy number.

Who interrupts it but a wicked witch of the west? We could get Ethel Merman for that. Dorothy tells Ethel she wants to get to the Emerald City, which cues Ethel to do her Mailgram number. Emerald City, it's only a day away by Mailgram. Get it?

All right, enough. I won't go on about the fantastic close-ups of the open-heart surgery performed on the Tin Woodman, who needs a heart implant, except to say that it'll take a strong man to sit through that sequence without fainting.

I don't hear anybody singing "Over the Rainbow" in this production. Songs like that went out with the Depression. I certainly don't hear Dorothy at the end telling everybody there's no place like home. We don't want the audience throwing popcorn at the screen.

I think Dorothy probably jets off to Europe in the last scene to get away from old fuddy-duddies who don't understand that a girl nowadays needs a convertible to escape middle-class tedium around the house.

I also don't think any movie people would make a wise-guy movie just to be wise guys. I think they'd make it because they're trapped in 1983, when hardly any little Dorothy anywhere can admit to thinking there's no place like home for fear she'll be thought soft in the head.

We can still go smiley-weepy when Judy Garland says it on old film, but if you say it nowadays, pardner, you'd better wink.

NO PEACE
FOR OLD PHARAOH

The mummy of Ramses II was flown from Egypt to Paris in 1976 to undergo medical treatment for a fungus infection. An honor guard of the French Air Force and the Garde Republicaine presented arms as the crated pharaoh was transferred from the airplane to a truck. He is 3,000 years older than the United States and may have known Moses.

Pharaoh had been in low spirits ever since arriving in Paris. "Here I am, an old man in a damp town, flung around in a crate like a shipment of cauliflower," he mused, as he looked up at the reporters, who looked down at him with curiosity and distaste. He knew all their questions.

They always asked how it felt to be the oldest dead man in the world. They would wonder if he had any tips for other dead people who wanted to stay in circulation for 3,200 years.

Ramses never answered these questions. Not because he thought them inexcusably stupid, which he did, but because he thought it undignified for a Pharaoh to be quoted in journals that were sold at supermarket checkout counters and devoted large headlines to UFO sightings. Ramses did not believe in the people's right to know. He did not even believe in freedom of the papyrus.

The reporters sensed that their distaste for him was fully reciprocated and always took mean little revenges by describing him in their stories as "emaciated" and "fungus-ridden." Naturally, it galled him to have to appear before these wretched people wearing last millennium's mummy wrappings, and when they began their listless questioning, he tried to shut it out by staring through them and thinking of how golden the sunlight was on the Nile when he was a lad in the land of the living.

"How's it feel, Pharaoh, to be the oldest dead man in the world?" asked a reporter. And Ramses remembered how, in life, the courtiers would awaken him each morning by singing a hymn to the sun.

"Do you have any tips for other dead people on how to stay in circulation 3,200 years?" asked another.

The utter indifference of this reporter irritated Ramses. This reporter, even more than the others, obviously thought that interviewing a Pharaoh was beneath him. Obviously, his idea of an important assignment was covering Franklin Pierce, Warren Harding, or whichever transient gladhander happened to be President of the United States these days.

Ramses could barely restrain himself from laughing. This poor dolt, he thought, really believed it was important to cover Franklin Pierce building the Teapot Dome. (Pharaoh's grasp of American history was weak, he knew, but he had decided not to worry about it unless America lasted another 2,000 years. "No use cluttering up the mind with trivia," he always mused.)

He gazed through the offending reporter with an absolutely silent contempt which said, "You poor pipsqueak. All Franklin Pierce will ever build is the Teapot Dome whereas I, Ramses II, built the Temple at Karnak." The reporter made some notes. They said "emaciated," "fungus-ridden" and "temple-dropper."

Ramses resolved to avoid further boasting in the presence of such people. There was a meanness of spirit here in the land of the dead for which his religious studies had not prepared him. There was a low-comedy ethos in this land. He had scarcely left for Abydos, the sacred city of the dead, beautifully mummified and encased in jewels, expecting to join Osiris, before grave robbers had stripped him bare.

After that, the denizens of the land of the dead had stuffed him in a forgotten tomb shaft in the Theban cliffs and left him there for a thousand years or two before hauling him out and carting him off to Cairo. "Some joke," Ramses had been musing for two or three thousand years.

And now Paris. Another joke. As Pharaoh, of course, he was scheduled to go to join Osiris. Some disgruntled shipping clerk had doubtless willfully misread the instructions and directed him to Paris. Paris. Osiris. The lout would plead a confusion of spelling. Paris was an eerie backwater, thought Ramses. People eating snails and frog parts. And the reporters, the inevitable reporters, with their desultory probing for a feature story.

"How did Cleopatra stack up against Nefertiti, Pharaoh?"

"Pharaoh, did you really know Moses?"

Moses? That name again. He could not remember a Moses, but there was somebody—what was the name?—Ahmose?—Utmose? A troublemaker of some sort. But so long ago. What did it matter?

The reporters left to ingest snails, frog parts and fermented grapes. Pharaoh was left alone in the darkened room. He wondered idly how much longer he would have to go on amusing them before they relented and let him finally join Osiris, but he was not impatient. He was beyond impatience now, and did not have high hopes when he heard approaching footsteps and looked up through a flashlight beam at a grinning figure in a blue suit with brass buttons.

"How's it feel to be the oldest dead man in the world, dad?" said the guard, and strode away whistling with self-satisfaction.

THE MALE WEEPIE

The popular success of "Chariots of Fire," a sentimental film about young men striving to become Olympic champions, puzzled me until an Englishman pointed out that the explanation is quite simple. "It's a male weepie," he said.

Of course. As masters of popular entertainment have always known, men in the audience like a good cry just as much as the women do. The difference is that men don't like to sob out loud. It embarrasses them, so they prefer something that makes them cry silently but doesn't reduce them to watery convulsions.

The well-made "male weepie" produces in the male that choked-up sensation in the chest called "a lump in the throat." "Chariots of Fire" gave me "a lump in the throat," and I'm not ashamed to admit it. If it had pushed sentimentality too far and reduced me to copious tears, I would have detested it. Wanting to cry was a delicious sensation; being pressed for outright sobs would have offended me, and I might have left the theater feeling the movie was ridiculous.

Oscar Wilde spoke for the male attitude toward "weepies" when, writing of one of Dickens's tear-stained passages about the death of a cardboard heroine, he said that only a person with a heart of stone could read it without laughing.

I used to have the same response to female "weepies"—also known as "four-handkerchief movies"—in which Barbara Stanwyck or Bette Davis or Joan Crawford had the women in the theater wailing damply in the dark. While all around me trembled with sorrow, I yearned to laugh aloud.

Those who say men would be healthier if they wept with less restraint may have a good point, but whether venting gales of tears at the movie house improves the hygiene is another question. It seems to me that crying is not at its best when you're paying $5 a seat to weep in harmony with a mass of strangers.

Still, the male pleasure in feeling a lump in the throat is undeniable. Moviemakers of the old school always understood it, always knew that men wanted to feel like crying without being brought to sobs, and cunningly exploited this hunger, even with their toughest heroes.

When John Wayne, the ultimate in hard-shelled masculinity, came up for retirement from the U.S. Cavalry, the director gave us a scene in which his troopers presented him with a watch at the final muster, then focused the camera on old Duke's face fighting to hold back the tears, while every man in the audience felt that delightful lump rising in his throat. If Duke had sobbed, we would all have started to sob and hated it and started to giggle, but the director knew where to stop. At the throat line, with lump rising.

Once in a while the director went too far, as when Cecil B. De Mille, having done a nice lump-in-the-throat job on Gary Cooper's death in "The Plainsman," spoiled everything with that ridiculous closing shot of Gary and Jean Arthur riding a buckboard in the sky, thereby suggesting a weepily sentimental reunion in a heaven full of cumulus clouds. Lump in the throat immediately yielded to smirk on the pan.

In recent years when films became technically and, often, artistically better, the lump-in-the-throat effect was no longer much sought. Maybe movie people thought it was too easy, too cheap, too false, too old-fashioned. In these good new movies, the audience was most often detached from the emotional turmoil of the characters.

You can watch Clint Eastwood, Marlon Brando, even Burt Reynolds with fascination, as a scientist might study his specimens, but it's hard to feel much kinship with the characters they play or to respond with anything except wonder, curiosity, envy or admiration for men so unlike yourself and all the other men you know.

In these movies there is a great deal of blood, gallons of blood, but it never seems to me as terrible as the tiny droplets of blood glimpsed briefly when John Wayne or Gary Cooper bled. In fact it doesn't seem like blood at all. It seems more like ichor, the inhuman substance that flowed in the arteries of the gods.

The box-office success of "An Officer and a Gentleman" interested the movie reviewers precisely because it is such an unmodern film. Except for the new-fangled obligatory sex scenes, it is pure 1943. It tells you what it's going to tell you; then it tells you; then it tells you what it's told you.

The audience knows what is going to happen from start to finish. We know that Mayo, the rat with women, will undergo redemption, learn humility, and marry the good woman. They don't make movies like this anymore, and maybe they shouldn't, yet audiences love it. Why? Well, it raises a lump in the throat, just as "Chariots of Fire" did. It's a "male weepie."

I suppose the success of these two films will tempt a lot of movie people and we'll see a run of new shows catering to the rediscovery of the fact that men like to feel the tears rise as much as women do. The trick will be to keep those tears from falling.

A BETTER COLUMN

The editor has imported a Japanese newspaper columnist. Apparently I am not cost-efficient. The editor has not said it in so many words, but the calligraphy is on the wall. Suddenly there is ominous talk about getting rid of outmoded old word guzzlers who consume high-priced newsprint at insupportable rates.

It is said that when the Japanese columnist comes into production he will be able to deliver an 800-word column idea in 150 words that can be easily digested in stop-and-go city reading. For highway reading, the same idea can be delivered in 129.6 words.

This is nothing compared to what is yet to come. I am told that in Japan they are already developing a miniaturized newspaper columnist capable of reducing an 800-word column to 25 words.

Thanks to the spreading popularity of speed-reading this means that Americans will soon be able to read as many as 128 newspaper columns in 60 seconds. Exposure to 128 newpaper columns, even over the span of a year, can do devastating damage to human brain cells; consuming 128 in 60 seconds, you might think, would be catastrophic.

Japanese newspaper-column miniaturizers, aware of the danger, have already perfected numerous safety devices. These include the newspaper-column bumper, which automatically stops the reader from colliding with a fourth consecutive column and bounces him off into the comic strips. An air bag is also being developed. Activated by the reader's physical collapse, this will spring out of the classified ads and surround the stunned column reader with life-restoring oxygen.

Costs of the air bag are still exorbitant, but Japanese industrialists are confident that they can be brought within the financial capability of the average American newspaper once Japanese technology produces a silicon chip to miniaturize the average American column reader.

The Japanese columnist on our payroll, I hear, will go into production as soon he passes the entrance examination of the American Newspaper Columnists Association. This requires applicants only to demonstrate that they are more qualified to be President of the United States than the President is.

I have moved that the association adopt more difficult rules. Specifically, these would forbid membership to any columnist who arrives at the job before noon, leaves later than 12:45 P.M. and refuses to use at least 800 words when writing a column about a 50-word idea.

My Japanese competitor fails on each of these tests. He sleeps on a cot in the office, rises at 6:30 A.M. and does 50 push-ups to prepare his mind for the work of reducing 800-word ideas to 150-word columns.

Instead of leaving for lunch at 12:45 P.M. and discovering it necessary to rendezvous with highly reliable sources at a movie theater and keep cocktail-hour appointments with invaluable Government insiders, he eats at his desk at 4 P.M.

By this time, he has already computerized 145 columns—an entire year's output for old, outmoded word guzzlers. Does he relax over lunch with the crossword puzzle? No. He asks other columnists to join him for an exchange of ideas about how their work can be improved and columns made even shorter.

My last good card is the union. As usual, the union is threatening to go on strike. "Do you have strikes in Japan?" I asked him.

"Certainly," he said. "We are very fond of strikes in Japan."

That made me like him a bit more. "We like strikes here too," I said. "Of course, I'm not crazy about walking round and round the building for weeks at a time, especially in rainy weeks, but yelling at people who cross the picket line is one of the great ways to let off steam."

"Americans quit working when they go on strike?" he asked.

"Why do you think we call it a 'job action'? Because there's no action on the job. Don't you have job actions in Japan?"

"In Japan," he said, "we have what I suppose you Americans would call 'job inactions.' When we strike, we put on armbands to show we are unhappy and we go into the plant and work twice as hard as usual to prove to the bosses how valuable we are."

I anticipate he will have some agreeable union problems which may save my skin. If he doesn't, Congress can just call me Chrysler and give me a pass to the Treasury. The economic significance of this Japanese invasion is obvious to ——.

Sorry, but it's 12:45. I must meet a highly placed source over a bottle of Bordeaux and a duckling.

FLICKING THE DIAL

Saturday afternoon with the TV set:

". . . and that's the scene here at the 12th hole in Dubrovnik, where Watson has just birdied his five iron to fall two runs behind Mario Andretti. Now we go to Lake Ladoga for the quarter-final competition in water skiing where beautiful Amanda . . ."

"Is that why you lied when you told O'Toole you felt a giant turkey brush past you after the lights went out for the séance?"

"You can't pin this rap on me, shamus. Myra Summers was killed by a peck from a giant turkey. If you check with my doctor, you'll find I'm allergic to turkeys. What's more . . ."

". . . bases loaded and two out here in the seventh inning. Look at that little fellow sleeping, Wally. Think he cares that Mario Andretti is walking up to the plate with the big lumber?"

"I'd like to get some shuteye myself, Harry. Boy, that hotel they got us in is murder for noise. All night long."

"Speaking of noise, Wally, remember that echo used to come off the rafters in Shibe Park?"

"Do I? But what about those wooden poles in the old Polo Grounds?"

"Yeah. You know, I got splinters in my hand from one of those poles one day."

"No kidding? Speaking of hands . . ."

". . . so don't wait another second. Rush right out and tell your hardware salesman Pete Petcock sent you, and he'll give you a special . . ."

". . . and lots more on Eyeball to Eyeball News at 6 o'clock with anchorman Ernie . . ."

"Do you see the same thing I see, Speedy?"

"It's a mummy, all right, and it's walking."

"But mummies come from Egypt, don't they? What's a mummy doing here in one of the craters of Jupiter?"

"That's what we're going to find out right now. Let's get into our space suits and . . ."

". . . from my fresh youthful skin that I am 57 years old, would you? The secret of eternally youthful skin is right here in . . ."

". . . and Goolagong breaks the world backstroke record! Her time is a fantastic . . ."

". . . of all the gin joints in all the . . ."

". . . scoring two runs ahead of him! Look at his teammates pour out of the dugout to congratulate him."

"Speaking of dugouts, Wally, that plane they flew us out here on yesterday smelled like a . . ."

". . . big heaping plate of fried chicken and a mountain of cole slaw that'll make the whole family lick their chops and shout for . . ."

". . . and you were lying when you told O'Toole that Mrs. Danvers had been secretly breeding giant turkeys."

"Just a minute, shamus. Have you seen this coroner's report? Myra Summers may have been pecked by a giant turkey, but the peck didn't kill her. Examination of her throat showed that she had inhaled lethal mummy dust. You know what that means?"

"Of course, somebody lied to O'Toole when they said there were no mummies in the room during the séance. Now we're getting . . ."

". . . crispy, crunchy, yummy, chunky goodies for gluttonous kiddies. Good for Fido, too, with twice as much tailwagging, meaty-tasting heartiness and oodles and oodles of . . ."

". . . international summer ski-jumping competition here in Marrakech. Now we switch you to Munich for the semi-finals in the Bavarian Cosmic Tennis Tournament for a purse of $750,000. Bjorn Borg is seeded . . ."

". . . with this unique roach poison. See how Mr. Cockroach walks right in and then . . ."

". . . turns into a giant turkey under the power of the full moon?

But where does he get the mummy dust that he forces his victims to inhale?"

"I'll ask the questions, Hoskins. Why did you lie to O'Toole when you told him Mrs. Danvers hadn't imported any mummies from Egypt during the past six weeks?"

"Because . . ."

". . . I need something to relieve the painful symptoms of hemorrhoids, doc."

"Well, why don't you try . . ."

". . . your New York Yankee baseball cap. Offer good until . . ."

". . . we get this mummy off Jupiter and get him back to Earth where Doctor Kinsolving can subject the wrappings to ionic scan."

"You mean we're gonna be locked into this spaceship with that mummy all the way back to Earth? I don't like it, Speedy. That thing looks . . . uncanny—like . . . like . . ."

". . . a grant from the Exxon Corporation. This afternoon our guests will discuss the evolution of lute music. Did you know that in ancient China . . ."

". . . they play this unique version of golf with pole-vaulting sticks, and we will bring it to you from Spokane next Saturday afternoon. Now, this word from Mario Andretti . . ."

". . . Round up the usual suspects . . ."

"Is that why you lied when you told O'Toole . . . ?"

ETC.

BACK TO THE DUMP

When I was a boy everybody urged me to get plenty of sunshine, so I got plenty of sunshine for a long time. One day while I was absorbing July sun as fast as I could, a doctor asked what I thought I was doing.

"Getting plenty of sunshine," I said.

"Are you mad?" he replied.

No, I was not mad, just slow to catch up with life's revisions. Getting plenty of sunshine had been declared dangerous while I was out to lunch. I revised my store of knowledge. Now I get only small droppers of sunshine extracted from the half hour just before sunset.

When I was old enough to notice that girls were pleasantly different from boys, my mother told me the fact of life. "You must always treat a woman like a lady," she said. So for a long time I went through life treating women like ladies.

One day while I was helping a woman into her coat, another woman asked me what I thought I was doing.

"Treating a woman like a lady," I said.

"Are you mad?" she replied.

No, I was not mad, but my interrogator was furious. I had been out to lunch during one of life's revisions and missed the announcement that it was swinish to treat a woman like a lady. I discarded another piece of my childhood education. Now I treat women like ticking bombs.

When I was 17 and for many years afterward, I admired Franklin and Eleanor Roosevelt as the ideal couple. One evening I had an encounter with a ticking bomb, and contemplated behaving like a fool, but rejected the impulse because we weren't married.

"What do you think you're doing?" she asked as I fled. I told her that someday I wanted to be half of a couple as ideal as Franklin and Eleanor Roosevelt.

"Are you mad?" she replied.

No, not mad. I had been out to lunch during another of life's revisions and, so, had missed the disclosure that Eleanor didn't get along well with Franklin and that Franklin fooled around when she was out of town. Another part of my youthful education went to the dump, but too late. By then, age had brought its inevitable energy crisis and I had begun to prefer napping to behaving like a fool.

Perhaps it was not age that defeated me, though. Maybe it was fatigue caused by the constant trips to the dump to discard everything I'd learned in the first half of my life. Life seemed to be an educator's practical joke in which you spent the first half learning and the second half learning that everything you learned in the first half was wrong.

The trips to the dump became more and more frequent. There I lugged the old precept that a hearty breakfast of bacon and eggs was good for me.

I also hauled away the old lesson that it was racist to refer to people of African ancestry as "black." One windy night, I hoisted up the cherished teaching that every American had a duty to drive a two-ton, eight-cylinder automobile with room enough inside for a steamer trunk and the whole darn family, and staggered off to the dump. That was a heavy night's work and left me bent in spine and spirit.

At about this time, movie actors began running for President, astronauts began flying around the planet to get from one desert to another and people began renting one-bedroom apartments for $2,000 a month. Out to the dump went important fragments of my education which had made me believe that movie actors existed to be browbeaten by Congressional investigators, that if you've seen one cactus you've seen them all, and that $2,000 a month ought to buy you a controlling interest in the Gritti Palace Hotel.

No wonder I was tired. And then, a terrible fear seized me. If everything I'd learned in life's first half had to go to the dump, wasn't it inevitable that everything I was learning in the second half would also have to go?

A crushing thought. I'm not getting any younger. I've had the stamina so far to heave out everything I learned in youth, but if everything I've learned since has to go in the next 25 years I'll be too feeble for the job.

I'm sitting here right now wondering what present certainties might have to be junked before the century is out. My conviction that President Reagan is a nice guy, for instance. Will some whipper-snapper someday say, "If you hadn't been out to lunch again, old-timer, you'd have read the recent book reporting that Reagan had to be dosed on jolly pills to control his passion for kicking orphans"?

And there's my present fear that the nuclear weapons race could kill us all. Some people already say I wouldn't have that fear if the Russians hadn't manipulated my brain. I think that's silly right now. Considering all the other people I know are manipulating my brain, I don't see how the Russians could get a crack at it. But you never know. Someday I might have to learn that I wasn't really afraid of nuclear war at all, but only under the sway of Moscow Svengalis.

It wouldn't surprise me. Live long enough and you'll eventually be wrong about everything.

THE ONLY
GENTLEMAN

The question of what books are fit for young eyes arose in unusually absurd form in the Washington suburbs recently when authorities fell to arguing whether the Mark Twain Intermediate School of Fairfax County should drop Mark Twain's "Huckleberry Finn" from the curriculum. My immediate question was, what's it doing in the curriculum in the first place?

It's a dreadful disservice to Mark Twain for teachers to push "Huckleberry Finn" on seventh-, eighth- and ninth-graders. I had it forced on me in 11th grade and, after the hair-raising opening passages about Huck's whisky-besotted "Pap," found it tedious in the extreme. Thereafter I avoided it for years. It had been poisoned for me by schoolteachers who drove me to it before I was equipped to enjoy it.

I had similar experiences with Shakespeare ("As You Like It" and "Macbeth"), George Eliot ("Silas Marner"), Charles Dickens ("A Tale of Two Cities") and Herman Melville ("Moby Dick"). Schoolteachers seemed determined to persuade me that "classic" was a synonym for "narcotic."

Ever since, it's been my aim to place severe restrictions on teachers' power to assign great books. Under my system any teacher caught assigning Dickens to a person under the age of 25 would be sentenced to teach summer school at half pay.

Punishment would be harsher for assigning "Moby Dick," a book accessible only to people old enough to know what it is to rail at God about the inevitability of death.

"Huckleberry Finn" can be partly enjoyed after the age of 25, but for fullest benefit it probably shouldn't be read before age 35, and even then only if the reader has had a broad experience of American society.

Unfortunately, this sensible reason for pruning the school curriculum was not advanced in Fairfax County's case for dropping "Huckleberry Finn." Instead of pointing out that assigning the book to adolescents damages Mark Twain, the authorities argued that Mark Twain damages the students.

John H. Wallace, one of the school's administrators, made the case in The Washington Post. The book "uses the pejorative term 'nigger' profusely." (It does.) "It speaks of black Americans with implications that they are not honest, they are not as intelligent as whites and they are not human."

While this is meant to be satirical, and is, Mr. Wallace concedes, it also "ridicules blacks," is "extremely difficult for black young sters to handle," and therefore subjects them to "mental cruelty, harassment and outright racial intimidation."

I suppose a black youngster of 12, 13 or 14 might very well suffer the anguish Mr. Wallace describes, and even white young sters of that age might misread Twain as outrageously as Mr. Wallace has in thinking the book is about the dishonesty, dumb ness and inhumanity of blacks. This is the kind of risk you invite when you assign books of some subtlety to youngsters mentally unprepared to enjoy them.

Mr. Wallace thinks Mark Twain aimed only to be "satirical," but only in the loosest sense can "Huckleberry Finn" be called satire. It is the darkest of visions of American society, and it isn't satire that makes it a triumph, but an irony full of pessimism about the human race and particularly its white American members.

Irony is the subtlest of artistic devices, and one of the hardest for youngsters to grasp. It requires enough experience of life to enable you to perceive the difference between the world as it is and the world as it is supposed to be. Many adults have trouble seeing that the world Huck and Jim traverse along the Mississippi is not a boyhood adventure land out of Disney, but a real American landscape swarming with native monsters.

The people they encounter are drunkards, murderers, bullies, swindlers, lynchers, thieves, liars, frauds, child abusers, numbskulls, hypocrites, windbags and traders in human flesh. All are white. The one man of honor in this phantasmagoria is black Jim, the runaway slave. "The nigger," as Twain has his white trash call Jim to emphasize the irony of a society in which the only true gentleman was held beneath contempt.

You can see why a black child nowadays, when "nigger" is such a taboo word that even full-blooded racists are too delicate to use it, might cringe and hurt too much to understand what Twain was really up to. It takes a lot of education and a lot of living to grasp these ironies and smile, which is why adolescents shouldn't be subjected to "Huckleberry Finn."

The sensible thing for the Mark Twain Intermediate School of Fairfax County to do, I thought, would have been to meet the race issue head-on, put aside some other things and conduct a schoolwide teach-in to help its students understand what Huck and Jim are really saying about their world.

When the great teach-in was over, a few might even have understood why Mark Twain, if he'd surprised himself by landing in Paradise, would be watching them and laughing and laughing and laughing.

BEING RICH

In this fantasy I am a poor, shabby, but upright young man and appear at the entrance of the flossiest restaurant in town. Don't ask me why I want to go to a fancy restaurant since actually I hate to eat out, but anyhow I am greeted—in the fantasy, that is—by a snooty headwaiter who bars the door, saying, "We do not traffic here with persons of your ilk."

Years pass, though for some reason they do not show on me, or the snooty headwaiter either, for when I reappear at the door I look just as shabby and poor as ever and he looks just as insolent and has not altered one word of his dialogue. "We do not traffic here with persons of your ilk," says he. To which I reply, "You do now, my good fellow. I have just bought this place. And incidentally, from now on you will be working as attendant in the washroom."

What has happened, you see, is that I have become immensely rich and control a financial-industrial empire powerful enough to make and break governments on four continents. In certain variations, I do not consign the snooty headwaiter to holding towels in the men's room, but keep him on the payroll at an exorbitant salary so I can strike my matches on his starched shirt front.

I first cultivated this dream as a boy, but stowed it away and forgot it after deciding it would be a terrible mistake to become rich. In those years social reformists and Christian apologists for maldistribution of wealth persuaded me, as they persuaded many another, that being rich was unworthy, intolerably troublesome and bound to lead to misery.

So firmly embedded in the national psyche was this claptrap that I even heard it from paupers, who not only keened incessantly about money's powerlessness to buy happiness, but invariably pointed to news reports about millionaires' divorces as evidence that riches bred misery, before going home to beat their wives.

I was far advanced in years before realizing how completely duped I had been. There is little doubt I would be rich today if instead of heeding this nonsense I had started after money earlier.

The Reagan Government has finally dissipated these old myths about the curse of wealth and once again made it fashionable and respectable to be rich. I confess to looking upon Ron's millionaires with more regret than malice. These birds obviously were never gulled for a minute by the more-is-less philosophy of money to which the great majority of us succumbed. My certainty that I might have been one of them is reinforced by the constant flow of letters from readers asking, "If you're so smart, how come you're not rich?"

The sad answer is: I would be if bad advisers during childhood had not cautioned me against it.

Well, it is still not too late to amass the bucks, and for a few months after the Reagan people arrived on the scene I toyed with the idea before discovering that it would not be worth the effort. The problem is that, coming to riches so late in life, I wouldn't know how to handle the daily routine.

There is a movie titled "Arthur," in which a rich man is confronted with the threat of having to live in poverty if he marries the woman he loves. Canny old advisers caution him against it. He's been rich too long. To live in poverty takes years of experience.

The same principle applies to coming into riches too late in life. Consider the restaurant fantasy, for example. In order to enjoy the great moment, the moment when you return richer than Croesus and tell the insufferable headwaiter you have just bought the place, you must have first bought the place.

The fact is, I have no idea how to buy a restaurant without

letting the headwaiter know in advance what is happening. People who have been rich since the age of 5 probably go through life buying and selling restaurants, and know all about it. You probably have to telephone somebody at a restaurant brokerage exchange and they'll buy it for you in two or three minutes, or maybe you call a lawyer, or maybe somebody in the crime syndicate. I don't know, never having been rich before.

What I would do would be to go to the restaurant to offer a lot of money to the owner. That means having to get past the headwaiter. Being unaccustomed to richness, I would tell him, "I'd like to see the owner as I intend to buy this restaurant." Which would give him the chance to toss me out, saying, "We do not sell here to persons of your ilk."

Even if you knocked him down, got inside and bought it, the pleasure of the thing would be destroyed because, knowing his new boss was going to be somebody he'd offended, he would probably quit before you could reassign him to the men's room. As a result, all you end up with is a restaurant, and who needs a restaurant? It's nuisance enough having a car without having a restaurant to worry about.

I suppose if you really had plenty of experience at being rich you would know how to blackball the headwaiter at every other eating spot in town so he would have no choice but to come back and earn his pay by having matches struck on him. But how do you blackball somebody at every restaurant in town? Do you phone a blackball agent?

It takes years to learn these things. You've got to start way down there when you're just a little boy. Now if somebody many years ago, instead of saying, "Money won't buy happiness," had just said, "And the way to blackball a headwaiter when you're very, very rich is. . . ."

SUMMER ACTION

I was thrilled. At last I was a summer bachelor. Tales of these lucky devils and their licentious sportings while the wife was away were part of American lore. Ah, to be affluent! Then can the family be dispatched to the waters for a hot sunburn while, back in town, the decks are clear for . . . action!

Action indeed. Yes, there is action. There is the bed to be made. At the start you think the big problem will be making the bed. Making the bed has always seemed peculiarly odious labor, perhaps because of its military resonances. It was a labor enforced by uncouth sergeants before dawn. Afterward, a lieutenant with two years of college would bring his intellect to bear upon your bedmaking and, if his silver quarter did not bounce respectfully from the sheets, would deprive you of Saturday night's beer.

The thought of having to make the bed took the pleasure out of bachelorhood before the family had disappeared over the horizon. Then, an inspiration! This, after all, was not the Army. The bed could be left unmade.

What's more, this being a double bed, its sheets wouldn't even have to be changed for—for who knew how long? You could sleep on one side until the sheets began to feel disagreeable and, then, move over and sleep on the other side for the rest of the summer.

The bedmaking problem having been solved, the cooking problem remained. What fun! One spent an hour at the grocery, then spent an hour in the kitchen and—presto!—one had a splendid meal, which took four minutes to eat. Then came another hour of clearing the table, washing the dishes, scraping pans and blotting grease from stove and kitchen floor.

After the first three evenings of this, the fun rapidly oozed out of it. By that time I had performed nine hours of culinary toil in exchange for 12 minutes of eating. Moreover, after the three hours of nightly labor, one's energy was too drained to support an evening of adventure on the town.

The alternatives, such as eating beans out of a can with a spoon, cut the labor satisfactorily, but did nothing to create the high spirits necessary to pursue the bachelor pleasures. After a dinner of beans spooned out of a can, I noted, my spirit was up to nothing more than a listless five-hour sprawl in front of the television set.

Restaurants. There was the alternative. The restaurants, however, did not like being an alternative. "Just one?" headwaiters would ask, in voices suggesting that I had just announced myself a typhoid carrier, when all I had said was, "A table for one, please." Some were willing to seat me in remote isolation, where I could be securely despised by waiters sentenced to a one-plate tip at a two-plate table.

The other diners, among them beautiful women of the sort with whom I had fancied myself at summer play, looked at me back near the kitchen door as a curiosity, possibly dangerous, almost certainly eccentric.

I took to spending evenings at home eating prodigious quantities of fruit, which never seemed to be ripe enough. In college nobody teaches you how to recognize a ripe peach. For a while, I fried eggs in the middle of the night, dreading the inevitable heart attack.

The worst part, however, was the absence of talk. It is amazing how much of marriage is devoted to conversation. And now there was nobody to talk to. Nobody in the kitchen, nobody in the parlor, nobody in the bedroom. Nobody to say, "What a day!" to. Or, "Let's watch television." Or, "Do you think it's going to rain?" Or, "My God! I can't believe these bills."

At first, I would say things like "Let's watch television," to myself. One night, I said, "Let's watch television" to myself, and myself said, "I don't feel like it." I almost retorted, "Well, you can sit here and read Cosmopolitan if you want to, but I'm going to watch television," but I didn't. I got a grip on myself instead.

The part of myself I got a grip on was a tuft of hair behind the right ear. I had been doing my own barbering for several years, and this particular tuft needed trimming. I got the scissors and trimmed it. This was the beginning of cutting my hair seriously, which became a substitute for talking. Very rapidly I shed the old habit of talking and took up the new habit of cutting hair. It passed the time. My hair became shorter and shorter.

Within 10 days I had scarcely any hair left to cut. I switched to cutting fingernails. Then toenails. The house was silent except for the snip-snip-snip of scissors. One evening, a woman of a certain reputation telephoned and suggested a rendezvous, but with my hair and nails so severely cut she would certainly, I knew, laugh at me. Cruelly. I declined. I had forgotten how to talk, anyhow.

Now I must stop. It is time to eat some unripe cantaloupe. Afterward, I shall cut the sleeves off some shirts.

BACK AT THE MANSE

Herewith, the full text of "Browbeaten Towers," the very latest Gothic novel.

A governess arrives at a sinister manse. It feels like the nineteenth century, not only because there are sinister manses all over the countryside, but also because the governess's bosom is heaving. There is also a lot of *embonpoint,* not to mention a fierce brooding laird striding the grim battlements, a pack of ravenous mastiffs and a suspicious excess of adjectives.

The governess's timid knock is answered by a tightly corseted housekeeper, Mrs. Rivers, who hates the governess for her youth and heaving bosom and because governesses are always trying to ferret out the manse's most dread secrets.

To crush the governess's spirit, Mrs. Rivers gives her a bowl of cold mutton soup and sends her to a tiny, unheated cell where she lives unnoticed for three weeks. At night she can hear the insane cackling of some tortured soul deep within the vastnesses of the great stone pile, but otherwise it is an uneventful existence except for the heaving of her bosom.

One day on the fog-shrouded staircase she encounters a beautifully muscled but suffering gentleman mounting the stairs on a mighty black stallion with fiery red eyes. He quickly covers his face with the saddle, but she instinctively knows it is the laird because of the telltale bellows-wheezing created by the flaring and unflaring of his passionate nostrils.

"I will na' ha' wenches waylaying me on my own staircase!" he cries, raising his riding crop to strike her. But before the fell blow can fall, an inner sweetness—some restraining memory of his gentle boyhood—stays his brutal hand. And in that ominous silence, so fraught with unspoken fraughtings, he hears the heaving of the governess's bosom.

"What a panic's in thy breastie," he murmurs with crinkling eyes.

"Wilt thou not vouchsafe to call me lass?" demurely inquires the governess. "And to remove the saddle from afore thy fierce laird's face that I might see thy cold, dark, cruel but manly features and glowering black brows which cannot conceal the suffering burning in thy coal-black eyes?"

Her soft plea sends the laird into an access of fury. Goading his spurs into the stallion's foam-flecked flanks fiercely, he and his noble steed plunge recklessly up the staircase with a cry of "Heigh ho, Tonto! Away!" All afternoon she hears the pounding of hoofs galloping back and forth across the rooftop.

"I must find the children and comfort them," she says, and then remembers that there are no children. There are only the laird, and his faithful foam-flecked Tonto, and Mrs. Rivers, and the manse maniac locked up somewhere in the depths. It occurs to the governess that her situation is absolutely pointless, and she is on the verge of asking to be assigned to another novel when, at midnight, she is summoned to join the laird for a gallop on the roof.

Riding side-saddle she makes her way up to the treacherous ladder connecting the attic to the battlements, her mind filled with forbidden anticipation of that moment when the laird will remove the saddle from his face and crush her to him until she can see nothing but that scarred, cruel, but tender face and the glowering black brows which separate the lairds from the boys.

"I could hear your bosom heaving two floors below!"

It is Mrs. Rivers, the housekeeper, gone insane with jealousy and mutton soup. Beside her stands a wizened, bent, gray apparition whose face is undistinguished except for a magnificent set of glowering black eyebrows.

"Yes!" cackles Mrs. Rivers. "It is the laird's Uncle Angus, locked up these twenty years past for insanity and having eyebrows the laird couldn't bear to look at!"

She has become an avenging crone. Seizing a timber, she mounts to the roof, fells the waiting laird with a stroke and removes the saddle masking his unconscious face. "See your precious laird now for what he is!" she shrieks. The governess stares and recoils in horror. The laird is completely hairless where his eyebrows should be.

"Something's wrong here," says the governess. "In the novel I'm assigned to, I'm supposed to win the love of a fierce laird with glowering black brows. Is this 'Aylechester Towers?'"

"Good heavens," says Uncle Angus, "this governess has wandered into the wrong novel. This is 'Browbeaten Towers.' 'Aylechester Towers' is going on in the sinister manse down at the bend in the highway."

The governess apologizes for her mistake but the laird, who is not amused, strikes her with his riding crop. Mrs. Rivers yawns and heads for bed. The next governess is due at breakfast time, and the mutton soup still has to be chilled.

THE PRESIDENT'S
PLUMBING

The best thing about being President is that it gets you out of American life. I don't know what the theory is behind this, but it is a fact. The first thing we do with a President is shunt him off on a siding where nothing American can ever happen to him.

This is why you never see a President waiting in the rain at a bus stop. Somebody decided a long time ago that this was too American for Presidents to be subjected to. After a while, Presidents quite naturally forget that there are such things as bus stops, and if they stay in office long enough they even forget that it rains. In some 20 years of watching Presidents, I don't recall ever seeing one get rained on.

In most respects, the Presidency strikes me as a thoroughly undesirable job, but periodically, when I reflect on the escape from America that goes with it, it seems mighty fetching. America is not only a place where it rains at bus stops, but also a place where pipes leak. In fact, I have had pipes leaking some place or other most of my life, and I believe that for the great mass of the population leaking pipe is a vital part of the American experience.

Probably pipes even in the White House leak now and then, but you can bet they don't leak on the President. It's too American. The White House probably has pipe examiners testing the plumbing daily. At the first drop of water, you may be sure, squadrons of repairmen are flung into action so as not to disturb the President with a universal American headache.

No wonder these fellows quickly come to believe that foreign-policy problems are graver than domestic affairs. Being sealed off in a world where domestic problems don't exist, they can hardly be expected to fret much about the American state of mind.

If a President had to cope with the American plumbing problem before coming to grips with the latest dispatch from Moscow, he might understand a bit better than Presidents generally do why Americans find it so hard to avoid excessive drink and ill-tempered use of firearms.

I suspect that most Americans could be as great as most Presidents if they did not have to wait in the rain at bus stops, struggle with plumbing, sit in traffic jams and worry how they can afford a new roof. If, that is, they were not afflicted with American life.

You always read about Presidents giving way to temper outbursts. Their advisers are said to be so fearful of upsetting them that they withhold good advice and bad news. This makes little sense to me. If I did not have to deal with leaking pipes, sit in traffic jams, get drenched at bus stops and worry about a new roof, I would be in excellent spirits all of the time. If I knew, moreover, that nobody was going to badger me with good advice or bad news, I believe I would be absolutely incapable of a tantrum.

What in the world can Presidents possibly find to get their tempers up? Wherever they go, everybody is polite to them. Unlike Americans, they never find their hotel reservations canceled, never get snubbed by waiters, never find themselves bumped from airline flights. They don't even have to slow down for red lights. They don't have to spend hours driving around in search of a parking place.

When is the last time you heard of a President showing up late for an appointment because he got stuck in traffic and then couldn't find a place to park? When is the last time you heard of a President catching a cold because he had to wait 30 minutes in the rain for a bus? When is the last time you heard of a President going to the theater and being sold a seat in the second balcony? When is the last time you saw a President seated in a restaurant back by the kitchen door?

Now, I concede that the work is unattractive, humdrum and arid, and does not bring a person into contact with the best class of people. Many Americans might say the same thing of their own jobs, yet no one would argue that this justifies being excused from full participation in American life.

Why it was thought wise to place the President completely out of contact with the American realities, I cannot say. I would ask my plumber, who is wise about democracy, but he has not been able to get here for months. He is in bed with a cold caught at a rainy bus stop, or perhaps still looking for a parking space, or, more likely, snubbing me for a thoughtless insult I offered his workmanship last summer when I was in sour spirits after being bumped from an airline flight.

BALL OF WAX

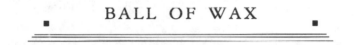

After paying my income tax I took the kid down to Washington so he could watch them spend it. The kid had been giving me a pain. He was always saying things. Things like, "When are you going to get smart and find tax dodges like all the other finaglers?"

Things like, "Smart guys don't pay taxes." I don't like kids talking that way. My old man would have given me a fat lip for talking that way, but this is 1983. We don't bop kids to get sense into them, we reason with them.

Without my taxes the Government was nothing, I told him. No space shuttle. No MX missiles to keep the Reds away. No bench for the Supreme Court to sit on. Nobody wants that kind of country, so I paid my taxes.

"Why don't we subscribe to Tax Shelter Digest like everybody else?" the kid replied.

So I took him to Washington. "You're going to get a lesson in the rewards of doing your duty," I said.

The Government man said he wished more people would bring kids in. He liked kids. If interest rates ever came down and college tuition dropped he might have some kids himself.

"I want the kid to watch the Government spend my money," I said.

He said the request was unusual, but since he liked kids——

He took my Social Security number and went away and came back.

"You're too late. Your money's already been spent," he said.

"That was quick," I said.

"We can move pretty fast when it comes to spending money," he said.

"It took me a whole year to earn that money."

"Ain't it the truth," he said.

"If you open your mouth," I said to the kid, "I'll give you a fat lip."

To the Government man: "I guess they needed a new M-1 tank right away and were just waiting for my money to get here."

"Not likely," he said. "Those M-1's were running two or three million bucks apiece last time I checked and you paid taxes of— let's see. . . ."

He looked at the figures and laughed.

"What can I tell you," he said. "Except that every little bit helps."

He winked at the kid.

"Don't try to corrupt the kid," I said.

"Sorry," he said. "Listen, why don't I look up what they spent your money for? It'll give the kid a sense of being part of the Government, knowing what his old man contributed to the country."

He went away and came back again with his hat on. "Come on. I'll show you," he said.

Pretty soon he stopped at a parking lot. Acres of cars. There it was, he said. My contribution to the United States of America during the past taxable year. "Those are all Government cars," he said. "Without them it would be hard for a lot of Government people to get out to lunch."

The kid was impressed. I was pretty impressed too, though it wasn't an MX missile or a space shuttle.

"Boy," the kid said. "You bought all those cars for the Government, and you can't even afford to get rid of that old '69 Buick you've got in the garage."

"The money didn't go for the cars," the Government man said. "It went for the wax."

"What wax?"

"Every one of those cars has to be kept waxed," he said.

"I worked a whole year to wax cars?"

"That's about the size of it," he said. Because of the deficit the Government was nine months behind in paying its car-wax supplier. My money had arrived just in time to help get the wax-bill collectors off the Government's back.

"I'm not even buying any wax for the current year?"

"You know how it is," he said.

"Could you show the kid a can of the wax I bought? It would give him a feeling of involvement with the Government."

"There's none left," he said. "We used the last can three months ago. All the new wax will be paid for next year by somebody else. It's unlikely they'll apply your money to car wax again next year. They don't often repeat."

"Cheer up," the kid said. "Maybe next year you'll be buying a piece of the MX missile."

"Could be," the Government man said, "but my guess is it'll be chrome-plated water jugs for the Department of Commerce."

The kid winked at the Government man. "It's a big government," the Government man said. "It takes a lot of car wax and water jugs to keep going."

"Don't take it so hard," the kid said when we got home. "If you're too proud to be a finagler at least you could hold your head high about keeping the cars waxed."

I gave him a fat lip.

RINGING
UP THE PAST

■   ■

The more advanced technology becomes, the more it baffles me. Take the telephone company's latest electronic miracle, which I recently had installed in a moment of weakness.

"Connect yourself with the past," the literature urged. "Phone back across the ages. Now, through the miracle of electronics telephone Abraham Lincoln on the eve of the battle of Gettysburg. Use our time-dissolving international punch-button code to ring Napoleon Bonaparte in exile on Elba. For a slight additional monthly charge, you can also make conference calls and hold three-way conversations with people like Grover Cleveland, Lucrezia Borgia and thousands of others."

Well, it was new technology, wasn't it? Also I wanted to talk to Henry James. I was reading chapter 17 of a Henry James novel and wanted to know if anything was going to happen before the end of the book.

I punched the time code, the area code and the number listed for Henry James. A woman answered.

"Virginia Woolf here," said a distinctly English voice.

"I'm trying to reach Henry James," I said.

"You've dialed the wrong time code. This is 1929," she said. "Try 1899."

"Hold on a minute, I've got an idea," I said. "With this equipment I can set up a conference call, and both of us can speak to Henry James."

"Don't you have anything to do?" asked Virginia Woolf, and hung up.

Unabashed, I punched the buttons again. "Yes," said a masculine voice, yes, Henry James was the name.

"You don't know me, Mr. James, but I live up here in 1983. How're things going? You had any rain lately back there?"

"I trust you will excuse me," he said, with a courtesy so exquisite that I knew he was the real Henry James, "but I happen to be writing chapter 35 of my new novel and would prefer not to be interrupted with requests for meteorological reports."

"Anything happen in chapter 35?" I asked.

With the author's irresistible enthusiasm for his own work, Henry James suddenly became voluble. "In fact, an immense emotional storm is in progress under my pen," he said. "A hostess has just sensed that one of her male guests senses that her gown is just a touch vulgar, and—here is the cream of the crisis—the male guest senses that the hostess senses that he senses it. Can you see how delicate the position is, with the guest sensing the hostess senses what he has sensed?"

Not wanting to seem slow-witted, I changed the subject. "I just spoke to Virginia Woolf," I said. "Reached her in 1929."

You could sense his enthusiasm fading, but he was too well bred to hang up. "And how are things going up there in 1929? he asked. "Have they had any rain lately?"

I evaded the question. No use telling him Virginia had hung up on me. "We really had a roofbanger of a storm here last week," I said.

There was a long pause. I sensed he was struggling to overcome some embarrassment. Moreover, he sensed that I sensed it, for he said, "I sense that you sense my sense of embarrassment, so I might as well put the question bluntly. You are telephoning from 1983, you say. Be good enough to tell me: What are you doing there?"

"Calling up people in the past. Thanks to the miracle of technology I can get Abraham Lincoln and Lucrezia Borgia on a conference call right now. Like to talk to them?"

"I am an artist, not a historian," said Henry James.

Well, I'm not a historian either, as I told Henry, but since the technology was in place, why not use it?

"Don't you have anything to do up there in 1983?" he replied.

So I told him about the miracles of technology. I had plenty to do. By flipping a switch I could condition the air. Twisting a dial allowed me to watch grown men playing boys' games thousands of miles away. Activating my computer, I could obtain the reading on my bank balance. Adjusting my video screen, I could play a game with little electronic figures while headphones clamped to my ears pumped music directly into my skull. With pills I could deaden my senses or achieve visions and frenzies———.

He interrupted. "But what do you do there?" he repeated. "Don't you have anything to do?"

I sensed that he sensed people at 1983 didn't know what they were doing here.

"You sense wrong," he said. "I sense that you pass your time playing with toys because you have nothing you believe to be worth doing."

I suddenly sensed it too, and what's more I sensed that he sensed that I sensed it, for when I tried to bluff it out by asking, "How's the family these days?" he hung up with the most exquisite courtesy.

BLOWING UP

Many years ago, I read that if you reduced a typical human body to its chemical elements and sold them across the drugstore counter their value would be only 89 cents. Maybe it was 98 cents, or 78 cents. I'm vague on the precise figures, but anyhow it was a trifling sum.

What impressed me about this wasn't the low value of the goods I was clothing and tending to, but the message that I was a mass of chemicals. A batch of calcium, a little oxygen, some hydrogen probably. Being weak on chemistry, I can't guess about the other stuff and don't particularly want to.

This knowledge disturbed me at the time and still has a marked influence on my behavior. Even as a child, I distrusted chemicals. One Christmas, somebody gave me a "chemistry set" containing some test tubes, litmus paper and various powders, and a nervous aunt, who was afraid I was going to blow up the house, put such fear of the thing into me that to this day I will drive miles out of the way to avoid getting close to a Du Pont factory.

Among the many imaginary self-portraits I carry around in my head is one which shows me as a seething caldron of chemicals which could go haywire and blow up the house at any moment unless kept in the most delicate balance. As an adventurous youth, I tested this idea a few times by adding a chemical compound called gin and found the theory perfectly sound.

As a result, I have always been wary of disturbing the chemical broth simmering within. Every three years or so, I take an aspirin tablet, but not before having a friend lock me into a windowless room.

I don't really expect the aspirin to affect me the way the full moon always affected Lon Chaney Jr. in those old "Wolf Man" movies, but on the other hand, feeling as I do about chemistry, I wouldn't be surprised if it did.

This brings me to cocaine. As the foregoing should indicate, I would no more pump a dose of cocaine into the works than I would carry a stick of dynamite in my hip pocket. Fortunately, you don't have to bear dynamite on your person this season to be one of the fashionable people. Unfortunately, you're hardly fit to be photographed at the fanciest soirees unless you've got cocaine bubbling in your interior retort.

Why you've got to put cocaine in your chemical stew to be fashionable nobody quite knows. Maybe because it's so expensive and shows you're rich enough to poke money up your nose. Being illegal doesn't hurt it much either. If cocaine were legalized and sold for 50 cents a pound, it would probably be as unchic as Royal Crown Cola at the charity ball.

The point, though, is that I do like to be fashionable. Shameful, but true. Why else did I wear blue jeans to the Plaza all through the 1960s and drink watered white wine at the cocktail hour all through the 1970s? (White wine at the cocktail hour is not a chemical; it's masochism indulged in for the sake of chic, like spiked heels for women and meeting the payments on a Mercedes-Benz for aspiring bunco artists.)

Refusal to stir in the cocaine has cost me dearly in the chic stakes. Friends who don't want to have to refuse to be seen in my company accuse me of crankish eccentricity. "You toss in tranquilizers to keep your aplomb at the office, Benzedrine to pick you up after thinking about Ronald Reagan, antihistamine to keep your nose from running when you've got a cold . . . ," one of them started to tell me the other day. I cut him off.

"Everybody else tosses in tranquilizers, Benzedrine and antihistamine," I said. "All I ever toss in is one aspirin tablet every three years."

"What about the gin?"

"It's true, whenever I want to blow up the house I toss in the gin, but if on top of that I started tossing in the tranquilizers, the Benzedrine, the antihistamine, the aspirin and the cocaine, I might blow up the whole city."

I am accused of not wanting to feel good. Cocaine, they all say, makes you feel good. It is true I don't want to feel good very often. I like to feel good about three times a year. Isn't that enough?

Not that I want to feel bad, of course. I hate feeling bad, but usually you can't help it. It's one of the prices you pay for being in the world, and there'd be no way to know you were feeling good if you never experienced feeling bad. There are thousands of other ways to feel, all of them instructive and most of them interesting. I'd like to feel them all, but if you're going to waste most of your time feeling good, there isn't going to be enough time to feel all the other possible ways.

In any case, it's unlikely that a dose of cocaine could make me feel good. Not in my state of mind about chemicals. I'm afraid I'd be too worried about the whole internal laboratory blowing up and taking a city block with it to feel anything but nervous. I do feel sad about being unfashionable, though. Maybe next year fashion will make easier demands. Something like wearing mashed grapes in your ears. I'd like that.

NO TEARS
FOR THE GIANTS

With the death of Mao Tse-tung in 1976 the age of giants ended at last. To mourn it would have taken a heart of stone, for it had been a barbarian's passage through oceans of blood and the charnel it washed on the shore makes Attila seem in retrospect as fetching as Peck's Bad Boy.

The giants who led it, or perhaps only made the trip first-cabin, were flamboyant egocentrics whose passion for power fulfilled their age's hunger for new societies organized on the principle of industrial efficiency. This carried most of them toward centralized government constructed around political godheads with mythic or divine characteristics being attributed to the leader, whether he was called Der Fuhrer, Il Duce, the Generalissimo, the Chairman, the Caudillo or the President.

The characteristic political creation of the age of giants was dictatorship, and the characteristic political philosophy, which still survives it in such vestigial artifacts as the C.I.A. and K.G.B., was that the end justifies the means. Not surprisingly, the citizenry for whom the giants labored became an inhuman abstraction—the masses or the people. Persons who made a to-do about their individuality became nuisances, eccentrics or menaces. The attitude varied from giant to giant, but on balance it was not a good time to be at odds with the will of the people, to be a person. The age gave us no persons' republics.

An exception should be made for Winston Churchill, the one giant of the age who was, in fact, not of the age at all but a creature of Victorian England, who was still able to sentimentalize war and visualize a future in which the masses would not insist on pressing their power too rudely. Britain rejected him as an antique as soon as the Nazis surrendered.

Time magazine once hailed Churchill as the man of the century. The accolade now seems as amusing as calling World War I the war to end wars. In the age of giants, Churchill was not even a very big giant.

From Lenin, who opened the age in 1917, to Mao, whose death closed it three generations later, there were giant giants, middle-sized giants, mini-giants, midget giants and false giants. The classic specimen of the last category was Chiang Kai-shek, who was inflated so alarmingly by Roosevelt and Churchill that it took Americans a generation to perceive that the castle housed only a mouse.

Francisco Franco was, to a degree, the similar creation of Hitler and Mussolini. De Gaulle sought the gift of inflation from Roosevelt and Churchill, was rejected, went away angry and came back years later to earn the seven-league boots for himself by restoring a France at the edge of a breakdown.

Hitler and Stalin, the purest specimens of the age's giant breed, were almost certainly political geniuses, which leaves little more to be said about politics in the 20th century. Lunacy harnessed to industrialism in the cause of mass uplift. Dreams of perfecting humanity with the bullet in the back of the head and the gas oven. Nasty stuff, and infectious to sanity. Twenty years later Americans were destroying Vietnam to save it.

The age of giants, of course, has been over for a long time now, and we are slipping into the age of caretakers. The giants were great biographies and good copy; the caretakers are mostly a yawn. Witness Carter and Reagan trying to persuade us that they are up to something vital. Witness Andropov, the committee chairman in Moscow. Name quickly the Prime Ministers of Italy, Britain, Japan and Germany.

There is scarcely a biography in the bunch. Carter and Reagan between them are hardly interesting enough to sustain a magazine article. And isn't it splendid? With no giants strutting around shaking the earth, something vaguely resembling peace has become palpable. Vietnam may have been the last gasp of the age of giants in America. A case can be argued that it was Kennedy's, Johnson's and Nixon's insistence on trying to preserve gianthood in the Presidency that accounted for the Asian fiasco, that they were men reluctant to accept the death of the age of giants, or too slow to perceive that it was over and that giants were no longer possible.

There is a glimpse of sunshine in this conjecture. If the giants, from Lenin to Mao, were not really giants but only expressions of a historic global impulse toward cataclysmic change, then maybe the rise of the caretakers reflects the arrival of a new epoch of stability in which societies that will give us the opportunity to use such gains as the bloodletting netted us to search for our lost individuality.

■ A PREVIOUS LIFE ■

The way I see it, I wasn't anybody you ever heard of in a previous life. This confession is prompted by a conversation with a woman at dinner not long ago. "I have the feeling I've known you in a previous life," she said. "Were you ever a duke at the Court of Louis XIV?"

It seemed improbable, considering my difficulties speaking French; it would have taken more than 300 years for a duke's accent to deteriorate until it was as bad as mine. "Perhaps," the woman suggested, "you were a high priest during the reign of the

Pharaoh Amenhotep." This woman apparently traveled only in the fanciest circles as she journeyed from life to life.

For all that, she didn't seem to have gone anyplace much. Oh, she may have danced with a pharaoh and powdered her wig at Versailles, but in all these lives she had stayed Earthbound, never able to escape this obscure little planet out here in a dim corner of the universe. I believe this is my first time on this planet, though you can never be too sure of these things, memory being as tricky as it is. I first heard of the place around 1916, 1917, maybe 1918, speaking in Earthly calendar terms, of course.

At the time, I was still eight or nine years from being born and had been barreling through the cosmos on a celestial version of the Wabash Cannonball when we stopped at a main junction depot about 10 galaxies west of here. I got off to stretch my atoms and odd bits of plasma—there wasn't much more to me then—and noticed an old gentleman in galluses, carrying a rifle, waiting on the platform for the outbound express.

He was my great-grandfather who had died 10 years earlier and was outward bound. "Where you headed, boy?" he asked.

"Some pipsqueak planet called Earth out in the boondocks."

"Well, you can't win 'em all," the old gentleman said. "I just been there myself. A mighty long spell, too. Eighty-seven Earth years. Just died 10 years ago. Feared they meant to send me around a second time as a hobo in that there Depression they've got coming up in a few years, but I was lucky."

Indeed he was. He was being assigned to the luscious strawberries-and-cream planet in Galaxy 217-30-4295, where people get born as beautiful hot-air balloons and spend their lives floating over the sapphire valleys playing the cello and writing poetry.

"What's that tool you're lugging?" I asked.

"A gun," he said. On Earth, he had been a gunsmith. Naturally, I had never heard of guns. "They shoot things," he said. "Tin cans sitting on fence posts, apples sitting on small boys' heads, and so on. Looks kind of foolish out here in the cosmos," he went on, "but after you're born on Earth, it comes in mighty handy and you get attached to it."

Just then there was a whoosh, followed by a spray of light. "The Eastern Galaxy express is now ready for boarding on track 29," said a disembodied voice. "That's my connection," said Great-Granddaddy. "She takes 8,000 years to get to the strawberries-and-cream planet, but when she pulls in I'll become a beautiful hot-air balloon."

"Could I have your gun?" I asked. "I'm due to be born in just eight or nine years, and nobody will believe I met you out here unless I've got some evidence to prove it."

"Boy," he said, "if you can work out a way to be born with a gun in your hand, welcome to it. They'll probably put your face on their postage stamps." He was off in a whoosh and a spray of light, but I noticed that another passenger who had been waiting nearby did not board the express.

Instead, when the Earth local pulled in he got aboard and sat down beside me. In Earthy fashion he started telling everything about himself, how he had died on Earth in 1905 and been assigned to the Planet of Velvet Doors in the 58th Galaxy, how he had learned the trick of outwitting the authorities and getting back to Earth each time he died simply by hopping on the Earth local every time at this depot junction.

"Don't you ever want to go someplace new and be a beautiful hot-air balloon or a gorgeous velvet door for a change?" I asked.

Not him. There was no place for him but Earth. There wasn't another planet in the universe where you could go out to dinner and have such a good time dropping names like Nebuchadnezzar, with whom he had once dined in Babylon, or the Pharaoh Ramses, who had once waved to him from camel-back, or Louis XIV, or President McKinley, who had once nodded to his wife in the life just concluded.

It sounded so tedious that I changed the subject by asking him how my gun worked. He lifted it and shot a passing comet. The outraged conductor asked to see his ticket, then had the train stopped while transferring him to the express to the Galaxy of Lavender Trees for rebirth as a gentle spring shower.

Due to the delay, I was a year late in being born, but nobody since has ever asked me if he didn't once see me dancing in the Hanging Gardens of Babylon.

ON THE SIDE
OF THE ANGELS

I went to the reverend precinct clubhouse for political guidance. This is a custom cultivated during the Vietnam War when I was shocked to discover that I was at odds with God's policy on that conflict.

I had been supporting the war with the usual religious fervor for the American side when one day I noticed that the reverend political clergy had started to oppose it. At the reverend precinct clubhouse the awakening was cruel.

As a student of World War I and a veteran of World War II, I had been taught to support American wars because God was on our side. Now apparently the political parsonage had inquired about the Almighty's war policy and there had been a shift. God wanted peace.

It seemed that a voter could get into really serious long-range problems such as having his credentials closely audited at the Pearly Gates if he failed to keep in touch with the folks who kept in touch with divine political policy.

So I went to the clubhouse to find out whether it was still all right to vote for candidates who favored racial desegregation, which, according to the men of the political cloth, had become the godly way to vote during the 1960s, or whether they had detected a change of signals from Heaven.

There had been a change of signals all right. The clubhouse was occupied by a new set of parsons whose interest in racial desegregation was minimal, to say the most. Their conversation left little doubt that they were privy to inside information that God had become a Republican.

Maybe I got the wrong impression, but when I inquired about which politicians to vote against if I wanted a warm welcome in Paradise, all the people they warned against seemed to be Democrats. Charts were produced—earthly charts, admittedly, but nevertheless charts compiled by men who trod the pulpit with confidence. These charts showed which politicians were against the family, which in favor of the equal rights amendment, which favored letting homosexuals enjoy constitutional rights and so forth, and all these villains were Democrats.

If the reverend political clergy could be believed, God had spent a lot of time considering American domestic policy, concluded that it was a mess and decided that this was the Democrats' fault. The question was whether the parsons were accurately representing the Almighty's cogitations on American domestic policy or whether there had been a communications breakdown.

There was no doubt among the clerics. They were sincere men, just as the clergymen who used to say that God was on our side in war were sincere, just as the clergymen who later said that God was not on our side were sincere.

Nor could you say for certain that they had gotten God's message all garbled up, although this conclusion was mighty tempting in view of the fact that there are so many people in the world who get God's message only to start quarreling among themselves about what it says.

All these people who get God's message, with the exception of certain mercenary frauds, are so absolutely certain they have heard it right that their habit of quarreling with one another about what it said makes you pause and wonder whether God isn't up to something more subtle than they are able to understand—like, for example, trying to teach them humility.

A proper respect for God might start with the assumption that He is a power surpassing all understanding and that to profess to grasp any message emanating from such a source is, at best, to give yourself airs about your own superiority and, at worst, an act of arrogance which calls for the corrective medicine of humility. I hesitate to commit such foolishness by stating flatly that God sends mortals so many contradictory messages to teach them how inadequate their auditory equipment is. In view of the low quality of our mortal talent for humility, such a lesson would probably be wasted on us anyhow.

Trying to teach humility to a race capable of treating God as if He were a ward heeler would be a divine waste of time, though whether God might, nevertheless, think it amusing to try, I will not presume to guess.

CIGAR-SMOKE
SCIENCE

Two leading Congressional scientists, Senator Helms and Representative Hyde, have been doing pioneer research in the nature of life. This has produced the Helms-Hyde theory which states that scientific fact can be established by a majority vote of the United States Congress.

Unfortunately, Doctors Hyde and Helms appear to be timid about pressing their theory to its limits. Is there any earthly reason, for example, why Congress should not pass a law declaring that 7 times 9 is 67?

For years we have had a barrage of propaganda calculated to make us believe that 7 times 9 is actually 63. Forty years of coping with the nine-times table has left me unpersuaded. When a pedagogue pounces out of the shadows demanding to know, "How much is 7 times 9?" I instinctively reply, "67." "Wrong," he says, "it's 63."

My proposal, long ignored in Washington, is that Congress pass a law declaring that 7 times 9 is 67 and specifying that severe penalties be imposed for pedagogues who hold otherwise.

Professors Hyde and Helms are moving toward my point of view, but only very gingerly. At present they would apply Congress's power to legislate scientific fact only to issues on which scientists themselves are in a muddle. Specifically, they propose a bill under which Congress would solve the knotty question of life's origin by voting that life begins at the moment of conception.

These pioneers of new scientific method deserve a salute for trying to solve this troublesome question with a democratic show of hands. Nevertheless, the slightest reflection will show how absurdly wrong they are in asking Congressional science to discover that life begins at conception.

The scientific fact—and I urge the professors to amend their bill to recognize it—is that life begins long before conception. The flaw in the Helms-Hyde hypothesis results from their myopic concentration on the parents of the impending child.

In their view, one male and one female participate in a biological transaction and, presto!, life begins with nine months of citizenship in the womb followed by an indeterminate term of exterior activity. If, dear reader, you ponder your own existence for a moment, you will see how short-sighted this view actually is.

Are you here solely because of two parents? Of course not. Each of those parents required two parents, which is why you have four grandparents. To obtain the necessary four grandparents, you needed eight great-grandparents.

And how in the world are you going to scrape up eight great-grandparents without the cooperation of 16 great-great-grandparents? Well you can get 16 great-great-grandparents if you are lucky enough to have 32 great-great-great-grandparents, but of course you are not going to get 32 unless you are lucky enough to have 64 great-great-great-great-grandparents.

If you are youngish right now, back around the time of the American Revolution, six generations ago, you had 64 great-great-great-great-grandparents, all of whom were engaged—not simultaneously, of course—in producing you. If you hadn't, you would now be in a condition of unlife.

Is it necessary to point out that any number of persons are at this very moment unexisting because in 1776 there were 63 people perfectly willing to cooperate in producing life by the late 20th century, but were unable to find a 64th?

In these cases, life in the 1980s failed to begin in 1776 because one member of the 64-person committee said, "To hell with the 1980s." If you are fortunate enough to be here, of course, it is because back around 1750 there were 128 people willing to cheer when somebody said, "Why don't we all get to work on a great-great-great-great-great-grandchild?"

In legislating the beginning of life, Congress will probably be unwilling to go back to 1750, since it would be treading on the territory of King George III, but legislating science from the date of the Declaration of Independence is perfectly constitutional. The obvious scientific fact, which Professors Hyde and Helms should be urging the Congress to enact, is that life for each American begins with great-great-great-great-grandparents in the last quarter of the 18th century.

Even with this starting team, of course, the threat of unlife lurked all along the route to 1983. I had many a narrow escape myself. One of my grandmothers, apparently weary of birthing after ten accouchements, paused for a terrifyingly long time before proceeding with my father. If she had said "To hell with it," you would have to look for me out there in the unlife.

My grandmother went on to twelfth and thirteenth children, but never produced a fourteenth. Hence, I probably have a couple of unexistent cousins, which would have sorely irritated the

64 people who, back in 1776, started them on the road of life.

The goal of Professors Hyde and Helms is to punish people who end life once it has started. My grandmother is beyond the power of Congress these days and, hence, cannot be clapped in irons. In such cases Congress may have to pass resolutions of censure.

■ BY ROYAL COMMAND ■

In the spring of 1953 I received a message from His Grace, the Duke of Norfolk, Earl Marshal of England, etc., etc., etc., stating that he had been commanded by Her Majesty, Queen Elizabeth II, etc., etc., etc., to invite my attendance at her Coronation at the Abbey at Westminster.

Thus began my first and last participation in a royal occasion. The Queen's command to the Earl Marshal could not have been issued very insistently, and the Earl Marshal probably gritted his teeth before obeying, for seats in the Abbey were being sought almost as eagerly as places in Heaven. Nevertheless, as one of the few American journalists lucky enough to draw an invitation in the scribblers' lottery, I accepted without worrying whether they really, truly, honestly wanted me.

The painstaking precision with which the British prepare their great shows extended even down to the grubbiest pub crawlers of Fleet Street. The mail brought elaborate directions about how to dress. Dress uniforms and medals were acceptable and tribal costumes were approved for persons from the more exotic realms of the Commonwealth, though not for journalists, for whom tribal uniform would have included a filthy mackintosh and a gravy-stained necktie.

The dress order in my case was quite explicit: white tie, tails, top hat. As a devotee of Fred Astaire, I was familiar with this get-up, but did not own such duds and had never worn them. No matter, haberdashery-wise Londoners said. "Go to Mossbross."

Moss Bros.—or Mossbross, as it was universally known—was the most redoubtable rental-clothes shop in the Empire, catering to belted earls and Fleet Street hacks alike and without noticeable discrimination. For a very small sum, they provided me with a fine fit and a splendid high silk hat.

Orders of increasing complexity, meanwhile, continued to pour in from the Earl Marshal. These dealt with such matters as which door of the Abbey to enter, when to make use of the specially installed toilet facilities inside the Abbey during the ceremony, and how to conduct myself while eating. (Discreetly.)

My orders required me to report at 6:30 A.M. Obediently, I arose at 4:30 in the morning and discovered a pouring rain. This was dismaying since, living only a half mile from the Abbey, I had decided to walk to the Coronation.

By 5:30 it was still raining fit to launch the ark, but I was gorgeously adorned in white tie and tails and addressing a large breakfast. At my insistence my wife took snapshots of me in top hat by the breakfast dishes.

During my boyhood the men of my family rose daily at this hour to start the farm chores, and I wanted photographic evidence that I, too, had once risen at this obscene hour of the night to dress like Fred Astaire.

At about 6 A.M. the downpour ceased and I bolted out of the house in bleak gray dawn, strode toward Victoria Station and turned into Victoria, the avenue leading to the Abbey. Here, for the first and only moment in my life, I suddenly discovered what it was to be a star and strut upon a great stage.

The sidewalks were packed with humanity, but the street was sealed against all motor traffic. Most of the people had spent the night partying and sleeping on the sidewalks. They were drenched and should have been miserable in their sleepless waterlogged state, but their gravest problem seemed to be boredom.

When a magnificently briefed policeman, checking my

assortment of passes, opened the barrier and let me stride down the center of the thoroughfare, the crowds rose from the sidewalk and began cheering. After hours and hours of wretched waiting in the downpour, they were getting their first glimpse of the great royal occasion, and they hailed me as happily as if I had been a Knight of the Garter in full regalia.

Fortunately the deluge did not abruptly resume to turn my great royal moment into high comedy, and as I proceeded up the long avenue to loud cheers and the waving of soaked newspapers I put aside timidity and here and there, in a gesture I hoped was worthy of the great Fred Astaire, I lifted my top hat and tipped it to the crowd.

I had almost reached the Abbey before I realized what had put them in such good spirits. There I noticed that several persons at the curb were pointing at my hand and laughing. Then I saw the higher light. In that hand, quite forgotten, I was lugging my lunch of two sandwiches and an orange in a brown paper bag. The crowd loved it. Here was this regular toff—top hat, white tie and all, mind you, at 6 o'clock in the morning—and he was brown-bagging the Coronation.

It felt quite wonderful to create such a stir with such democratic plainness, and in an uncharacteristic seizure of stage presence I tipped my hat again, then lifted my brown paper bag and waved it, and was washed with the sweet thunder of applause. It was a sublime moment. The rest of the day was rather long.

A HEY
NONNY GEORGE

Every time the teams go south for spring training I think back to the year George Steinbrenner bought Sweet Will Shakespeare from the Globe Theater Cats. In those days, of course, we didn't go down to Florida or Arizona. Our idea of fun in the sun was Lyme Regis.

We'd all gather down there around the middle of March—still cold enough to freeze a foot right off your hexameter—and start warming up our dactyls and spondees. At least, that's what the press boys said we were doing, but mostly we were drying out after a long winter of hoisting the tankards around the Mermaid Tavern. Getting our heads cleared up for the new season, you might say.

George owned the Loch Ness Monsters in those days, a sad outfit. They still had a couple of old-timers who had been good once. One of them had pitched "Ralph Roister Doister" and the other later went into the Hall of Fame for "Gammer Gurton's Needle," but by the time George bought in the rest of the staff was so thin that the team's motto was "Ralph Roister Doister and Gammer Gurton's Needle and pray for rain."

George wanted a winner and was willing to pay for it. That's how he got Kit Marlowe—"Mighty Line Marlowe," the scribes called him—from the Leeds Loons, for three butts of sack and a cask of doublets.

The next year he bought O'Rare Ben Jonson from the Canterbury Cassowaries, but O'Rare didn't come cheap. "I wouldst not play for the Loch Ness Monsters though they paid me in ships to the number of 900 and 99," Jonson told George.

"Suppose I make it a thousand," said George. To which O'Rare said, "It's a deal."

Naturally, Marlowe didn't take to Jonson and Jonson didn't take to Marlowe after Kit, being introduced to O'Rare at spring training down in Lyme Regis, asked, "Is this the face that launched a thousand ships?"

So there was bad blood on the team, and it got worse the next year when George bought Sweet Will from the Globe Theater Cats. Will was coming off a thirty-sonnet season: the hottest thing to hit the league since the Venerable Bede and a cinch to cop the Jeff Chaucer Award once he licked his weakness for serving up the old mistaken-identity plot.

You can guess how George and Marlowe felt when word got around that George was paying Will all the perfume in Arabia with a bonus guarantee of ten percent of all the perfume in Paris if Will could win the Series in four straight tragedies.

When time came for everybody to show up at Lyme Regis that spring, both Kit and O'Rare were absent. This was a disappointment to the press and especially to the woodcut carvers, who had hoped to make woodcuts of George's three mighty stars embracing and showing each other their quill pens.

Instead, they had to be satisfied with woodcuts of Sweet Will warming up his soliloquy lines. Will obligingly posed for the carvers delivering a practice soliloquy that went, "Should I be or not? Hey nonny nonny."

And when they cried, "Just one more, Will!" he wound up and delivered, "You know what the problem is? It's whether I want to exist with bare fardels or bear this bodkin, nonny nonny no."

"Just one last one, Will!" cried the woodcarvers, but George tossed them out in a fury, which was caused by the arrival of heralds bearing tidings from Kit Marlowe and Jonson.

"Dear George," said Kit, "I cannot get to Lyme Regis before May, possibly August, due to an inflamed rotator cuff in my writing arm which makes it impossible to deliver two lines of iambic pentameter without intense pain."

Jonson's tiding was rambling and incoherent. A business crisis created by dry rot in his thousand ships required immediate attention, and what's more there were mice in all his writing doublets, and moreover his mother who was ailing and needed expensive bleeding almost daily was pleading with him to give up poetry and accept a high-paying offer to write sermons for the Bishop of London.

Enraged, George cried that he was sick of being abused by money gougers. "When I get through with those two schnorrers," he cried, "they won't have enough left for a six-line tetrameter."

Sweet Will, who was always genial, said, "Prithee, good George, thinkst thou there is something rotten in the town of Lyme Regis?"

George showed him missives borne by heralds from his liege men. "Hm," said Will, "what they will, Will dost well know, and well wilt thou do, wilt thou take Will's most willing word."

"Speak English," said George.

"Put money in their purse," said Will.

This sent George through the roof and when he came back he glared and shook his head at Shakespeare.

"Shake not thy Georgey locks at me!" cried Shakespeare, striding out of camp. George persuaded him to return, but it was a bad season. Shakespeare wrote "Measure for Measure" instead of "King Lear," and George was so disgusted that he took a carrack to New York where, finding that somebody had already bought the island, he settled for buying the New York Yankees.

NODDING
BY THE MIRE

Now the golden rays of July burnish the verdant hillside and the croak of the trout vies with the mewling of the spotted sapsucker and the snarl of the nocturnal tomcat to remind us that nature is not to be trifled with.

This is July's message, as ancient as the button-down collar, as eternal as the moss's refusal to grow on the rolling stone. Man turns deaf ears to nature's message only at his peril, for man too is part of nature, as is woman, and to trifle with nature is to trifle with himself, as well as herself.

As Thoreau observed after watching the great blue owl take

wing across the blasted heath, "to trifle with nature is as pointless as having your nose bobbed." But man, the trifler—and woman, the trifleress—are slow to learn, as the popularity of surgical tucks in the buttocks and the dewlaps attests all too expensively.

What of the magnificent summer tides relentlessly tugged and hauled by the richness of the lunar glory and the fullness of the nature writer's prose? The tides know that nature is not to be trifled with. Not for the tides the gleaming slash of surgeon's scalpel. The tides do not trifle with their wrinkles, shift their navels hither and yon like buttons on a checkerboard. The tides know the wisdom of nature.

So does the mighty elm. So does the mighty hen cackling in triumph at her daily ovate emission. Not for the mighty hen such trifling speculation as whether she or the egg comes first. She knows too well the inexorable decree of nature that the egg comes first, being served at breakfast, while the chicken is re-served for dinner.

This is the meaning of July, that mirth-maker and mocker of man's speculations, as well as woman's speculations. Its sun-drenched days are diurnal and its shortened nights nocturnal, its dewy mornings matutinal and its scorching afternoons postmatutinal. This is nature's message.

Who among us is not humbled by the matutinality of a July morn with the whooping crane becoming extinct against the gathering sky and the gathering houseflies whooping in delight at a fragment of lobster, now extinct, unguarded in the balm of perfumed kitchen air?

Even Voltaire, who claimed to find nature the most tiresome subject in French journalism, conceded that he was always moved by the spectacles of a giant oak falling on his unassuming cottage and a wild boar sinking his tusks into a hunting aristocrat. Such is the power and the whim of nature in July as this ancient planet, older than Bing Crosby and the Rhythm Boys, once again continues in its poignant perennial journey around Old Sol, a journey that will bear it through autumn, winter and spring, and fructify the earth with the variegated seasonal fruit of the nature writer's toil.

And what fruit July will produce when the earth has come full circle once again! Watermelon. Watercress. Water chestnuts. Polluted water. Ice water. Polluted ice water. This is the message of July.

You can hear it in a bosky glade when the cicadas salute the rumbling brook with their immemorial melody, not at all like the sound of a hog eating slops by a waterfall, as the nature-hater Nietzsche once described it, but rather like the whine of a power saw devouring a forest of redwoods.

In fact, this haunting music, the characteristic fugue of July in all bosky glades, is thought to be either the mating cry of the cicada or a warning call emitted to caution fellow cicadas of a spider approaching their encampment.

Yes, this is the message of July: a spider is approaching the encampment. Sometimes, of course, it is a shark approaching the surf; at others, a slug approaching the lettuce patch, the elm blight leaping from tree to tree, the scorpion crawling into a temporarily vacant shoe. Sometimes it is the insurance salesman approaching the front door.

Thus are we chastened by the miracle of July when nature's primordial symphony goes to bat like a ton of bricks throwing caution to the winds and takes the bull by the horns to pull out all the stops. This is nature's message. The bull knows it.

And what of the dim-spotted lapwing moistening its parched beak in the crepuscular bilge of soft purple down that gathers at the edge of the gorse as the sun sets like a scalding orange pot beneath the restlessly heaving bosom of the timeless yet primeval oceans with their mysterious swaying to the power of the primordial moon?

What of the lowly milk cow? What of her timeless chewing of the ancient cud? Does the cow know what the dim-spotted lapwing knows, what the cicada knows, what the slug approaching the lettuce patch knows, what the insurance salesman approaching the front door knows?

Whittlestein knew, knew all too well when, dying of thrips, he said, "Nature simply is." We shall not see his like again.

■ BEING MEAN ■

In this television commercial Mean Joe Green, who is a football player, is limping into the locker room looking bruised, sullen and mean enough to kick the stuffing out of a teddy bear, and he is accosted by a male moppet extending a bottle of carbonated water. Mean Joe scowls at the intruding little busybody and limps on, then suffers a change of heart, turns back, takes the proffered bottle and gives the tyke the biggest, sweetest smile you ever saw in your life.

Do you get the message? Mean Joe Green isn't mean at all. Beneath that mean exterior lurks just another pussycat waiting for tiny tots to make him purr with soda pop.

I know nothing about Mean Joe Green except that he plays professional football for the Pittsburgh Steelers and is always called Mean Joe Green. I like the idea behind that name and am disappointed to discover that it is misleading, that Joe Green is soft on little tykes, soft as goose down on soda pop. I'm also disappointed when the kid answers Joe's smile with a smile of his own, instead of bursting into tears at the sight of Joe's happily flashing incisors and crying, "Say it ain't so, Joe."

But the kid doesn't cry. He smiles. He is happy to discover that in Mean Joe there is no real meanness. The kid is on his way to becoming a confirmed believer in the modern creed that there is no such thing as a mean man. Twenty or 30 years from now that kid will sit on juries that give not-guilty verdicts to people who shoot their wives and four children because

E T C.

somebody left the cap off the toothpaste tube.

As I say, I know nothing about Mean Joe Green. Maybe he never had an ounce of decent meanness in him. Maybe the name was just another one of those publicity frauds so common in professional sports. The point is that American youth needs models of human meanness just as much as it needs heroes. For a famous mean man to get caught smiling at moppets is just as bad as for a hero to get caught swindling widows and orphans.

A great deal is made nowadays about the lack of heroes, and what a pity it is, and how everybody, as a result, is going to grow up and get rich by swindling widows and orphans. But the lack of mean men has effects just as evil on society.

Until very recently it was widely thought, on the basis of overwhelming evidence, that the world contained a certain percentage of people who were just downright mean, almost no good at all and likely to behave, given half a chance, like rotten human beings. Being aware of the probability, you kept an eye out for such customers, gave them wide berth whenever possible, just as you would skirt a viper, and, if compelled to deal with them, kept your dagger unsheathed.

Nowadays, however, the meannest of people find it almost impossible to commit any act of redeeming social vileness. A policeman who shoots an unarmed boy is not allowed to become a useful symbol of that public menace, the rotten cop; instead he is declared mentally ailing and tucked away among psychiatrists. Parents who maim their small children are not allowed to be flogged in public, but are turned over to social workers to find out what's troubling them.

Even when someone like the late Gary Gilmore succeeds in getting himself executed as a model of unmitigated meanness, he is frustrated by social diagnosticians insistent on finding out how society wrought such dreadful perversities in such a commonplace lad.

It is enough to make a genuinely mean man give up in despair. How can he ever commit a deed exemplary enough to caution youth about the dark side of human nature when his most revolting cruelties are belittled by psychiatrists as the work of a humdrum psychosis? When sociologists deny him credit for his own cussedness and award it, instead, to society? When lawyers diminish his capacity for bestiality by reducing courtrooms to tears with testimony about the anguish he has suffered on life's harsh road?

Americans seem determined to abolish the mean man in spite of himself. The ancient saw that there is a little bit of goodness in everybody has been distorted. Nowadays it is: There's no real meanness in anybody.

And Mean Joe Green is soft on kids. Soft on soda pop. What a flabby world. For relief I reopen Dickens—"David Copperfield"—and spend a therapeutic hour with Mr. Murdstone and his sister, Jane Murdstone, playing twin monsters upon poor young David. The Murdstones were mean, no good, rotten human beings. They didn't fool Dickens for a moment. Dickens knew about the world. Mr. Murdstone would have shown Sweet Joe Green how to deal with a kid offering him a pop bottle. He would have locked him in the cellar, turned in the kid's bottle and kept the deposit money. That's what meanness is, Mr. Green.

BARNUM LIVES ON

There is a natural affinity between a used-car salesman and a Congressman. Neither one wants you to know what's under the hood.

For this reason there was nothing surprising about Congress's rejection of Federal rules that would have forced used-car dealers to tell their customers about serious defects in their merchandise. Do Congressmen advertise the cracks in their brains? Why should a used-car salesman have to advertise the holes in his radiator?

I don't think it was all those campaign donations from the

used-car lobby that made Congress toss out the proposed rules. I think a surge of natural brotherly sympathy would have been enough to carry the day for America's Honest Harrys, Smilin' Sams and Upright Ulrics.

Put yourself in your Congressman's shoes. One of these days he is going to be out of office. Defeated, old, tired, 120,000 miles on his smile and two pistons cracked in his best joke. They're going to put him out on the used-Congressman lot.

Does he want to have a sticker on him stating that he gets only eight miles on a gallon of bourbon? That his rip-roaring anti-Communist speech hasn't had an overhaul since 1969? That his generator is so decomposed it hasn't sparked a fresh thought in 15 years?

You know and I know what he wants. When Happy Harvey brings a buyer over, he wants Happy to be able to say: "Now I've got to tell you this is a used Congressman, but he's better than new. Had only one owner—a little old oil industry who never used him for anything except to go to church on Sundays."

I'm sympathetic to that used Congressman. Having the Federal Government protect consumers is well and good, but there are a few areas where the consumer has traditionally been expected to fend for himself. Choosing a Congressman is one of these. Buying a used car is another.

Admittedly, they are not perfectly analogous. Nobody, for example, tells you it's your citizen's obligation to buy a used car, whereas people are always telling you it's shameful not to vote for a Congressman. This is why I always vote for a Congressman, even though I'd rather not.

I'd never dream of buying a used car though. I've always classified people who buy used cars along with people who handle rattlesnakes. They're people who are eager for surprises and will go out of their way to enjoy one.

Voting for a Congressman is slightly different. You know you're going to get a surprise all right, and you'd probably rather not, but good citizenship compels you to stick your hand in the box and pull the lever. Then you howl for the next two years, or the next six years if it's a senator.

I expect to howl after voting for a Congressman, and I'd expect to howl if I bought a used car. People running for Congress and used-car salesmen are expected to make you howl. They're among the last few breeds left in the country who survive by their wits, and the country needs them, not only to give us something to howl against, but also to satisfy the millions afflicted with an incurable rage to gamble.

The extent of this compulsion can be judged from the numbers who flock to Las Vegas and Atlantic City under the delusion they can beat the house. The more such lunatics we can satisfy at the ballot box and the used-car lot, the better for the country. Better to have them playing politics and helping the auto business than squandering their time and wealth in fleshpots.

As for the used-car salesman, the legend of his chicanery has become part of the fabric of America, like Roy Bean, the hanging judge, and P.T. Barnum, who is cherished in the American soul for having enunciated the national faith in a sucker's being born every minute. By keeping alive the memory of the Old West horse trader in a thousand concrete cities, the used-car dealer keeps us in touch with our roots.

We should not be trying to endanger his species. We should be enacting measures to preserve him for posterity, so that no American will ever have to grow up without being tempted to match wits with Integrity Irv, Principled Pete, Good Guy George or Cheery Charlie.

I hope never to see the day when an American child will walk onto a used-car lot and be told, "I wouldn't dream of taking your money, kid, before telling you that heap you like so much has two broken axles, a motor full of sawdust and a frame so badly bent it would take a team of elephants to align the front end."

That would be almost as bad as having a Congressman say, "Before voting for me, you must realize that I cheat on my wife and income tax, am on the secret payroll of two very large corporations whose interests are not yours and heartily dislike people who can't waltz.''

I think Congress understood the importance of protecting our ancient frauds when it voted down the restrictions on used-car dealers. Of course the campaign gifts from the used-car folks probably didn't hurt, either. It helped remind both parties how much they had in common.

EAT WHAT YOU ARE

There's hardly ever any good news from the eating front anymore. I use the word "front" on purpose, because eating, which used to be one of humanity's sublime pleasures, is nowadays more like walking through a mine field.

I blame this on the phenomenon of health chic, that intense preoccupation with our physiques that compels fashionable people nowadays to boast how regimens that would have made a Spartan beg for mercy leave them feeling aglow with robust hygienic delight.

The dream of these people is to live forever, and in order to do so they will submit to any hardship—except growing old, of course. They are particularly fond of pouncing on you just when you have your mouth opened for a good meal, and pointing out every item on the menu that will kill you.

In the past 20 years the compendium of fatal foods has, at one time or another, included everything consumed by the human race. The only way to live forever, it seemed, was never to eat again.

I have no wish to live forever, but I would like to go as long as Methuselah, who lived 900 years, on condition that I wouldn't look a day over 27. Accordingly, some years ago, I quit regarding the table as a place of delight and treated it as something at which

I would have to suffer for the next eight and a half centuries.

I fancied myself being interviewed by the reporters on my 900th birthday, being asked: "What's the secret of living to be 900, old-timer?" And I would answer: "Haven't touched a meal that was fit to eat since Hector was a pup."

I relished the idea of giving them this line, since, considering the present decline in educational standards, I figured that by the year 2825 when the interview would be held, nobody else on earth would know who Hector was, and it would give me a chance to show off my classical education. I could even imagine the headlines: "Old-Timer Recalls Hector's Puphood."

As the 1970s progressed and more and more foods were declared fatal, it began to look as if I'd have to starve my way to 900. Bacon, eggs and milk were gone from my table because of their lethal cholesterol. Same for nice juicy meats and gravy. Then coffee, tea and soda pop. Everything that had sugar in it.

All I drank anymore were carbonated liquids with noncaloric sweeteners that left my mouth tasting as if I had gargled a mouthful of pennies. Nothing that contained nitrites passed my lips, of course, and almost everything contained nitrites.

Next went salt. "You'll never make it to 900 if you use salt," everybody said. This was a bad time because about the only thing left to eat was vegetables without nitrites.

I could make do with that as long as I ate at home, since I'm passionately fond of raw vegetables and could satisfy myself leaning on the counter gnawing on raw carrots, raw potatoes and raw broccoli and, for dessert, raw tomato slices placed sandwich-style between two wedges of raw cabbage.

Going out to dinner was the problem. Hostesses, to put a good face on the meal, felt obliged to cook the vegetables, except that having heard that overcooked vegetables will kill you, they didn't really cook them. They'd steam them for just a few seconds, not long enough to cook them, but just long enough to take all the taste out of them. Then you had to eat them without salt.

Just when it looked as if I'd have to stop eating forever in order to extend my days on earth, there was a terrifying development. A new generation of nutrition scientists emerged from medical school with a new message.

While it was true that too much cholesterol, sugar, salt and gravy could kill some people, they said, a lot of other people were killing themselves by not eating enough cholesterol, sugar, salt and gravy.

A few weeks ago a high-blood-pressure expert warned a convention of his colleagues that the fad for salt-free eating could harm more people than it helped. "Salt is the number one natural component of all human tissue," he said. "The concept that you don't need much is wrong."

Here was a direct challenge to the food philosophers who had been saying: "You are what you eat." The new philosophy was: "Eat what you are."

The people who say: "You are what you eat" have always seemed addled to me. In my opinion, you are what you think, and if you don't think, you can eat all the meat in Kansas City and still be nothing but a vegetable.

Following my own principle that you are what you think, I conclude that at this stage of life I am pure confusion. Having read all the advice on how to live 900 years, what I think is that eating a tasty meal once again will surely doom me long before I reach 900 while not eating that same meal could very well kill me. It's enough to make you reach for a cigarette!

FROM CHAIRPERSONS ■ TO TOTAL PERSONS ■

I recently met a chairperson. That is one of the advantages of living in the present age. You can meet a chairperson. Grandfather couldn't do that. I remember him sitting by the potbellied stove in the parlor one day in nineteen-ought-six moaning about the disadvantages of being born too soon.

He had tramped all the way across the Short Hill Mountain that day and walked almost to Harpers Ferry. "Nary a chairperson in the whole county," he said. "It looks like I'm going to die without ever seeing me one." He did. He was born too soon.

"You're lucky, boy," he used to say when I wandered into his blacksmith's shed to watch him beat out a horseshoe on the anvil. "There's a great day coming in this country, and you're going to live to see it."

"What'll it be like, Grandpa?" I would ask him.

"There's going to be chairpersons all through the hills and down in the hollows," he said, "and you're going to see them."

"That'll be some day, all right."

"And that's not all," he said. "There's also going to be co-chairpersons."

"You're spoofing me," I said.

"Co-chairpersons, boy. Mark my words, you're going to live to see real live co-chairpersons."

"What about couchpersons, Grandpa? Will I live to see couch-persons?"

"You're going to live to see wonderful things," he said. "Maybe even couchpersons. Who knows? Maybe even co-couch-persons."

I thought about Grandfather when I met that chairperson recently. "My granddaddy told me I'd see something like you one of these days," I told it. "But what I'd really like to see is a co-chairperson."

The chairperson said the best place to see those was in Washington or New York, since the co-variety of chairperson was still very rare in the hills and hollows. I'm going up to New York next summer and look around and while I'm up there I'm going to look for a total person. My grandfather said this creature was coming in my lifetime just as sure as the Model T Ford and the spaceship.

"One of these days, boy," he said one afternoon while patching a horse collar, "you're going to live in a world that's got total persons. Won't come in my time, won't come in your daddy's time, but you're going to live to see it—the total person."

"What's the difference between a person and a total person?" I asked.

"Well now," he said, "the total person is going to be person all over. Head, feet, arms, innards—every part will be person. That'll be something to see."

"What's the difference going to be between somebody like you and a total person?"

"Your total person isn't going to spend the time making horseshoes and patching horse collars and answering silly questions from little nose-pickers. Total persons are going to be jogging and interrelating in meaningful ways and fulfilling their selfs."

"Total persons are going to have selfs?"

"Just as sure as man is going to walk on the moon," he said. "Just as sure as the war budget is going to be defense expenditures and just as sure as marriage is going to be a sociocultural interface, total persons are going to have selfs."

"Honest?"

"Sure as shootin'. They're all going to have these here selfs and they're going to fulfill them."

"I'd sure like to see that," I said.

"You will," he said.

"What would you use to fulfill a self with, Grandpa?"

"Beats me," he said. "I went out to Spring's store and asked if they could order me a self from the catalogue, and Bernard Spring told me they're not making selfs yet, but you'll live to see total persons that have got selfs and they'll be all fulfilled, too. Wait and see."

The old gentleman was a prophet. The self hit the market in the 1960s and sold like horseshoes in nineteen-ought-six. It wasn't until a month or so ago, however, that I first heard of a total person.

There was a letter to a newspaper editor from somebody boasting about being a total person. From the tone of it, I guessed that this personal totality also had a self fulfilled right up to the brim.

It made me sentimental about Grandfather way back there making those horseshoes. Born too soon, he was doomed to be only a partial person, but there was enough of him to have a vision of future American greatness.

THE BOYS
OF AUTUMN

The Pitcher is old and canny and full of wisdom, though sometimes he is young and cool-headed under incredible pressure.

His office is the mound. He bestrides the mound. He tamps the mound. He comes down off the mound and goes to his mouth. Upon ascending the mound again, he toes the rubber. Other mound chores include going to the resin bag and keeping the base-runner honest with a good pick-off move.

The Pitcher's tools are good velocity and excellent location. He can go the distance unless he is the sort who tires after six good innings. If so, he must participate in a conference on the mound.

The Pitcher keeps the ball low but also, now and then, serves one up. Sometimes when he serves one up, the batter takes him downtown.

Do you know what The Pitcher wishes after a batter has taken him downtown? He wishes he had that one back.

Does The Pitcher become rattled upon finding himself downtown? Not likely. If he is old and canny and full of wisdom, he has been taken downtown before and knows that the game is never over until it has ended. He knows he has a great team behind him. It is a team that never quits.

And why does it never quit? Not, as people ignorant of baseball say, because the players would rather go on playing forever than face all that surgery that will be inflicted on them as soon as the season ends.

Facing surgery is as much a part of baseball as hitting the cutoff man, being fooled by the change-up and spiking the second baseman.

The Pitcher faces elbow surgery without fear. Ever since medical science a few years ago discovered something called the rotator cuff, The Pitcher also faces rotator-cuff surgery without fear. The Pitcher knows that all this surgery may prolong his brilliant career on the mound.

No, it is not fear of the knife that keeps the team from ever quitting. It is character. The team has character. So much character. Its members have pride. That pride will not let them quit. With so much character and so much pride, they cannot be counted out. They will never choke.

The Catcher will not let them give up. Though full of aches and bruises, The Catcher is too scrappy to let them give up. Inning after inning, game after game, week after week, he uses his whole body to block the ball. His arm is a rifle aimed at second base. Though tired and battered, he reaches back into hidden reserves of strength to battle The Pitcher's dancing knuckleball.

The Catcher calls a brilliant game. The Catcher gives up his body to block the plate. He can do no less, for he is The Catcher. He is the backbone of the squad, and courage is the name of the game, as well as the backbone.

Without The Catcher there would be no one to steady the young but cool-headed Pitcher who has just been taken downtown.

Without The Catcher who would there be to tip off The

Manager that the canny, wise old Pitcher was losing the dip on his greaseball?

Not The First Baseman. Snitching on The Pitcher is beyond The First Baseman's duties. It is The First Baseman's job to be big and powerful but lithe as a cat and hold the runner close to the bag and, later, when it is his turn to hit, to take The Opposing Pitcher downtown the instant The Opposing Pitcher serves one up.

Only The Catcher can tip off The Manager when The Pitcher begins losing his Stuff. At a signal from The Catcher, The Manager goes to the mound for a conference. "How much of your Stuff have you lost?" he asks The Pitcher.

If The Pitcher says The Catcher doesn't know what he's talking about and insists that he still has all his Stuff right there in his hand, The Manager is in a quandary. Shall he call for his Fireman or risk letting The Pitcher serve up another one?

The necessity to make such decisions makes The Manager controversial or brilliant, depending upon whether his team loses or wins. The Manager's other field duties include standing on the sidelines looking grim and leaping up and down on his hat while denouncing The Umpire.

The Manager's office duties also include being fired if the team is defeated. This is because it is cheaper to hire somebody else who can jump up and down on his cap than to hire new Pitchers who never lose their Stuff, new Catchers willing to give up their bodies to block the plate and new First Basemen who can take The Opposing Pitcher downtown.

This explains why The Manager is always seen committing acts of jubilation immediately after his team has won The World Series. The victory means that he, of all The Managers in the world, is the one Manager assured of another year of work.

ADVERSITY

Nightmares by a roaring television screen:

I am wandering in the desolate wilds of the American stomach. It is located at the southern extremity of the American esophagus, and it would be hard to imagine a more forlorn place. Stomach acid sloshes about at all hours. The entire landscape is obscured by impenetrable vapors, which I instantly recognize as the notorious "stomach gas."

From far above I hear the esophagus shouting to the stomach. "Potato chip with cheese dip coming down!" it cries. The stomach groans furiously. In an instant there is a thunderous roar overhead. Potato chip and cheese dip shoot through the gas like meteors from blackest space and plunge into the acid.

Then, without warning, a drenching torrent pours down upon me. The stomach snarls in rage at the esophagus. "Why didn't you warn me this bum was about to drink half a martini?" it cries. "I'll fix him."

In a murderous act of treachery, the stomach produces a dense mass of stomach gas and forces it back up the esophagus. I am caught in the updraft and am forced up, up, up, until I am wedged right under the breastbone. There, trapped, I hear the esophagus calling again. "Brace yourself down there! A whole anchovy coming down!"

Looking up, I see a gigantic salted fish plummeting upon me. I struggle to race back down the esophagus, but my feet are stuck in cheese dip, and the anchovy is gaining rapidly. . . .

I am jolted briefly into blessed wakefulness, then doze again. I have retained a baby sitter named Mrs. Marsh for the evening. She has brought a huge suitcase containing toothpaste, toothbrushes, sticks of chalk, glasses filled with dyed water and a

Thompson submachine gun, which she is pointing at me with one hand while dipping chalk into dyed water with the other.

She is determined not to let me go out to the movies until she has shown me how deeply her toothpaste will penetrate the enamel of my children's teeth. She is demonstrating with the chalk sticks. Sure enough, the dye is turning the chalk bright hues all the way through.

"You wouldn't do that to my children's teeth!" I am pleading. She cackles insanely. "Hah!" I cry. "Your toothpaste may penetrate chalk, but chalk isn't tooth enamel!" Mrs. Marsh fires a burst of machine-gun fire over my head to remind me to keep my hands up.

"My toothpaste," she gloats, "will penetrate anything. Look!" And she rubs it on the television set, which turns bright purple.

Is there nothing I can do to stop her mad plot? One thing, she tells me. If I agree to stay home and sit with her until midnight while she demonstrates her toothpaste's penetrating power on the Queen Anne chairs. . . .

I open my eyes and close them again, then reopen them wide because, standing right there before me, is my blue pinstripe suit. It is in an ugly mood. "I've got something to tell you, stupid," says the suit.

"What's holding you up?" I ask. "Do you have the invisible man inside?"

"I wish I did," says the suit. "He's probably got enough sense to realize a man needs twice as much protection."

"Where do you talk from?" I ask the suit. "Your voice seems to be coming from your right pocket, but I don't see the flap moving."

The suit says it has not come there to talk about suit anatomy. "Well, flip off then," I say. "I don't hold with wool that talks."

The suit makes a terrifying grimace with its left lapel and calls for reinforcements. In an instant, I am surrounded by angry clothing—sweaters, underpants, socks—all prancing around the room and jabbering furiously. I swing a right hook at a pair of socks, and miss, and in the next moment the clothes have all leaped on me and are about to break my arm, when I awake.

Breathing heavily, I lumber off to bed and put out the light. There is a stranger in the room. I demand to know what he is doing there. He says he is looking for the washing machine so he can surprise me next time I do the sheets by showing me a soap that gets white things twice as white. I lead him to the cellar. He thanks me. On the stairs I am mugged and robbed of all my vacation cash. When I get back to bed Karl Malden tells me always to carry traveler's checks.

A COLD HARD NET

The only Santa Claus I saw last December was wearing a blue suit and a badge, and he was being interviewed on television in Penn Station where he worked as a railroad cop. It was in the morning's wee hours, the time when Santa traditionally performs his ancient charities, and the station had a silent, abandoned look.

When the camera scanned the interior, though, you could see that while it was quiet all right, abandoned it wasn't. All around, down long corridors and against silent walls, people were snuggled—well, not deep in their beds, to be sure, but wrapped in their coats on floors of stone.

Sure, the cop said, if you went by the book you ought to throw them all out onto the street, but he didn't do that. Couldn't do that. Out on the street these late December mornings temperatures go down to 25, to 15 degrees. Sometimes lower.

Bedding on a railroad station floor might not be a heated water bed under eiderdown, but it was better than frostbite. His policy was to let them dream for a couple of hours, then wake them, tell them to move on and watch them shuffle to another corner, another corridor, and bed down again.

The reporting for this Christmas story was done by Gabe Pressman, one of the few ornaments of the local television news industry in New York, if only because he so often seems to be covering a real city rather than Mindless Fluffland, which absorbs most of his colleagues.

In a minute or two, though, Pressman's line to the real world was cut off, and there was a gent peddling mink Christmas gifts at $4,000 per coat. It is tempting to fall into error and view this as an abrupt transition to the unreal world, but it isn't.

The $4,000 Christmas package is as real in New York, and most other places in the country, as people sleeping on stone floors. A few nights after the Pressman story, the network news did a story on homelessness in America. With more and more people being dumped by the failing economy, homelessness may soon become almost as popular with TV news as arson and touring film stars.

The network story dealt with a Congressional hearing, and there was film of two or three articulate street people trying to tell Congressmen what it was like sleeping on railroad station floors. This was followed immediately by a commercial for a wristwatch built into a gold coin. The price was not mentioned, probably on the theory that if price was a consideration, you couldn't afford it.

How are we supposed to respond, sitting in the parlor, when we are jerked without benefit of decompression chamber between these two visions of America? Yes, this is a country where people would freeze to death except for the kindness of decent cops, and of course we know there are plenty of you out there so anxious to be rid of excess money that you'd be ecstatic to splurge on a new mink, another watch.

My guess is that most of us don't respond at all. We've been too numbed by television's constant flow of images juxtaposing misery with luxury cars and new improved panty hose.

I probably wouldn't have noticed either if I hadn't been on Fifth Avenue the day before watching shoppers hurry home with their treasures and noticed that they were impeded by having to step around the reclining bodies of homeless people at rest on the sidewalks.

If we had film of this sort of thing from Moscow, wouldn't it be widely screened as evidence of the failure of Communism? Does the juxtaposition on television of stone beds and gold coins for wrist decoration tell us something depressing about the failures of capitalism?

In a large part of the world outside the Communist zones, the message surely wouldn't be helpful to our cause, but we
can always fall back on the explanation that while capitalism may not be perfect, it's still better than anything else on the market.

This may go down successfully in some countries struggling to survive, but it's embarrassing to have to settle for such faint self-praise here at home. Even President Reagan, the St. George of embattled capitalism, once thought he could rescue it without causing misery and desperation.

His famous "safety net" would see to that, he promised. It was a restful idea, the safety net. It suggested lying in a gentle hammock, secure until the great engines of capitalism recalled everyone to work. The reality is a patch of stone floor in a railroad station and a decent cop willing to let you dream for two hours before waking you up. Some safety. Some net.

THROUGH
A GLASS DARKLY

What is the Situation?

The Situation is bad. The crisis has become acute. Time is running out. The outlook is grave. This may be our last opportunity.

What must we do when the Weather Bureau says the air quality is unacceptable?

Avoid breathing and all other exercise until the All Clear is sounded. If it is 10 P.M., find out where your children are. Curb your dog. Fight drug addiction. Watch out for deer. No littering or spitting. Don't be fuelish. Use your ashtray.

What are the origins of the present Situation?

Violence on television. Cigarette smoke. Sex education in the schools. Cholesterol. Drought. The Warren Commission.

How can we survive?

Get a regular dental checkup. Give to muscular dystrophy. Do not park unless you have diplomatic license plates. Support your police. Get a chest X-ray. Check tire pressure twice a month. Fasten seat belt. Don't walk. Give to the Heart Fund. No left turn. Avoid wetness twice as long. Make love not war. Check blood pressure once a month.

What about the big oil companies?

The oil companies and the Arabs are in it up to their necks. This is because they were raised by permissive parents. As a result, the supply of big oil companies will be exhausted before the year 1996 and the last of the Arabs will be used up before the year 2010.

Is there hope in science's recent discovery of rings around Uranus?

It is too soon to tell. Some scientists believe the Uranian rings may provide a rich new source of ionospheric patching material to plug holes around the earth caused by aerosol sprays. Most students of science, however, believe science will discover that the rings cause cancer in mice.

What is the immediate outlook?

For America's forgotten senior citizens, grim. For the permanently unemployed, bleak. For disadvantaged minorities, oppressive. For the young, higher taxes. For Social Security, bankruptcy. For the middle-aged, despair. The only hope is a dramatic breakthrough in solar energy or new sugar-substitute research—and, in the long run, lasers or development of synthetic pets with sharply reduced nutritional requirements.

Would the Situation improve with a drop in coffee prices?

Not unless it were accompanied by a sharp drop in the consumption of cream, sugar, fried foods, marbled beef, gravy, big automobiles, cigarettes, alcohol, barbiturates, candy, chemical sprays, carbon monoxide, heroin, asbestos fiber, cocaine, pistols, shotguns, bald eagles, pornography, welfare funds, mugging victims and stolen Indian lands.

In the moment of crisis, what can the individual do to help?

File by April 15. Avoid mediciney breath and baggy panty hose. Don't carry cash.

Where is the safest place to be when time runs out?

There is no safe place, but some places are safer than others. Federal crisis analysts say it is better to be in the Sun Belt at the critical moment than to be a hostage in a hijacked airplane. Do not be on the streets when disgruntled snipers are struggling to achieve television stardom. Stay a safe distance from careering oil companies, nursing homes run by racketeers, large corporations fleeing to the suburbs and lawyers of all varieties.

What is Federal policy on the Situation?

It is bold, imaginative, new and dynamic, as well as timid, devoid of new ideas, stale and tired. The Government has at last met the challenge, although it is too little and too late. In his dramatic appearance before the Congress, the President declared that the Situation had become almost as complex as the tax law. Congress is moving swiftly to add new complexities to the tax law so that it will maintain its present lead over the Situation.

How much time is left?

It depends on the Russians and insecticides. A breakthrough in pothole-patching technology could also give us more time, as could a solution of the African problem, a sudden decline in greed, easier-to-understand insurance policies, a rise in reading skills among high-school students or development of a horse capable of cruising eight hours at 55 miles per hour to replace the automobile. Otherwise, as the Babylonians were the first to point out, it's all going to be over almost any day now.

▪ IN BED WE LIE ▪

Have you ever noticed, friend, that when you are sleeping happily and the telephone rings and you reach an arm from under the blanket and say "Hello" into the mouthpiece, the voice on the telephone always says, "Did I wake you up?"

And have you ever noticed how you immediately and invariably reply? You lie. "Of course not," you say, or, "Are you kidding? I've been up for hours."

Scientific studies with laboratory mice have not yet shown how many persons will answer candidly—"Yes, you woke me up, and I hope you're satisfied"——but I bet it is fewer than three in a million.

For some reason, being peaceably asleep in your bed is looked upon as a deed so degrading that people are ashamed to confess it over the telephone. Most murderers of whom I have had knowledge could scarcely wait to get to the police and confess their guilt, but imagine any one of them deciding to pause for a nap before going to the police station, and imagine the chief of detectives interrupting his slumber with a phone call.

"Did I wake you up?" the chief would surely ask.

"Of course not," the murderer would lie. And perhaps, to show that slumber was of no interest to him whatever, he might garnish his answer by saying, "In fact, I was just brushing my teeth before calling you up to confess a murder."

Why is it easier for people to confess to murder than to being asleep when the telephone rings?

An equally mysterious question: How does the caller always know that he has awakened his victim? Through decades of being telephoned out of sleep, I recollect not one case in which the caller did not know instantly that he had awakened me.

Think for a moment of your own experience. It is 8 A.M. and you have been up since 6. The telephone rings. "Hello," you say. Does the caller ever, under this circumstance, say, "Did I wake you up?" Of course not. He knows—don't ask me how—that you have been up for at least two hours.

The same person calling at 10 A.M. the next day when you are sleeping merrily will immediately say, "Did I wake you up?"

He knows he woke you up. What's more, you know he knows you were sleeping, knows just as surely as though he had television monitors in your bedroom. Why do you insist on lying about it?

The lie makes you feel inferior and rotten and gives the caller psychological superiority. He realizes he has power to make you lie. He feels superior, for he is not the one who has lied over the telephone. He has merely asked a harmless question.

Or is it harmless? I believe this question is maliciously framed to give the caller powerful psychological advantage over his victim. Since he obviously knows he has awakened you, why does he bother to ask? Why not do the civilized thing and immediately hang up with a quiet, "Sorry, I'll phone later when you're awake"?

Instead, knowing fully you are addled and possibly suffering from hangover, he takes the opportunity to subject you to a humiliating cross-examination. "Did I wake you up?" He knows you will lie. He lies himself when people wake him up by jangling his telephone.

This reflexive tendency to lie about sleeping probably reflects some ancient American belief in the virtues of early rising. Benjamin Franklin held that, coupled with early bedding, it made you healthy, wealthy and wise. Like so many of Franklin's sayings, this makes little sense today. Nowadays it is lawyers that make you wise enough to become sufficiently wealthy under tax shelters to afford a place in healthy air far from the city.

The early bird gets the worm, goes another old aphorism, and I suppose all Americans sleeping after 6 A.M. may feel subconsciously guilty about enjoying themselves instead of getting worms.

This does not explain, however, why most people are just as quick to lie about being asleep when the phone goes off at 3 o'clock in the morning and the inevitable question comes out of the earpiece. "Did I wake you up?"

At 3 o'clock in the morning? You must be kidding. I've been up since midnight getting worms.

Witty reply, even of this ham-handed quality, is never possible from a mind summoned out of sleep by clanging machinery. Even if it were, it would lead to greater humiliation than an admission of being caught at sleep, for the caller would almost certainly turn out to be Aunt Isabel phoning in tears to report that Uncle Norman had been gravely stricken with the boll weevil.

So we lie. Wake me up? Not a chance. Everybody is wide awake here in the U.S.A. Twenty-four hours a day.

▪ I REMEMBER PAPA ▪

Yet another collection of anecdotes about the literary giants:

One afternoon in Paris, Ernest Hemingway and Morley Callaghan challenged Scott Fitzgerald and me to a bout of team wrestling. Hemingway, who was vain about his half nelson, became enraged halfway to the first fall when Edna St. Vincent Millay jumped into the ring and broke her umbrella over his skull, crying, "You monosyllabic brute! Get that half nelson off the finest American writers of our generation!"

Ernest was so stunned—possibly by the umbrella blow, possibly by hearing Scott and me described as his literary superiors—that he grabbed his partner, Morley Callaghan, and was about to pin him with a body slam when Morley flattened him with a right hook to the jaw. Ernest never forgave Scott and me.

John O'Hara and I were drinking late one evening in Tim Costello's when Ernest Hemingway came in to do some betting. "See that blackthorn walking stick hanging over the bar? I'll bet $5 I can break it over your skull," he told John.

"You're pretty good at breaking sticks," O'Hara said, "but not worth a damn at knitting."

"Oh, yeah?" said Ernest. "I'll bet $10 I can knit a pair of baby bootees faster than you can."

O'Hara accepted the challenge and they went at it. Hemingway was furious when O'Hara completed two masterfully crafted baby bootees before Ernest had even learned to hold the knitting needles. In his rage, Hemingway seized the blackthorn walking stick and broke it over my head, so I sued him for the hospital bill and the courts made him pay. Ernest never forgave me.

One day I was having tea with T. S. Eliot at the Plaza when Ernest Hemingway dropped in with Dorothy Parker. "Meet the wittiest woman in the world," Ernest said to Eliot.

"Delighted," T. S. said to Dottie, rising, hooking his umbrella over the back of the chair and shaking her hand. "Say something witty."

"Tell me Calvin Coolidge is dead," said Dottie.

"Gladly," said Eliot. "Calvin Coolidge is dead."

"How can they tell?" said Dorothy.

"Can you top that?" Hemingway roared with appreciation, until I pointed out that Coolidge had been dead for 25 years and that General Eisenhower was now President.

"So what?" scowled Ernest.

"So ask me what they call the White House since Eisenhower moved in," I said.

"What do they call the White House since Eisenhower moved in?" asked T. S.

"The tomb of the well-known soldier," I said.

I got to Eliot's umbrella one step ahead of Ernest and broke it over the teapot. Ernest never forgave me.

Once, at lunch around the Algonquin Round Table, Noel Coward challenged Ernest Hemingway to drink a double martini out of Gertrude Stein's slipper. I was dismayed when Ernest accepted the challenge because Gertrude had phoned me the previous night to ask if I could recommend an effective ointment for athlete's foot.

"Ernie," I whispered, as he lifted the gin-filled slipper with an olive toward his lips.

"Don't interrupt, or I'll never forgive you," he growled, draining the slipper and smashing the olive over Noel Coward's head.

After that, Hemingway started growing his beard to conceal a skin problem. Ernest never forgave me.

Herman Melville and Petroleum V. Nasby called on me one afternoon while I was lying under a beach umbrella at Key West. They wanted a favor

"Neither Herman nor I have ever met Ernest Hemingway," said Petroleum.

"Better keep quiet about it," I cautioned. "If Ernest finds out you haven't met him, he'll never forgive you."

"The problem," said Melville, "is, if we never meet him, we will never have the chance to be involved in a Hemingway literary anecdote, and our names will disappear from the history of American literature."

Naturally, I wanted to give the poor devils a shot at fame so I hailed Hemingway, who happened to be in his boat just offshore hunting for Nazi submarines.

He was in an uncharacteristically genial mood and could not have been more charming. He said he thought Herman was one of the finest writers in the language and he told Petroleum that any man who could make Abraham Lincoln laugh was all right with Papa.

"That's all very well, Ernie," I said, "but these fellows need a little anecdotal action. Why don't you break the beach umbrella over their skulls?"

Ernest absolutely refused. "That wouldn't be very polite to fellows who came all the way to Key West to shake my hand," he said, and walked away with a cheerful wave. Herman and Petroleum never forgave him.

SEALED EARS

Dr. Harold Liverworth, the syndicated sociologist, is under the impression that Americans want someone to listen to them. Hence the title of his latest book, "How to Make People Shut Up and Listen to You," published by Quack & Blurb at $19.95.

It may be, as Dr. Liverworth assumed, that the country is teeming with people yearning to be heard. On the other hand, how many of us are so desperate for an audience that we would go out to dinner wearing a ring in the nose?

"Mrs. J.T., the wife of an autoparts executive, had gone out to dinners for 17 years without once being listened to by a single guest," he writes. "She was desperate when she came to me for help. 'I'll do anything if, just once, I can make somebody at a dinner table listen to me,' she said."

What did Dr. Liverworth recommend? That's right: a ring in her nose. "No one," he writes, "not the most resolute, egomaniacal blabbermouth, can ignore your conversation when you show up for dinner with a ring in your nose."

This passage clears up a mystery that has bothered me since last September when I went to a dinner party attended by a woman with a ring in her nose. "Why is that woman wearing a ring in her nose?" I asked the host. Not having listened to me, he explained, "That reminds me of a long-winded anecdote about something brilliant I did the other day."

This is an extreme application of the basic Liverworth theory, which holds that most people are not listened to because they are uninteresting. "If your talk is hopelessly dull," he writes, "turn yourself into a conversation piece. Wear a bottle of fine Bordeaux instead of a necklace or necktie. Have your hips whittled away and wear a transparent skirt or trousers to elicit curiosity."

All this advice and much more in a similar vein makes me suspect that Dr. Liverworth doesn't go out much. If he did he would know that dangling a bottle of Chateau Margaux in your cleavage is not going to daunt the millions of Americans determined to listen to no one but themselves.

With all due respect to Dr. Liverworth's scientific credentials, I consider myself the world's foremost authority on being ignored in what passes for American conversation. No one has listened to me in a conversation in the last 20 years, and, far from whining about it, I find it enjoyable.

At first, of course, it was depressing. This was at Washington dinner parties. Seated between two women who had been officially certified orthodox by the United States Government, I would be asked three questions in sequence by the woman on the right:

"What do you do?" "Where did you go to college?" "What school are your children in?"

Then it was the turn of the woman on the left: "What do you do?" "Where did you go to college?" "What school are your children in?"

Having answered twice, I turned back to the one on the right. "What do you do?" she always asked.

One night I replied, "I have just slain the butcher's wife with a broadsword."

"Where did you go to college?" she replied.

"Because she threatened to expose me as an agent of the K.G.B. unless I abandoned my family and ran away with her to Samoa," I said.

"What school are your children in?" she inquired.

Since then I have found the pleasures of not being listened to so exhilarating that going out to parties has again become the joy I remember from youth, when there was always the chance the woman of your dreams might walk in and say yes to a stroll in the moonlight.

If the women are gathered in the corner to ask each other where they went to college and what schools their children are in, and the men are thumping their chests, I often cry out, "I have just slain the butcher's wife with a broadsword," and know that the other men will compete to be the first to say, "It's interesting you should say that because when I went to the bank the other day this profound insight occurred to me, which, if you don't mind a very long story . . ."

While all the others are waiting for him to fall dead so they can talk, I shout, "Shut up and let me talk, will you?"

"That's true," someone will be bound to say, "but you wouldn't be wearing polyester shirts today if the Supreme Court had ruled . . ."

I never listen to the ends of these conversational gambits, of course. I am too busy being the fascinating rogue I can be only in a typical American conversation. I am looking for the opportunity to cry, "Aha! I have just punctured the hostess's girdle with the very épée that Basil Rathbone wielded in 'Captain Blood.' "

This is much more pleasant than having your hips whittled away, and just as ineffective for getting an audience.

MASTER
OF THE CHAINS

For a long time I resisted the feminist argument that I was an oppressor. It was not because I found the suggestion altogether distasteful. Most people harbor secret urges to do a little oppressing now and then, and I was no exception.

At one time I had even yielded enthusiastically to the urge and spent a great deal of energy trying to oppress certain adolescents who were infesting my house, making a mess of the bathroom, wearing the phonograph to a frazzle and running up big repair bills on the car. I oppressed them as vigorously as I could, without result.

Either they were irrepressibly unoppressible or I was utterly lacking in oppressor know-how, like Louis Calhern in "Duck Soup," whose efforts at beastliness resulted in such futilities as getting the tails of his morning coat scissored off by the Marx Brothers.

A childhood spent at the movies had persuaded me that while oppressors always came to a bad end, they had a good bit of pleasure getting there. The typical oppressor of this era was usually a big man around old Rome. Slaves waited on him hand and foot and beautiful women danced for him in Fredericks of Hollywood flimsies while he sprawled on a sofa and ate grapes.

If the grapes disagreed with him, he would clap his hands and have Victor Mature brought in in chains. Obviously, I could see, being an oppressor was a rotten thing, but if it was your destiny, it was not without compensations. Having Victor Mature brought in in chains, being surrounded by dancing girls and slaves, lying around eating grapes—these were only part of the reward.

By themselves they would have afforded no pleasure at all, but really top-drawer oppressors, I noticed, were blessed with a singular freedom from the curse of middle-class morality, which made it possible to savor their blessings without the slightest pain to conscience.

When Victor Mature was brought in in chains, the oppressing grape eater did not succumb to spasms of guilt and buy 10 places at a charity banquet for the relief of oppressed Christians. He enjoyed himself. Oppressing was in his blood and he exulted in it.

The experience of my one big fling at oppression—the case of the adolescents—had persuaded me that oppressing was not my line. When I had an adolescent brought in in chains, the sight turned me to jelly. Was this any way to treat a wretched adolescent who, after all, had merely torn two wheels off the new car?

The grapes turned to ashes in my mouth. Instead of consigning my victim to the mercies of the gladiators, I would content myself with breaking his new Beach Boys record, and then spend days feeling guilt and inadequacy.

Alas, though I did not then realize it, feelings of guilt and inadequacy are the sure signs of the true oppressor. The feminists have shown me this light. When they first came to me, denouncing my oppressing ways, I laughed at them.

I showed them that I had stood up when they entered the room instead of reclining on my sofa. I showed them that I was not eating grapes. Nor, I pointed out, was I attended by slaves, dancing girls or anybody at all brought in in chains.

They were intelligent, too intelligent to laugh at the asininity of my defense, too intelligent even to try to rebut it. When I told them that I would actually enjoy being an oppressor, but had tried it and failed because oppressing made me feel guilty and rotten, they calmly explained the modern world to me.

The great old oppressors like Charles Laughton and Basil Rathbone are a thing of the past. And yet, oppression goes on. Women are not the only people oppressed. Children are oppressed. The

GETTING MIGHTY SMALL HERE

poor are oppressed. Whole races and large parts of whole continents are oppressed.

Obviously, somebody must be doing the oppressing, and it isn't
Charles Laughton or Basil Rathbone, nor anybody else eating
grapes and enjoying the work.

Perhaps, I suggested, it was Victor Mature. The feminists dismissed this explanation as unworthy of a person of my keen
perception, brilliant intellect and vast guilt capacity. The people
doing the oppressing, they explained, were people who had deceived themselves with the fiction that they were not oppressing
anybody.

These people differ from almost everybody else by practically
never feeling oppressed themselves. This is because, like Laughton and Rathbone, they thrive on exploiting the oppressed
classes.

It is true that I do not feel oppressed and I accept the logic of
my victims. It is no good to say that I don't want to be an oppressor. I am. It is despicable, which wouldn't be so bad, if only you
could enjoy being despicable like the great old timers. But you
can't anymore. Nowadays all you get out of it is a miserable sense
of guilt and the permanent sense of being unworthy of the human
race. Progress takes the fun out of everything.

GETTING
MIGHTY SMALL HERE

Here is a curious new development in physics: As things become
bigger and bigger, the results become smaller and smaller.

Note the phenomenon at work in oil. Oil companies grow
and grow and become vast international conglomerates with
revenues of billions and billions. What is the result? The cars
served by these oily mammoths become smaller and smaller.

Here is a classic instance of bigness producing littleness.

The phenomenon is also visible in cities. In New York, for example, the buildings where people work become increasingly gigantic while the apartments in which people live shrink down toward the size of prison cells.

The strange relationship between money and size has long been familiar. The more money a person amasses, the smaller that person becomes.

It is the poor who are the biggest and fattest. When people start to accumulate money they take to dieting. The poundage slips away. As their wealth becomes bigger and bigger, they grow smaller and smaller.

Shops that cater to the richest women, you may have noticed, rarely carry dresses larger than a size 8.

Restuarants follow the same law. More yields less. Go into the most expensive restaurant, the one where it's going to cost you $50 to get out, provided you don't have the wine or the à la carte bread or the butter or the fish knife and the escargot fork, and what are you served?

Not a rib-stuffing poundage of pasta or a tonnage of pork chops lost under a mountain of home-fries. Not in this restaurant. This restaurant is for people who have the biggest bucks in town.

What you get are three or four courses so light, so small, so tiny, so minuscule that they couldn't put an ounce on a humming-bird's hips.

What is the biggest thing in the world if not the Pentagon? And what is the problem at the Pentagon? If the present Government in Washington can be believed, as the Pentagon spends more and more money every year, its ability to whomp the bejeebers out of foreign upstarts becomes smaller and smaller.

Though the Reagan people say you can't solve problems by throwing money at them, they plan to make an exception in this case and heave several hundred billion more at the Pentagon. Unless the law that more yields less proves wrong in this case, we'll probably end up with an Army, Navy and Air Force that can't whip Liechtenstein.

Movies become longer and longer, more and more costly to produce and more and more expensive at the box office. As a result, fewer and fewer movies are made and fewer and fewer of those that are made are as good as movies that used to be made when studios were turning out several hundred a year and charging a mere 50 cents to let you see them.

Books become fatter and fatter and contain less and less. The general rule of thumb about books is: The bigger the book, the less likely it is to hold your attention or rouse your brain.

Speaking of brains, the educational system, which has become bigger and bigger and bigger since World War II, now appears almost utterly incapable of producing an American who can tell Hecuba from Aruba, isosceles from Hercules or Natty Bumppo from Button Gwinnett.

The one thing that may be even bigger than the Pentagon, at least in the United States, is sex. Since the 1960s, sex has been spreading like crabgrass in August. Sex is now a multibillion-dollar business, according to The New York Times.

And what result would you expect? Exactly. The American family has been getting smaller and smaller.

So here we sit in the dusk of the century of progress serving giant corporations in gigantic workshops. At the end of the day we get into our tiny little cars and return to our tiny little living quarters to be with our tiny little families.

Perhaps we will pick up a gigantic book and toil for hours in search for a mouse of an idea, or maybe we will go out to a $20 million movie that lasts three hours and sends us out wishing we had stayed home and watched the old Bette Davis flick on television.

Maybe we will stay home with television. Television is so big now, especially if you have cable. Think of it: 587 channels to twist for and, most nights, nothing on any one of them worth looking at.

Well, maybe there's a new docudrama to help kill the week. That's the trick about docudramas. They take eight hours to tell a ninety-minute story. They give you so much less for more.

We exist with one foot in Lilliput and the other in Brobdingnag, our lives split daily between the extremes of tininess and grotesque giantism, and everyone hungers, if only subconsciously, for a return of proportion, the human scale, the golden mean, the happy medium, which is to say for another century. The 18th perhaps, though nobody would be very happy back there either, with that awful dentistry and no electric lights. Still, how much schizophrenia is tolerable?

■ MY ADOLESCENT BED ■

Presenting his new designs for bed and bath fabrics in an advertisement in The New Yorker, Oscar de la Renta says, "My designs are for the woman who believes her bed and bath should be as well-dressed as she is . . . the woman who makes as much of a personal statement with her room décor as her wardrobe."

I had become edgy about being seen in the company of my bed. It had recently fallen far below my own standards of sartorial elegance, and I was fearful that persons who saw the two of us together might be offended, assuming that the bed was making a devastating statement of my own indifference to good grooming.

This was, in fact, far from the case. I had always prided myself on keeping an exquisitely dressed bed capable of making an eloquent statement of my good taste to anyone who dropped in during my absence. Recently, however, there had been a distressing decline.

Thanks to my experience at dressing adolescent sons, I recognized the symptoms. The bed had begun lounging around in dingy, faded clothes, looking like an unmade adolescent. This was to be expected, since the bed was 14 years old, I would not have been surprised to find a dead salamander in its pillowcase or an empty tube of acne cream under its mattress.

The trail of unsightly dandruff on the pillow and the unrepaired rip in the seat of the sheet where the sharp end of an unsprung spring had once broken the fabric left no doubt what the problem was: Adolescent bed.

I made the usual mistakes. Coming into its room one night, wearing my finest sharkskin slacks, hounds-tooth check jacket and regimental necktie, I was appalled at the slovenly statement the bed was making. "I am sick and tired," I told it, "of having a bed sitting around this house telling the world I am nothing but a slob. Shape up or ship out."

The bed merely sulked in that infuriating adolescent manner, but as it did not put a record on the phonograph and turn the amplifier to peak volume, I assumed it was ready to listen to reason. "Tomorrow," I said, "you're going downtown and buy a new wardrobe."

Naturally, it did not buy a new wardrobe. When I came home next evening, it had bought a new faded-denim spread which was much too big for it because it had tried on the new spread without bothering to take off its old spread. After that, it had become bored and, instead of buying new sheets, ruffles and pillowslips, had joined a gang of other adolescent beds to spend the afternoon standing on a street corner throwing empty beer bottles at passing cars.

What's worse, it had come home and made a mess of the bathroom, leaving soapy streaks on the shaving mirror and a soggy pile of frayed towels on the bathroom floor. As chance would have it, Oscar de la Renta had come home with me to hear what the bathroom had to say about me, and he immediately left in a huff.

Needless to say, I tried to persuade him that the statement being issued by my bathroom was not my statement at all, but the statement of my bed, which no longer spoke for me. This only compounded my offense. I was having guests that evening, so was unable to proceed immediately with my plan for sending the bed off to a good stern military academy.

Instead, I ordered it to stay in its room all evening and keep the door closed. While dressing in a style that would leave the guests in no doubt that they were dining with a person who gave away nothing in fastidiousness, I was alarmed to discover that my last pair of socks was missing.

"Have you been wearing my socks?" I demanded of the bed. It was a ridiculous question, of course, because the bed had quit wearing socks several years ago, but I was in such a rage that I rummaged furiously through its secret hiding places and, lo and behold, found it had hidden all three of my socks under its sheets at its foot. They were entangled with an empty beer bottle and the third volume of Marcel Proust's "Remembrance of Things Past."

I was so enraged that I took off my silk suspenders and slashed them across the headboard. One of my guests, a lawyer who had arrived early, bounded in to see what the commotion was about. He immediately informed the bed that it had the basis for a suit. "You're wasting your time," I said. "It refuses to buy a suit." "That's not what I mean," he told the bed. "The Supreme Court has O.K.'d teachers' beating children, but it still hasn't authorized whipping beds."

The bed has taken me to court. My lawyers urge me not to contest. If the bed takes the witness stand, they tell me, no jury in America will fail to be horrified at the statement it will make about me.

ADDALS OF MEDICID

There seemed to be several fish hooks lodged in my throat. All teeth in the upper jaw throbbed with pain, and unaccustomed pressure behind the eyeballs threatened to pop them right out of the skull at any moment. I went to the doctor.

"I could take out that old heart and put in a plastic one," he said, "but it wouldn't help your head cold one bit. I suggest you take two aspirins and go to bed."

The bed was a furnace made of sheets; the pillow, an iron vise clamped against my head. From the bedside telephone I reached a second doctor.

"I see, I see," he said. "You're burning up and your head is being crushed. Now, one thing we can do for you is to create a new baby in a laboratory pan, but that's not going to relieve cold miseries, is it?"

"I don't want a baby manufactured in a lab, and I don't want a plastic heart either. I want help."

"Stay well covered up and try not to catch a chill," the doctor said.

Until that instant the idea of catching a chill had not crossed my mind, but immediately after hanging up I felt my body temperature drop 40 degrees. On the phone, the third doctor offered a wide range of possibilities.

"If your brain stops working, we can keep the rest of your body functioning on life support systems for another 20 or 30 years," he said. "We can also give you a liver transplant if your liver gives out. Alternatively, if you become suicidally depressed, we can brighten you up with some quite miraculous drugs."

"What can you do for a bad cold?"

He hung up. The night that ensued was a thousand hours long. Phantasms appeared at the foot of the bed and jeered. One was my grandfather, dead these 75 years past. "Didn't I always tell you, boy, that man would find it a lot easier to travel to the moon than to cure the common cold?"

"How could you possibly have told me that? You died 20 years before I was born."

"And didn't I tell you there'd come a day when doctors would start prescribing plastic hearts instead of mustard plasters, and second-hand livers instead of camomile tea, and that when that day came and you went to them with a bad cold they'd offer to make you a baby in the laboratory?"

Released from nightmare by dawn, I stood beside the bed and discovered that Gestapo agents had spent the night beating the backs of my legs with iron bars. What was more disturbing, my entire head was becoming liquefied.

"Whole head seems to be undergoing watery meltdown, eh?" remarked the doctor I'd picked at random out of the Yellow Pages. "By George, you might be a candidate for the first head transplant. Could make us both famous if it worked. Even if it didn't I'd get a lot of ink for pioneering a process that's bound to come sooner or later."

At this stage I was perfectly willing to try a head transplant. "Tell me something more about your symptoms," the doctor said.

I told him the Gestapo had beaten the backs of my legs through a thousand-hour night.

"Sounds to me like it's just a cold," he said.

Just a cold? I was willing to undergo a head transplant, and he called it *just* a cold?

"I'm offering to put my head in your hands," I said. "If it works you will go down in the annals of medicine as the man who discovered the cure for the common cold."

Sorry, he said. Nobody in medicine had been interested in the common cold in the last 30 years. If his colleagues ever caught

TO CATCH A TRAIN

him working on it, he'd be laughed out of the profession for pursuing unglamorous research.

"Just suffer agony for a few days and you'll soon be good as new," he said.

In midafternoon my head abruptly stopped gushing away through eye slits and nostrils, and an immense but invisible chain was suddenly cinched tight around my chest. Death seemed imminent. I was gasping for a final breath of air when a research professor of medicine, an old friend of mine, dropped in for a chat.

"Of course you feel like you're dying," he smiled, "but statistically speaking, death in these cases is very rare." While I went purple with coughing, he chatted about the latest developments in genetics. Did I know, for example, that by putting a rat gene into a mouse, science could now produce a mouse twice as big as mice normally are?

I offered him a chance to help mankind. "Take a gene from a mouse with a head cold and put it in me," I urged, "and maybe you can produce a man with a cold 10 times smaller than he used to get."

"In medicine," he explained, "nobody gets the big ink for work on the common cold. Just take a couple of aspirins and get into bed."

■ TO CATCH A TRAIN ■

Henry is afraid of flying, so he set out by train for New Orleans, and we met him there next day. Afterward we headed for Florida by car. Henry is also afraid of driving and refuses to learn, being persuaded—possibly correctly—that he will kill many people the first time he tries to operate heavy machinery in hot-tempered traffic.

E T C.

So Henry sat in the back seat while the rest of us took turns driving and joking about Henry's being obsolete. Henry took it like a good sport, and the rest of us felt fine and superior about being the kind of organisms that could guide dangerous machines past fast-food parlors or sit strapped in metal containers eating unspeakable messes while being shot through the sky at 500 miles an hour without brooding on man's tendency to mortality.

After driving for seven years on a highway that was bearing the entire populations of Ohio and Michigan south to great blue herons and warm swamp water, we came to rest on a brilliant green island in the Gulf of Mexico. There we watched game shows on television and ospreys on treetops and real-estate men on the rampage, and reminisced about fried-chicken drive-ins we had driven past at two miles per hour, and felt modern and fit for survival and shattered around the nerve ends, and joked about Henry's not having the good twitches and tics which showed you were a blooded travel person.

Well, it came time to return to cement-colored New York, and we joked about having to put musty old Henry with his pathetic lack of thrillingly high blood pressure on the train, and felt good about being able to stay a full day longer than Henry on account of our ability to be strapped without terror into containers and shot through the sky eating messes.

Problems arose. The American transportation industry despised Henry, hated his lack of tics, his maddeningly normal blood pressure. It was determined to discourage him from ever trying to travel again. "Won't spend three days coiled around a steering wheel, eh?" industry leaders had said. "Wants to go by train, eh?" There must have been cackling in the board rooms as they prepared to settle Henry's hash.

The scheme they devised was like this: They would run one train a day from a point 80 miles north of Henry's island, but it would leave before breakfast, and the only bus connection would leave Henry's island at tea time the previous night. This would require the lout to spend a night in a hotel, take a three-hour bus ride, tip cab drivers and bellboys, and teach him the folly of trying to catch a train.

Or—they would place an early-afternoon train stop 100 miles away in central Florida. This would require a three-hour drive for one of his motorizing companions to take Henry to the station and, of course, a three-hour drive back to home base.

Third choice: They would arrange a noon train stop at West Palm Beach. If one of Henry's companions was willing to join him on the train, he could rent a car, rise at 5:30 A.M., drive across the width of Florida, leave the car and board the train. To spice the situation, the schemers had added amusing complications on this option. There would be a $20 additional charge for leaving the car at West Palm Beach. And the rental company would insist that the car be left not at the railroad station but at the airport, which would mean a $3.50 cab fare back to the station.

In toto, getting Henry to the train required two hours of dickering with car-rental agents and six hours of travel time and cost $52.50.

Henry underwent these trials with serenity, a generous purse and infuriatingly unsettled blood pressure, but the rest of us were throwing coconut husks at "The Price Is Right" and shouting at telephones by the time Henry was out of sight. We hoped he would stay out until he learned to travel like a man.

It is hard to know what to do about Henrys. From the travel industry's viewpoint, they are dispensable people, and the travel system encourages sharing its contempt for them.

Heaven only knows how many Henrys there may be. Judging from the amount of whisky sold on airplanes and the number of acquaintances who cannot go to the airport without prior sedating pills, they must be as common as coronary patients. They have other possibilities, of course. The interstate bus and the bicycle are workable provided you have a strong back, but even these are useless for transoceanic travel.

One Henry I know remains determined to see the great world abroad and will even board an airplane for the purpose. I have been in parties that boarded him for Europe. It always takes a full team to get him up the ramp on account of the heavy sedations of alcohol he needs to forget he is human and, therefore, mortal. In his hand he clutches a vial of narcotics to anesthetize himself in midocean when the whisky wears off.

It is an interesting evolution for the species to have developed a transportation system so marvelous and swift that, for significant numbers, it leads to drug and alcohol abuse and strains friendship. It is probably a way of breeding weaklings out of the race. On the other hand, why is it that we the strong are the ones with the tics?

▪ TO WRACK AND ROME ▪

Oxford was enchanting in the old days. Everyone carried Teddy bears and dined on plover's eggs and got sent down for wearing grubby off-the-rack suits. Afterward we drove around in lovingly preserved antique cars and learned to distinguish Chateau d'Yquem from Montrachet and they sent us up again.

"Been sent down again, eh?" my father grunted the night I called at his Bayswater flat to ask for an increase in my allowance.

"Actually I'll be sent up again if I can find the scratch to pay my poultry bill," I explained.

"How are you doing in English Lit 101?" he asked, with his infuriating knack for changing the subject whenever I sought to bleed him for a few pounds.

"You know very well we're above things like English Lit up at Oxford, father."

"Why do people always say 'up at Oxford'?" he asked. "Oxford isn't up. It's out there, that way, or possibly that way. Why don't you say 'out at Oxford'?"

"Could you lend us a few quid to pay off the don who brings the plover's eggs?" I replied.

"Plover's eggs always remind me of my cousin Algernon," he said. "He detested them almost as profoundly as he despised grown men who carry Teddy bears."

Fortunately Sebastian cabled just then and invited me to go up to Venice. I could tell he had been drinking heavily again, for no one ever went up to Venice. One always went down to Venice. I went anyhow, since Sebastian was paying the freight.

There we were photographed in stunning pastel light dining with his father, Lord Muchmanger, who had been sent down from England in disgrace because of his scandalous attachment to an Italian Teddy bear. I was delighted by the grossly ursine appetites betrayed by the sparkle that lit his eye when it fell upon my own Teddy bear and would have stayed in Venice another hour or two, but Sebastian said it was boring, so his father sent us back up to Oxford and Oxford sent us down to Groomskull.

I adored Groomskull with its 359 rooms, 10,000 acres of good fox-hunting land and hundreds of servants who opened and shut the doors behind me without the least noise or the slightest complaint about being paid only six shillings a month. Poor Sebastian did not share my passion for the place, and I soon saw why.

"It's my mother," he said. "She's always trying to make friends with my Teddy bear and lure him away from me. She'll try to take you away from me too, Roger."

I didn't point out that my name was Charles, not Roger, for he was terribly headstrong after opening his second quart of Scotch and it was idle trying to correct him. But it was not only Lady Muchmanger who crushed his spirit. The house was also occupied by his unhappy-looking elder brother, the Earl of Groomskull, whom they all called "Groomy."

Gloomily, Groomy sat about the drawing room in his tuxedo after dinner threatening to read aloud from the classified ads on the front page of The Times of London. The rest of us sat about in our tuxedos watching Sebastian deteriorate by the great fireplace.

Matters came to their inevitable anticlimax one day during a

magnificently photographed fox hunt when the hounds flushed
Sebastian in a local pub where he had gone to deteriorate quietly.

"I can't stand deteriorating in front of my drearily tuxedoed
family in the drawing room every night," he had told me. "I've
got to escape to the anonymity of a pub."

I pleaded with him, arguing that Lady Muchmanger didn't look
the least bit dreary in her tuxedo. He refused to listen. When the
hounds bayed him down there was the very deuce of a row.

When I was sent down to dinner that night I knew that neither
Sebastian nor I would ever go up to Oxford again and be sent
down as we were in the old days. It was Groomy who told me
how dreadful things had finally become.

"Mother has ordered all the Teddy bears locked up," he said.
"However, if you'd like yours later, the servants will bring it to
you in your room."

This brutal gesture, unmistakable in its implications for his
future, left Sebastian no alternative. He deteriorated completely
right there at the table and Lady Muchmanger sent him up to bed. I
knew that though she might send him down again in the morning
she would never send him up to Oxford unless he promised to
start attending classes, which would destroy all his beauty.

The next morning I was sent from Groomskull and knew I
would never revisit it until Socialism had been sent down from
Westminster to denude it of its marvelously underpaid servants.

That is how I became a Catholic.

THE
WELL-BRED MUMMY

As always when "The Mummy" is shown on television, I was
riveted to my armchair the other night when the rotting casket
containing the Scroll of Thoth was excavated from the sands of

Egypt, along with a linen-wrapped object that looked suspiciously like Boris Karloff.

What has always fetched me to "The Mummy," a film which dates from the Administration of Herbert Hoover, is the high-society poise maintained by the principle characters in situations that might make even the Duke of Edinburgh forget to shave.

On first encountering the film, as a shabby but ambitious lad eager to learn how the swells lived, I marveled at the cool savoir-faire with which, despite murder, hypnotic spells and an ambulatory mummy in their midst, the leading characters always found time to don evening gowns or tuxedos for dinner and dancing. In recent viewings, however, my attention has centered on the truly exquisite manners of the mummy.

Somehow in spite of 3,000 years or so of lying buried out of touch with Emily Post, the mummy has become a master of the social graces, and where once I watched to learn how the upper classes did things, now I watch to learn from the mummy.

Coming back to it the other night, I hoped to discover how the mummy had dealt with a social problem that has stumped me for years; namely, how to get respect in a snooty haberdashery when you go in dressed like a bum.

After being exhumed, you will recall, the mummy comes out of his sarcophagus looking perfectly dreadful, what with dust and cobwebs all over his linen wrappings, and stumbles off toward Cairo with what look like filthy ragged bandages dangling from his heels and elbows.

From previous viewings I know the mummy is going to turn up a bit later looking like something off the cover of The Islamic Gentlemen's Quarterly in a stunning tarboosh, silk shirt and gorgeously tailored knee-length coat, suitable for indoor wear on cooler evenings.

How did the mummy, with not a thing on his back but those odious old mummy rags, manage to walk into the fanciest haber-dashery in Cairo and persuade the salesman to give him threads like those? When I walk into such places, though my wardrobe is several cuts superior to 3,000-year-old mummy wrappings, salesmen always take one glance and suggest I'd be happier shopping the vendors' stands on Canal Street.

Obviously the mummy knows the right thing to say, and when I tuned him in the other night the purpose was to learn the secret words. Unfortunately, the confrontation with tailors and salesmen was omitted from this night's screening, which reminded me that I didn't recall it in any of the versions seen since my attention had shifted to the mummy's social conduct. Perhaps the director cut it out of the film in the 1930s. If so, what a loss.

In any case, no night with "The Mummy" is ever a total educational loss, so swallowing my disappointment, I viewed on. Reward was soon forthcoming in a scene I had never before noticed.

In this scene the mummy is strolling about a museum in his smashing new haberdashery when he encounters the archeologist who has dug him up. Naturally the archeologist doesn't recognize the mummy in those elegant clothes, nor does he notice anything odd about him although we, the audience, have noticed that the mummy's eyeballs tend to glow like the high beams on automobile headlights now and then.

What does the archeologist do? Being a real toff, what can he do but invite the mummy to come to dinner some time? Suddenly I am totally engaged in the mummy's social problem. I can see that the mummy, like me, really doesn't like to go out to dinner very much. I can see that the mummy, as I do in similar predicaments, has sized up the archeologist as a colossal bore. But how does he escape the dinner without seeming rude?

Can he say, "Thanks, but I much prefer to sit home alone and read the Scroll of Thoth?" I don't think so. I know I am never able to say, "Thanks, but I'd rather stay home and watch television." All I can ever think of to do is lie, which is terrible.

If you say, "Unfortunately, I am tied up every night this week," you are confronted with, "Well how about next week?" If you say, "Thanks, but I'm planning to be in Europe for the next year or two," you don't dare show your face publicly for a year or two for fear of being exposed as a liar.

I watch the mummy in total absorption as he contends with this most trying of social problems, and the mummy does not fail me. Without blinking an eye, he replies suavely, conclusively, with the only response that brooks no argument.

"I regret," says the mummy, "I am too occupied to accept invitations."

Too occupied to accept invitations. It is magnificent. It is perfect. Why didn't Amy Vanderbilt feed us these lines?

DELIGHTS OF
THE TIME WARP

It is 2 A.M., but you can forget about the hot chocolate and bedtime for me, folks, because Kirk Douglas and the aircraft carrier Nimitz have just slipped through a time warp, and when people slip through time warps it takes wild horses to drag me away from the television set.

One moment, Kirk was steering the Nimitz through 1983 Pacific waters; the next, he was cruising off Pearl Harbor in December 1941, and guess what imperial fleet shows up on the radar preparing for a sneak attack on what famous Hawaiian naval base. Right you are.

Suddenly Kirk is in a position to undo 42 years of absolutely monstrous history because the Nimitz, of course, has all these jet airplanes and atomic weapons which the attacking Japanese have never heard of. It will be like shooting turkeys on a fence rail.

I do not give the plot away by revealing that nothing of the sort is done since time-warp fans know from bitter experience that nothing useful is ever done by people who slip through time warps. Instead of seizing their great opportunity they always fritter it away by staring bug-eyed at one another and saying, "I can't believe this is happening," and, "What a crazy situation."

We time-warp freaks don't expect anything valuable to be done, to tell the truth. The pleasure of time-warp plots is their power to gratify our desire to cheat. When you slip back through a time warp, you are like a person playing poker with a stacked deck.

Kirk and his officers are not only holding a royal straight flush (dealt them by the screenwriter), they also know that the four kings in the Japanese hand won't stand up and that the 1941 senator they fish out of the water will have to fold after drawing to an inside straight.

The sport is in watching the old-timers' jaws drop in amazement while people who are 40 years ahead of them toy with them and give them the know-it-all treatment. It is a joke about power, about the power that comes from knowing far more than people who think they are powerful.

The essence of it consists in the delusion of these foolish 1941 people that they are living in the present, when Kirk and the Nimitz crew and we know that the poor fools are actually living in the past.

This situation produces highly satisfying feelings of superiority, which is why I am so fond of time-warp stories. Knowing that nothing truly interesting is ever going to happen in them, I let them divert my mind into personalized time-warp plots in which I push around superior men.

In one of my favorites, I slip through a time warp immediately after the Republican Party has buried Theodore Roosevelt in the Vice Presidency and find him moaning that his career is ended.

"Chin up, Teddy," I tell him. "You will be President before the year is out."

Teddy's jaw drops in astonishment. "How do you know that?"

I do not explain. I am too occupied feeling superiority to this ignorant fellow. I am thinking, "Theodore Roosevelt, you overrated cowboy, you are now in the hands of a master."

"After serving a second term," I tell him, "you will pass the Presidency to Taft and then try to win it back in 1912, but you will never beat Woodrow Wilson."

You will note that in this plot, though I have the power to save President McKinley from assassination by telling him the name of the man who wants to shoot him, I do not do so. Inhumane? A reluctance to tamper with history? Not at all.

I do not fool around in time warps in order to do good or to reshape an unsatisfying universe. I am there strictly for the pleasure of feeling superior to Theodore Roosevelt, to get back at Teddy, who—in unwarped time—has always seemed so vastly superior to me.

Coming across him in a time warp, I am pleased to observe that Teddy was too dense to realize he was living in the past.

Kirk Douglas's uneventful journey into 1941 was ending just as Teddy was giving me a stupefied look, having just heard that he would not be the last Roosevelt to sit in the White House.

Contentedly, I went off to bed, and passing through the parlor, noticed two oddly dressed persons of indeterminate sex staring bug-eyed at each other.

"I can't believe this is happening," said one.

"What a crazy situation," said the other.

I instantly recognized the symptoms. "You have slipped through a time warp, I presume," said I. "Whatever you do, don't tell me what's going to happen over the next 10 years."

"Are you O.K., Dad?"

But of course. . . . It was my daughter in the latest boutique wardrobe. She introduced the other oddly dressed person, a male. They had just decided on matrimony, she said.

"But nobody gets married nowadays," I said.

"Dad," she said, "you are living in the past."

I went to the kitchen to recover with hot chocolate. Fortunately, Theodore Roosevelt was there.

RAIN OF TERROR

Naturally President Reagan went to war against leaks. They all do. Maddened by leaks, President Nixon created the Watergate plumbers. It was like stopping a faucet drip by putting dynamite down the sink drain.

President Johnson's technique was slyer. He combed newspapers inch by inch looking for leaks and made the papers look bad by proving them wrong. If his plan to appoint Biff Coombs ambassador to the Court of the Imperial Swan leaked into print before he announced it, he fooled everybody by announcing that Biff Coombs would retire to private life and Chip Lomax would become ambassador to the Court of the Imperial Swan.

The Johnson technique made life difficult both for Biff Coombs, who was utterly unfit for private life, and for Chip Lomax, who didn't know the Court of the Imperial Swan from a ballet by Tchaikovsky. Still, it shows how spooky a President can become about leaks after he's been in the White House awhile.

President Reagan's method is to strap suspected leakers to the lie detector. Naturally reporters phoning the Agriculture Department to talk about the winter wheat crop are already finding that no one will return their calls.

I phoned there several days ago to ask what winter wheat is. They said I'd have to speak to Ab Peck, but Peck's secretary said he was busy and would call me back. He didn't. Being on deadline, I looked up winter wheat in the encyclopedia.

The day after my definition appeared in print, Peck was on the telephone.

"Who leaked?"

"No reporter of integrity ever reveals his sources," I said.

It would take a writ upheld by the Supreme Court to make yours truly betray his encyclopedia.

"Never mind," Peck said. "If it was someone in my office I'll know by evening."

"You have ways of making them talk?"

"The lie detector," he said.

Fortunately everybody in Peck's office would come off the machine clean, but it had been a close call. Nobody would lose his job because of my reporting. Moreover, Lyndon Johnson was fortunately no longer in power. If it had been Johnson in the White House, winter wheat from now on would have to be grown in the summer.

I resolved to move cautiously and abstain from leaks until the heat was off. Not long afterward the phone rang and an unfamiliar voice said, "I'm on the White House staff and I hear from people at Agriculture that you're a guy who can cover his trail."

I said, "If leaking's your game, Mac, you've picked the wrong place to drip."

It did no good to hang up. Those White House operators have ways of making you answer the phone. They tracked me down at a booth on East 52d Street. "If you give me a hot story and this phone booth turns out to be tapped, they'll ferret you out, pal," I pleaded. "Let me give you a break and hang up."

He reached me next in a soap store in Greenwich Village.

"You know that story about the Administration okaying tax-exempt status for schools that teach racial discrimination?"

Did I know that story? The sound of the old Dixiecrats standing in mighty tall boll weevils crooning their joy about at last having a President with a head on his shoulders could be heard all the way to Harlem.

"With my own ears," said the caller, "I heard the President say he is not a racist."

I hung up and ran for a taxi to get out of town but a limousine pulled up to the curb on the Triboro Bridge. The driver leaned out with a telephone. "The White House wants to speak to you," he said.

I yelled into the phone: "I don't want to be leaked to. I'm at a limousine on the Triboro Bridge. The chauffeur might be a Federal agent. . . ."

"Not might be," said the man on the phone. "He *is* a Federal agent, and he's got orders to take you back to the office right away so you can get this leak into the next edition. That business about the President wanting to aid schools that teach racial discrimination was a stupid mistake somebody made without consulting the President, got it? Like the time some nitwit called ketchup a vegetable without consulting the President, got it? The President loves people of all races, got it?"

"I don't dare print that. They could fire you for leaking."

"It's dynamite, all right," he said, "but I trust you to protect me. Any man who can keep his lip buttoned about who spilled the beans on winter wheat is a man I'm willing to go to the well with."

"Speaking of which," I said, "could you tell me the difference between soybeans and black-eyed peas?"

There was a long silence at the White House end of the line. Finally: "I'll get back to you on that." So far he hasn't.

COWERING
BEFORE OMOO

Most people choose to be ignorant, and I am no exception. This is why, after 40 years of putting it off, I still haven't learned what "contumely" is.

I first encountered "contumely" in a Shakespearean passage in which Hamlet, musing about life and death, complains of having to endure "the proud man's contumely." My response was not an immediate trip to the dictionary, which was 100 feet away and up a flight of stairs, but a surge of sympathy for Hamlet.

"I don't blame Hamlet for finding the proud man's contumely insufferable," I said to myself. "I couldn't put up with contumely myself, least of all from somebody proud of his ability to dish it out."

Off and on as the years passed, I was briefly troubled by my ignorance about what "contumely" really was, but never, mind you, never troubled enough to open a dictionary. With middle age's arrival, I rationalized my failure to do so with the argument that an overstuffed head would make it pointless.

"There's no point in looking up 'contumely,'" I told myself, "because with my brain as packed as it is, I'll forget what it means within 30 minutes of looking it up."

This is what I have just told myself again when deciding once more not to look up "contumely" in the dictionary. Obviously, we are dealing here with a common case of willful ignorance. I am not simply ignorant on the point, but determined to remain so.

Nor does my will to ignorance limit itself to "contumely."

Who came first in the order of Presidents—Franklin Pierce or Millard Fillmore? I neither know nor care enough to look it up.

For years I've had a periodic yen to know the correct pronunciation of "congeries," but I've never asked anyone. Come to think of it, I don't even know what "congeries" means, but now that I've come to think of it, I have also decided not to find out.

To do so would take time that might be better spent reading "Omoo," a Herman Melville novel that was assigned reading in college and which I pointedly avoided reading then and ever since. I know I should read "Omoo" and know, even more surely, that I shall not read "Omoo," except at the point of a gun wielded by an insane Melville scholar.

What's more, I know this refusal to read "Omoo" is depriving me of an enriching pleasure not to be found in the thousands of issues of The National Enquirer which I have been able to read, thanks to all the hours I have not spent reading "Omoo."

I do not know what "Parsifal" is about. Nor the War of the Spanish Succession. Nor what a Trifecta bet is, how to pump gasoline from a self-service tank, when Nebuchadnezzar built the Hanging Gardens of Babylon or whether you should stuff a cold and starve a fever or vice versa.

I could go on, and would do so without shame, for the truth about the willfully ignorant is that we are not simply entertained by our own ignorance, but proud of it. How often have you heard some self-satisfied boob announce, "A little learning is a dangerous thing" while gazing in contempt upon someone struggling to escape the ignorance we all bring into the world and which so many treasure as a precious birthright?

Like everyone else, I consider myself different from everyone else in this regard. When I meet someone endangered by a little learning, I try to teach him humility by demonstrating that he is even more ignorant than I.

Recently such a man tried to open a discussion with me about "Omoo," which he had just read. " 'Moby Dick' is far superior," I replied.

"Ah, a Melville expert," he murmured. "Then how would you rank 'Bartleby the Scrivener' as against 'Typee'?"

"One is to the other as Millard Fillmore is to Franklin Pierce," I said.

"Surely you mean, as Franklin Pierce is to Millard Fillmore," he replied.

We were having this conversation at a self-service gasoline pump where he was waiting for me to get on with it.

"You seem to be as confused about pumping gasoline as you are about Pierce, Fillmore, 'Bartleby the Scrivener' and 'Typee.' Let me help you," he said.

"Have you read Tolstoy?" I snarled.

"Only in the original Russian," he said. "Now give me the hose."

I could have struck him with a jack handle if only, years ago, I'd got around to learning what a jack handle looked like and where to find one, and I told him so.

"Yes," he said, "a little ignorance can be a very safe thing for all concerned."

While he filled my tank I was tempted to cry, "I will not abide the proud man's contumely," but was afraid he'd tell me "contumely" meant "willingness to fill an empty tank" and cut off my gas.

TALES FOR CATS

My cat refuses to jog or diet and has no interest at all in tracking down Nazis. I mention this only to explain why I have become disgusted with best-selling cat books.

I bought three—"Jogging for Cats," "Dr. Pussikins's 18-Day Cat Diet" and "How to Trap a Nazi With a Cat"—and Primrose (which is the name of my cat) turned his nose up at all of them.

Primrose was perfectly willing to go jogging, so long as I did the jogging and he was carried in my arms, but the minute he was set down on his own four paws he slunk into a thorny bush and sat there motionless, and no amount of shouting about how cholesterol-clogged arteries would kill him could make him come out.

I should note that Primrose is 15 years old and weighs slightly more than an overpacked suitcase. Dr. Pussikins's 18-day diet promised to shrink him down until he could once again get into a size-8 cat skin. We got his weight down all right, but after we did there was no way to get him out of his old size-38 pelt. As a result, a tiny little Primrose was left in such excessive folds of sagging hide and hair that he looked more like a rug than a cat.

Fortunately, he wandered away from the house, was mistaken for a castoff rug and sold at a flea market. The buyer's wife said it didn't go with her other furniture and threw him out in the trash and garbage where Primrose was able to eat his way back to normal before wandering home again.

I was delighted to see him, since I had just bought "How to Trap a Nazi With a Cat" and was eager to train him for useful work. I had him out in the yard one day trying to train him to pounce when he spotted a swastika, and grandmother came out.

"What kind of foolishness is this?" she asked. I showed her the book. The chapter about how a cat, once properly trained, could track down and bring in the biggest Nazis in the book-publishing world.

"Imagine what a coup it would be if Primrose brought in Martin Bormann," I said.

"Martin Bormann!" she cried. "I've read about that fellow in several hundred best-selling novels, and he'd just as soon slit your gizzard as have a second beer with his sauerkraut. If Primrose is going to bring Bormann back here, I'm clearing out."

She had a point. I checked the book for suggestions on what to do with a Nazi once a cat had tracked one down and brought him in, but the author had ignored this problem.

In his youth Primrose had often tracked down birds and brought them in by mouth, proudly depositing them, half dead, on the parlor rug, then striding away and leaving them for me to deal with. That had been bad enough. Imagine him bringing me a Nazi, badly lacerated with cat bites and doubtless in an evil temper because of them, and dropping him on the parlor rug.

Primrose was happy about giving up training, and I was not terribly depressed either, since Nazis had gone into temporary literary eclipse by this time and the new best-selling subject was investment.

I bought a copy of the fantastically selling "How a Cat Can Survive the Coming Financial Catastrophe."

"According to this," grandmother said, "Primrose ought to be converted into gold or collectibles."

"It's the only sane defense against the coming financial catastrophe," I agreed.

"But if you do that," said grandmother, "we're going to have the house overrun with burglars as soon as news of the conversion gets around. If Primrose is converted to gold, I'm getting out of here."

This proved unnecessary. Primrose had been seated in the best parlor armchair during the discussion, and before it ended he climbed down, stalked out of the house and disappeared for several weeks. Grandmother, who believes Primrose has more sense than I have, said this proved that he was against being converted to gold.

During his absence I purchased the very latest best seller by the eminent psychologist Hugo Furrlein, "Conquer Your Enemies With Cat Power." I was mesmerized in the chapter explaining how to maneuver opponents for power into a chair covered with cat hairs so that when they stand up everyone will laugh at them trying to pick the hairs off their blue serge suits, when in walked Primrose with a best-selling author clamped in his jaws.

Primrose dropped the author on the parlor rug. He was exultant. "Primrose and I," he announced "start work at once on a best-selling as-told-to opus to be entitled 'I Was Hitler's Barn Cat.' Of course, we'll have to change Primrose's name to Fritzkin. Artistic license, you know."

"I always knew Primrose had more sense than you do," said grandmother, as Primrose carried the author off and began turning himself into gold.

WHERE HAVE ALL THE ULCERS GONE?

The papers say the American stomach ulcer is becoming an endangered species. The incidence of ulcers, both peptic and duodenal, has declined so notably in recent years that doctors can no longer assemble enough patients to obtain significant data about causes and treatment.

As one who grew up in the age when stomach ulcer was the badge of success, I lament this news as another symptom of a world changing for the worse, in a category with the death of John Wayne, the baseball strike and the passing of the Democratic Party.

In my boyhood, which was not that long ago, the stomach ulcer was so widely held as evidence of success that people who didn't have one often faked it. President Truman once destroyed a critic with the sneer that he held only a three-ulcer job. Everybody understood that twist of the knife. Important men had jobs that gave them 10 or 12 ulcers. Only pipsqueaks could be fulfilled in three-ulcer jobs.

The assumption was that ulcers were caused by tension and heavy bouts of dynamic decision making. The more ulcerated your gastrointestinal organs, the more respect you deserved. Among the male elders in my family, there was living competition about who could validly claim the worst ulcers, and despite the otherwise excessively good table manners which were enforced in our household, thunderous and indecorous belching was justified on grounds that it indicated an honorably parlous state of stomach ulceration.

In recent years, heart attack has replaced the stomach ulcer as the medical badge of the overworked male. Except that it eliminates belching as a form of social boasting, this strikes me as a definite step backward.

The stomach ulcer is not the only medical problem in decline. Acute appendicitis, once almost as common as athlete's foot, appears to have become a rare affliction. Thirty years ago or so, every other boy in the locker room flaunted an appendectomy scar on his abdomen, and every adolescent bellyache posed the terrifying possibility of surgery.

I recall the family doctor, after two or three visits to treat me for the green-apple agonies, announcing, "If this happens again, we'll take him in and have that appendix out." After that, I kept mum about stomach cramps and avoided the knife.

For older women, the great ailment was "gall bladder." Someone was always headed for the operating table for "gall bladder." I took it for granted that one of the miseries to which middle age doomed the female sex was gall-bladder surgery. In the past 15 or 20 years, however, I can't recall meeting or hearing of a single woman who was having her gall bladder removed.

Could this be because surgeons have become so fascinated with their marvelous new operations that they have no interest in such sophomoric stuff as appendix and gall-bladder removal except in the most critical cases? That would surely be too cynical a supposition about a noble and dedicated profession. Still, I now know a lot more people who have recently had open-heart surgery than have recently had a gall bladder or appendix removed.

Another medical problem that seems to be on the wane is broken arm. In my boyhood, it was hard to assemble nine boys for baseball without having at least one with an arm in a cast supported by an over-the-shoulder sling. When was the last time you saw a boy with his arm in a sling? I have to think back to the Eisenhower Administration.

Part of the explanation may be that new bone-setting techniques have eliminated the cast and sling, but part also, I suspect, is that boys no longer climb things like trees, cliffs and buildings for amusement. In my observation, admittedly limited to New York, gunshot wound is a far more common ailment of modern boyhood than broken arm.

This may also help explain the almost total disappearance of black eye. At one time, a boy who reached the age of courtship without ever having had a black eye would have been ruled off the course of romance on grounds that he had not yet undergone the rites of manhood. Nowadays, you can travel among hordes for months without ever seeing a young man sporting a shiner.

I assume this does not indicate a decline in the nation's virility level, but only a change in the ways in which youth expresses its exuberance. Very likely, I suspect, the reason the boy on the subway doesn't have a black eye is that he has a handsomely patched stab wound concealed by his shirt.

But let us not think on in this unhappy vein. It was bad enough in the old days when such thoughts could give you an ulcer. Now they could lead to a heart attack. Such is medical progress.

■ WIGGY ■

Confessions of Buck Bascom, reporter for the C.I.A.:

■ CHAPTER ONE ■

I, Buck Bascom, ace reporter, was recruited into the C.I.A. while interviewing the late Albert Einstein one afternoon at Princeton. After fielding my questions about the size of the universe for several hours, Einstein suggested we break for tea. I watched him take three teaspoons of sugar. "You're not the late Albert Einstein," I said.

"Of course not," he said. "Einstein has been dead for seven years."

"What's more," I said, "he never took sugar in his tea."

"We need men of your perspicacity," he said, drawing the blinds. "Allow me to introduce myself. I am Allen Dulles of the C.I.A."

■ CHAPTER TWO ■

My first mission was assigned in a musical code that had been written into the woodwind passage of a Franck symphony played over an FM radio station in Buffalo. It was January. My decoding machine froze and had to be thawed in a hot tub.

While waiting, I fell asleep. When I awoke, the decoder was hopelessly rusted.

There was nothing to do but swallow the cyanide capsules the agency provided for desperate emergencies.

■ CHAPTER THREE ■

I met my control, as always, while covering a warehouse fire on a pier which burned down with suspicious regularity. "Those weren't cyanide pills you gave me for the Buffalo job," I said.

"Naturally," he said, "and what's more, there wasn't any message coded into the Franck symphony. We were testing your reliability." I realized I was in the big leagues at last.

■ CHAPTER FOUR ■

One day at the office, a copyboy said, "The late Albert Einstein wants to see you by the water cooler." It was the start of the job every reporter for the C.I.A. dreams of.

"You are to attend President de Gaulle's next press conference in Paris," he said, "and send him up the wall by asking the following question: 'Mr. President, why is it that France can't cut the mustard anymore?'"

I told the managing editor I had to be assigned to Paris at once. "Who is this nut?" the managing editor asked the city editor. "Buck Bascom, ace reporter," said the city editor.

"I like his gall," said the managing editor. "Put him on the police beat for four or five years, and then send him to the Caribbean."

■ CHAPTER FIVE ■

It was my first visit to C.I.A. headquarters at McLean and I was disguised as the late Clara Petacci. C.I.A. scientists gave me a glass vial filled with powder.

"When you get to the Caribbean," they instructed, "pour this powder into Fidel Castro's shoes."

"How will I do that?" I asked.

"Ask Castro a question," they said. "It will take him an hour and a half to answer. Everyone else will go to sleep and Castro will be too lost in his own eloquence to notice anything. Get down on all fours and pour the powder in around his ankle bones."

Then the chief came to see me. "Bascom," he said, "you have the power to crush Communism in the Caribbean forever. This powder is a fantastic new depilatory which, taken up by the body through the feet, makes the victim's hair fall out. Within two weeks, Castro's beard will molt and he will become the laughing stock of the hemisphere."

■ CHAPTER SIX ■

At home, I placed the glass vial on the bedside night table by the telephone. At 3 A.M. the phone rang. I fumbled for it in the darkness. It was the night city editor. "Get over to Elm and Main right away," he ordered. "Two cats have just gone up a tree to rescue a fireman."

Groggily, I put on my shoes and sped to cover the story. Returning home at dawn, I was horrified to see that the glass vial had been overturned and was empty. I had knocked it over grabbing the telephone in the dark. But where was the powder, I asked, already knowing the answer.

Near tears, I slowly removed one shoe, then the other. The first dense batch of hair fell out at dinner that evening.

■ CHAPTER SEVEN ■

At McLean I demanded to see the late Allen Dulles. They said it was impossible. Dulles was allergic to bald heads. I pleaded to be allowed to come in from the cold, and they gave me an ill-fitting red wig to help me look like E. Howard Hunt and some fresh cyanide pills in case my newspaper fired me.

The pills were fakes. "Naturally," the C.I.A. told me. "The agency is forbidden by law to operate within the United States."

FATHERING

Good fathers go right into the delivery room nowadays and assist in delivering their own babies. There they have wonderful experiences.

A friend of mine who is an actor and a director of films and plays was assisting at his wife's labor not long ago when the doctor decided a Caesarean was indicated. Surgery began, then came the sublime moment when his new daughter was being lifted into life in our universe.

The anesthetist looked at my friend whose face was transported with the ecstasy of fatherhood and asked, "Did you ever work with Henry Fonda?"

Yes, he had worked with Henry Fonda, he murmured, trying to preserve the miracle of the moment intact despite the invitation to talk shop.

"His daughter's kind of kooky, isn't she?" said the anesthetist. Afterward, that's what my friend remembered best about his daughter's birth and he wondered whether, if he'd been an auto mechanic, the obstetrician would have asked if he'd ever done a front-end alignment for less than $65.

My father didn't help out when I was born. His mother was there and chased him out of the bedroom. At the time, it was thought healthier for grandmothers to do what we now know fathers ought to do at such times. I often wonder if I would have been a more normally adjusted person if he'd been there, especially since with advancing years I find myself acting more and more like a grandmother.

The grandmotherly mentality hadn't set in by the time my own children were born though, so I didn't insist on lending a hand. As a result, the obstetrician didn't have to be distracted trying to revive a sissy who faints at the sight of blood.

At that time it was very hard becoming a father in hospitals and there was very little instruction in how to go about it. Since my own father had died when I was a toddler and I'd been reared by matriarchs, I had no family male models to emulate. All I knew about the glorious experience had been learned from the movies.

For example, I knew that when labor began the husband was supposed to get plenty of boiling water. Movie doctors at this moment always shouted, "Get me plenty of boiling water!" and movie husbands went off to fire the stove.

I wondered for years what doctors did with all that boiling water. Boiling water was for brewing tea, doing laundry, cooking lobsters. Surely they weren't pouring it on the laboring mother or dousing the infant in it, were they? In any case I rushed to the hospital to be of help in case the doctor needed some water boiled.

The doctor didn't, of course. I suspected he wouldn't. I'd seen enough movies of fathers racing to the hospital in these circumstances. I knew they were supposed to sit in waiting rooms and smoke cigarettes, drink coffee, loosen their neckties, perspire heavily and rush into the corridor periodically to ask, "How is she, Doc?"

That's what I did. It seemed absurd but I did it anyhow because nobody had told me anything else to do. And didn't Jimmy Stewart do the same thing whenever he had a baby?

Now and then nurses came into the waiting room and smiled in amusement at the foolish uselessness of us fathers. I knew we were supposed to be smiled at by hospital people, so it was all right. I'd seen movie obstetrical nurses smile condescendingly at some of the greatest male stars of Hollywood. I knew that at the moment of birth no man was supposed to be too great a star to play the sap.

Anyhow, what else was there to do? "Go home and get a good night's sleep," an obstetrician told me in the midst of my third attempt to win an Academy Award for playing fifth wheel at a parturition. "The baby won't be born before morning."

Officially pardoned, I did something Jimmy Stewart would never have done and went home. I've been ashamed of that deed ever since. Spencer Tracy would never have gone home. I knew that when I returned at 6:30 A.M. to learn that my son had been born while I slept. The nurses' accusing eyes said, "Spencer Tracy would never have gone home," and having convicted me, refused to let me hold my son until afternoon.

Of the many father models I studied, Spencer Tracy was the one I most admired. I feel that if Tracy had lived to see the new age of fatherhood he would be right there in the delivery room, nowhere near fainting when the Caesarean began. If the doctor interrupted to ask, "Did you ever work with Clark Gable?" I wonder if Spencer Tracy would punch his nose.

I guess not. I think Spencer Tracy would quietly order him out of the room and deliver his own baby, though it would be disappointing if he didn't yell, "Get me plenty of boiling water!"

■ GRANDPARENTING ■

It's nice being a grandchild. You're sitting on the floor being screamed at by Mommy for shaving the Oriental rug with Daddy's razor, and the phone rings, and it's Granddaddy saying, "Bring the kid over here so I can love him up."

Go over to Granddaddy's, and he and Grandma show you their

teeth and lick you and say, "My, isn't he smart for his age," when you rub jelly on their eyeglasses. To show them just how smart, you pull a book off the shelf, rip out six pages and chew each one.

When Grandma looks at Granddaddy and says, "Don't you think he's a little young to be eating 'Sex After 80'?" Granddaddy picks you up and says, "Let's take a nice walk." And you take a nice walk with Granddaddy, and the beauty part is, if you cry, Granddaddy carries you all the way.

It's nice being way up there in his arms. You can stick your finger in his mouth and loosen his false teeth without getting hurt, because Granddaddies never bite. Before long, you're back at his place and he's on the phone telling Daddy, "O.K., I'm through playing with the kid. Come take him away."

When Daddy takes you away, it's different. You're not a grand-child then. Just a child under siege by Mom and Dad. Mom is always saying something like, "Fail physics again this semester, and we're not going to buy you that secondhand Chevy from Uncle Mike."

And Dad's always disagreeing with your peer group. You can't help liking Dad, but it sure would help if he'd move into the 20th century and learn about peer-group pressure. "I don't care if everybody in your peer group is smoking opium in front of their parents," he's always saying. "I don't want you smoking in my dining room."

Is it any wonder that you get older, get married and become a father yourself? After all those years of being a child, you've got to make somebody pay, don't you? And the people in your peer group are too big to be pushed around. Your wife has the same urge.

"If we had a child," she says, "we could treat it with love and understanding and make up for all the suffering our insensitive parents once inflicted on us."

"Or if the child didn't behave like we wanted, we could work off a lot of hostility by treating him as mean as our parents treated us," you say.

GRANDPARENTING

You learn fast after you become a father. You learn that all the love and understanding in the world can't stop you from screaming when your lovely little daughter uses your razor to shave the antique mohair settee. And you learn to love your old Dad when he calls up and says, "Bring the kid over here so I can love her up."

Good old Dad. Oh, maybe once in a while he did get uptight when you used to smoke opium in the dining room, but he had a right to because you were really a pretty awful kid. And he's really sweet, the way he lets your precious daughter smear jelly on his eyeglasses and keeps right on smiling and licking her.

In the same way, you learn to grind your teeth when Mom calls back two hours later and says, "O.K., Dad's tired of carrying the kid around the neighborhood with her finger under his lower plate and wants you to come take her back."

You'd think grandparents could spend at least 12 happy hours with their own granddaughter, wouldn't you? Of course, once she's old enough to fail physics and smoke illegal cigars smuggled from Havana, you can't send her to her grandparents anymore, even for two hours. They'd find out what a rotten job of child rearing you'd done, and you'd never hear the end of it.

You know the line: "If we'd done as bad a job with you as you've done with yours, where would this country be today?"

So you're driven to tyranny. "One more failure in biochemistry, Miss, and it's no Paris trip for you next summer. And what's more, I don't care if every soul at Hudson High is smoking illegal cigars from Havana in front of their parents, I'm not going to have illegal cigars smoked at this dining-room table."

Is it any wonder that the child gets older and gets married to a man who calls you one day and says, "Congratulations. You're grandparents"?

Now what do you do? You call up your daughter and hear your son-in-law in the background screaming at the baby for using his razor to shave the towels. "Bring the kid over here so I can love him up," you say.

They bring the kid over and you show him your wrinkles and lick him, cheer his skill at smashing the geraniums with a broomstick, and take him out for a long walk, and worry about whether he was born with sound reflexes and, if so, why he is using his finger to puncture your eardrum instead of to pry your lower plate loose.

When his weight becomes backbreaking, you phone your daughter. "I'm through playing with the kid. Take him away."

It's nice being a grandparent.

THE JOY OF ANGER

I'm tired of advice on love and of books and lectures and television panelists who preach the wonder of love and how to make love to women, men, animals, plants and dining-room furniture and the joy that comes of loving all humanity. Love is nice, love is swell, and I'm in favor of it, but these love bores constantly telling us, "Love is everything," are creating a terrible distortion of emotional values.

What about anger? Why don't any of these experts on human emotion tell us something useful about anger? Judging from the news, there's at least as much anger as love pumping through the American bloodstream.

Pick up any day's newspaper, and there it is: "Angered Parent Kills Spouse and Four Children"; "Angered by Firing, Man Slays 10"; "Angry Son Mails Mom a Letter Bomb"; "Angered Citizen Punches Supreme Court Justice," and on and on. It's senseless to say the problem with these people is that they don't know how to love.

When you're angry, as these people are, you don't want somebody shoving Leo Buscaglia's "Living, Loving and Learning" or Michael Morgenstern's "How to Make Love to a Woman" under your nose. As the Book of Ecclesiastes must say somewhere, there is a time for love and a time for anger, and when it's time for anger you don't want either bromides or technical manuals about love; you want some way to let everybody know you're sore without having to slay spouse and four children.

What we need is not another volume on "How to Make Love" but some foolproof advice on "How to Make Anger."

I was struck by the lack of sound advice on the subject when, one day this summer, I found myself shouting and pounding the desk in front of an airline clerk because a flight had been oversold and he refused to permit standing in the airplane aisles. I was astonished by my outburst, for I am so ignorant of the art of being angry that I haven't let myself enjoy a refreshing public outburst in 20 years.

Fortunately for the airline clerk, I am one of those odd Americans who never carry a sawed-off shotgun or even a handgun, so he was able to sneer at my rage with impunity. Fortunately for the passengers who were not being left behind, none approached me with counsel on the joys of loving, for I was furious enough to kick luggage to pieces with tennis shoes.

What still burned in my soul after a sedative four hours in the airport waiting lounge was the utter calm with which the officious devil at the airline desk ignored my show of anger. I realized he must have seen anger in all its forms, including the great masters of rage so skilled at outrage that he had quaked, gone aboard airplanes to haul off passengers already seated and given their places to those of whose anger he stood in awe.

I was not one deserving such respect. He had seen thousands like me. The trembling voice, the purple face, the bulging eyeballs, the quivering hands. He had sized me up perfectly, had said to himself, "Utterly ineffectual when abused by airline, hotel and car-rental clerks: hasn't the slightest notion how to make anger; can be easily crushed by my calm, superior manner which I shall use to give him a twist of the knife by showing that not only do I not love him, I don't even respect him."

Because the Leo Buscaglias and the Michael Morgensterns of the world have concentrated solely on improving my competence at love, I can find no useful tips on how to sharpen my competence at being angry with airline clerks.

Because of this weakness, over the years I have found it wiser to confine my expressions of anger to long bouts of sullenness and sulking. The immediate rewards are not bad. Once the people with whom you're angry—a wife, say, or a child—notice you are sulking, their curiosity will stimulate questions.

"All right, what are you sulking about this time?"

Answer (very sullenly voiced): "I'm not sulking."

"Of course you're sulking. You've been sulking for days. Now get it off your chest."

The one thing you mustn't do at this point is get it off your chest. This is not a friendly invitation, but a trap designed by the other party to make your voice tremble, your face turn purple and your eyeballs bulge. "How childish" the object of your anger can then say, luxuriating in the sense of being calm, unchildish and superior to a person whose anger is so incompetently expressed.

All I can recommend is continued sulking, and I recommend it with grave reservations. Years of quiet sulking, whether at a wife, a child or an airline clerk, often build up a residue of poison which calcifies into hate, and we all know what an unhappy effect hate has on love, don't we?

There will probably be a new book about it published soon. "Love Your Way Out of the Sulks." Just thinking about it makes me grind my molars, quietly, sullenly.

GOING FIRST CLASS

Five days away from inevitable death, William Saroyan telephoned the Associated Press to issue his official last words. These were:

"Everybody has got to die, but I have always believed an exception would be made in my case. Now what?"

As last words go, these are hard to beat, and my cap is off to Saroyan, not in ritual reverence for the dead, but for the simplicity, courage and wit with which he handled his exit line.

Last words are always a problem for people who want to do life properly. By coincidence, I had been trying to compose some of my own when I read of Saroyan's death. Not that I anticipate departing any time soon. Far from it. Like Saroyan, I rather expect an exception to be made in my case.

Nevertheless, it never hurts to be prepared. I had been reminded of this by an article in the current issue of Harvard Magazine about the final words of famous people. It contains a large sampling of these farewell remarks, most of which sound as bogus as the lines press agents feed gossip columnists on behalf of publicity-crazed entertainers.

Could Samuel Gompers, savoring his last few breaths, have possibly said: "Nurse, this is the end. God bless our American institutions. May they grow better every day"?

Could President William Henry Harrison have closed by telling his doctor: "Sir, I wish you to understand the true principles of government. I wish them carried out. I ask no more"?

My limited experience of sensing death's approach makes me doubt it. I recall too well waking at 4 o'clock one morning some years ago absolutely persuaded that death was at hand. Not for one instant did it cross my mind to cry, "God bless our American institutions." Nor did I wake my wife to say, "I wish you to understand the true principles of government."

Though the occasion was extraordinary and called for eloquence, all I could think of to say was: "I'll never mix brandy and pepperoni pizza again." Fortunately, a bicarbonate of soda cheated the Reaper that morning, but I have been aware ever since of the need to have something ready for his next pass.

President McKinley is said to have made a musical departure by singing two lines of the hymn, "Nearer My God to Thee," and

ETC.

Robert E. Lee is supposed to have died with a military command: "Strike the tent!"

The Lee line is hard to improve upon, but as a writer—if I may give myself esthetic airs in preparing for the ultimate moment—I would have to adjust it slightly. I have three variations under debate: (1) "Strike the dangling participle!" (2) "Avoid tautology, redundancy and ambiguity!" and (3) "Get rid of those adjectives!"

A musical exit in the McKinley manner seems risky for someone who can never remember the second lines of song lyrics. One could take the rock 'n' roll way out—the easy way—by singing the first line, "Yeh, yeh, yeh!" in reasonable confidence that the second line would also be "Yeh, yeh, yeh!"

On the other hand, this would surely tempt some unctuous elegist to describe you as "a man who said yeh to life." I much prefer to follow Daniel Webster's lead. Approaching the final moment, according to one account, Webster summoned a large audience, and the dialogue went as follows:

Webster: Friends, wife, doctor, son, family, are you all here?

Chorus: We are here.

Webster: Have I on this occasion—have I said anything unworthy of Daniel Webster?

Chorus: No, no! (Webster expires peacefully.)

The difficulty here is that it is nearly impossible to muster such an audience, particularly of family people, unless they are guaranteed that you are really going to depart.

Many children are likely to think the summons is a ruse to get them to come over for dinner with their parents, so unless you really die the first time you assemble them it is going to be hard to get them back for a second appearance.

This raises one of the major problems of delivering a truly fine exit speech; namely, the difficulty of knowing for certain when the final moment is at hand. It is much too easy to assemble a large crowd; to ask, "Are you all here?"; to demand whether you have in your dying hour said anything unworthy; to be told, "No, no!"; and then be forced to lie there feeling better and better until somebody says, "That wasn't death calling, it was just the brandy mixing it up with the pepperoni."

If it were possible to call the tune, you could arrange to have a straight man present, as Ethan Allen is said to have had in a convenient minister who said, "The angels are waiting for you, General Allen." With this cue, Allen could then rise and shout, "They are, are they? Well, God damn 'em, let 'em wait!"

Historians say this story is, unfortunately, false.

THINGS PASSED

At 3:37 in the afternoon of October 10, 1982, I read the final page of Marcel Proust's "Remembrance of Things Past." I had started it 35 years earlier on a warm October night in 1947, and had read steadily for a year or two before realizing that I faced a monumental task.

By that time I had nearly finished Volume One, and with remarkable self-control had restrained myself from turning to the last page of Volume Seven to see how it turned out. It irked me, then, when one of the children, complaining that she hadn't seen me for a year or two, took down Volume Seven, scanned the final pages and said, "What happens in the end is, there's this big party and everybody's gotten a lot older, so what about coming downstairs and watching the football game with me?"

"I can't sit in a drafty stadium and watch football," I explained. "I might catch cold and be delayed in getting on to Volume Two, which the translator has mysteriously titled 'Within a Budding Grove,' though the French title is quite clearly 'Shadowed by Young Fillies.' "

"You don't have to go to a stadium now that we have television," she said.

"What! They have perfected television while I was reading?"

"Now we watch football right in the parlor."

"I'd like to see that someday," I said, and resolved to, as soon as I finished "Remembrance of Things Past." This was my New Year's resolution for 1950, but though I finished Volume One, I collapsed into deep sleep in April during a 35-page passage about clouds.

I was roused by two hairy brutes knocking down the door to my room. "If you want the money it's in my sock," I told them, "but please don't take my Proust."

"He doesn't recognize us," said one.

"We're your sons, Dad," said the other.

"You lie," I snarled. "My sons are sweet little boys in knee pants with cute cowlicks, while you are huge bearded brutes in blue jeans."

The bigger boy turned surly. "You'd better finish that Proust fast, old-timer, or you'll be as out-of-date as tail fins on a Chrysler."

They tossed me a calendar, shouted "Happy New Year!" and lumbered off. So—it was 1964, eh? No wonder the boys had swelled up so. That year I resolved again to finish Proust. On I plowed, reading steadily night and day, never resting, never sleeping, feeding on nothing but enormous chunks of "Shadowed by Young Fillies." The suspense was nerve-racking. Would the young filly, Gilberte, invite young Marcel to her tea party?

One day an aging woman entered the room. "The movers are coming today. Do you want them to pack you in the van with the rest of your room?"

"I'm busy reading. Talk to my wife about those housekeeping details."

"I am your wife," she said.

Yes, it was 1976, but that was all right because I was 47 pages into Volume Three. "You should read this magnificent book sometime," I urged my wife.

"I'll wait until they raise female life expectancy to 250 years," she said.

So my wife had turned into a cynic about literature, had she? What did I care, after all? I was approaching Volume Five. Albertine was sick and tired of Marcel's possessive ways and might leave him in another million words or two.

My room and I were deposited in a strange city. Outside I could hear motorists shooting at each other about parking space. How well it fitted the violent mood that Proust had spun with his portrait of Parisian sidewalks in World War I.

It was so invigorating that I opened the door one month and called to my wife. "Shall we walk to the corner grocery and buy a nickel candy bar?" I shouted.

"The corner grocery has turned into the 50-acre shopping mall and nickel candy is now 35 cents plus tax," she shouted back. "What's more, your suit hasn't been pressed in 34 years so you've got nothing fit to wear."

If her 34-year figure was correct, then it was 1981. Time to embark on a crash program. I read through Volume Six like Patton roaring through France, and the momentum swept me through Volume Seven in a scant 10 months. As I finished on October 10 last, a gentle knock came at the door and two small children entered the room.

"My children are young again," I cried. "Proust was right. Time *can* be recaptured."

"I thought you'd like to join the party for your grandchildren," said the elderly woman, introducing herself as my wife. A party —why not? Proust was right. In the end there was this big party and everybody had gotten a lot older.

Following are the dates of the issues of *The New York Times* in which the columns in this book appeared:

REGIONS OF THE PAST

A VISIT WITH THE FOLKS   June 21, 1980
THE BOY WHO CAME TO SUPPER   August 31, 1980
HECK ON WHEELS   November 14, 1978
GROSS ROOTS   August 29, 1976
RIGHT SMART O' WIND   January 23, 1982
ANY HUMANS THERE?   October 7, 1981
THERE IS NO THERE HERE   May 2, 1981
THE UNWELCOME WAGON   May 6, 1981
A MEMORY OF ROPE   July 6, 1976
MOSEYING AROUND   September 20, 1981
A PATCH IN TIME   February 26, 1983
MAKING IT   June 26, 1983

URBAN GOTHIC

BEASTLY MANHATTAN   May 27, 1975
THOSE PRUSSIAN WHEELS   September 10, 1980
THE FAR SIDE OF STYX   November 25, 1975
THE LULL IN LULLABY   March 5, 1983
SUCH NICE PEOPLE   January 29, 1983

OF DUDS, WOGS, MAE WEST ET AL.

THE DREAMER'S PROGRESS   February 15, 1981
THE DUDS DOLDRUMS   December 4, 1979
NOW IT CAN BE TOLD   September 19, 1981
MARRIAGE À LA MODE   January 14, 1981
ELEPHANT'S-EYE HIGH   May 31, 1980
A GOTHIC TALE   February 3, 1976
A LITTLE SANITY, PLEASE   February 25, 1981
CRANK AT THE BANK   March 16, 1983
MOON OF CUALADORA   January 4, 1981
HOW SHALL I DEAR THEE?   April 15, 1981
FEAR OF FOSSILS   January 13, 1982
THE CRUELEST MONTH   September 21, 1980
BYE-BYE, SILVER BULLETS   September 4, 1979
EGG ON THE FACE   August 30, 1981
GHOST STORY   October 18, 1981
THERE SHE IS   September 6, 1980

MERRILY WE PENTAGON
UNIVERSAL MILITARY MOTION
Composed of five 1981 columns, here merged; they are, in order:
UNIVERSAL MILITARY MOTION (April 4);
MERRILY WE PENTAGON, PENTAGON, PENTAGON (April 25);
NOTHING BUT THE TRUTH (May 16);
GREASE FOR THE GANDER (May 27);
and AND SAUSAGE ON THE SIDE (June 10).
MAIL-ORDER TANKS   July 12, 1981
THE $138 MILLION MISTAKE   August 23, 1981
BRASS HAT IN HAND   April 17, 1983

ENGLISH UTILIZATIONAGE
BABBLE, BABBLE, GLUB-GLUB   December 13, 1977
VANISHING BREED   March 21, 1982
CRASHING INTO CROSSWORDLAND   January 19, 1975
DOCTOR OF THE INTERIOR   April 22, 1981
LOSS OF FACE   September 12, 1982
THE ENGLISH MAFIA   April 26, 1981

MEDIA: OR, WHAT'S THAT ROTTING MY BRAIN?
COMPLETELY DIFFERENT   March 28, 1982
TOOTH AND MAN   December 4, 1982
WAITING FOR 11 HOUR   April 7, 1982
FOREVER EMBER   October 18, 1980
THE LEGAL PITCH   March 1, 1981
THE SCRUTABLE KREMLIN   November 17, 1982
THE ROAD TO APEVILLE   March 15, 1977
RICHES OF THE TUBE   March 15, 1981
AND THE REICH GOES ON   November 11, 1981
ROCKED   December 5, 1976
MIND OVER BLATHER   April 25, 1982
THE MUSHROOM BLUES   April 10, 1982
TAKING HEROES SERIOUSLY   December 20, 1981
NO PEACE FOR OLD PHARAOH   October 2, 1976
THE MALE WEEPIE   October 3, 1982
A BETTER COLUMN   May 3, 1981
FLICKING THE DIAL   June 13, 1981

ETC.
BACK TO THE DUMP   February 27, 1983
THE ONLY GENTLEMAN   April 14, 1982
BEING RICH   August 2, 1981

THE RESCUE OF MISS YASKELL